71258

Poetry & Dogma

POETRY & DOGMA

The Transfiguration of
Eucharistic Symbols in
Seventeenth Century
English Poetry

Malcolm Mackenzie Ross

RUTGERS UNIVERSITY PRESS
New Brunswick, New Jersey
1954

MANUFACTURED IN THE UNITED STATES OF AMERICA
BY BOYD PRINTING COMPANY, INC., ALBANY, NEW YORK

For A. S. P. Woodhouse

Foreword

THIS BOOK is an attempt to present some of the consequences for religious poetry in England of the Protestant revision of Eucharistic dogma. My argument rests on the assumption that the dogmatic symbolism of the traditional Eucharistic rite had nourished the analogical mode of poetic symbol, indeed had effected imaginatively a poetic knowledge of the participation (each in the other) of the natural, the historical, and the divine orders.

The capacity of the Eucharistic symbol in poetry to function simultaneously at the levels of the natural, the historical, and the divine is threatened and eventually lost in the course of the seventeenth century. In poetry, "The Blood," "The Body," "The Sacrifice," are reduced to metaphor and below metaphor, finally to cliché. "Fact" and "value" disengage and draw apart. A Christian "spiritism" holds itself aloof from the order of things—and event. The course of English poetry is thereby divided. One direction will be that of the utterly secular, under the sign of rationalism and materialism. The other will be that of the romantic idealisms and "psychologisms," the pseudo-sacred as against the real profane.

Few, I think, will doubt that this declension and this division did in fact occur. The aesthetic phenomenon—if you like, "the dissociation of sensibility"—has engaged the best skill of the "new" critics. The scholar has gone beneath and beyond the aesthetic fact in an effort to explain the phenomenon. Thus we have been led to speculate about the impact of the new science, or Descartes, or the rebirth of scepticism or the "Counter Renaissance," or the social and political revolution. It is none of my purpose to challenge the validity either of the "new" criticism or the history of ideas. My debt to critics like T. S. Eliot and Allen Tate and to scholars like A. S. P. Woodhouse, Douglas Bush, Basil Willey, Marjorie Nicolson, Louis Bredvold, and Arthur Barker is real and, I hope, evident. Yet there is a mystery in the air of the seventeenth century which is perhaps only apprehended in a mystery. An incredible motion occurs in the firmament of poetry which cannot quite be explained by reference to any extrinsic motion of ideas, events, or gadgets. I have argued in this book that the drastic transformation of central Christian symbol in the poetry of the period can be fully understood only in terms of an intrinsic motion—a motion in the very heart of Christian dogma itself.

My study is admittedly limited. I have not attempted anything like an inclusive comment on the entire range of Christian symbolism in seventeenth century English poetry. My concern here is with the heart of dogma—with the Incarnation as extended in the sacrificial act of the Mystical Body—and with the analogical act of the poetic imagination nourished by Eucharistic dogma, starved by the fleshless abstraction which is sometimes offered in its stead. For, heretical as this may seem to our sophisticated apostles of the absolute autonomy of poetry, I am persuaded that the dogmatic symbol may inform and sustain the poetic symbol as such without losing its proper dogmatic identity and without tyrannizing the specifically poetic process. The change which certainly does occur in the poetic function of Christian symbol in the seventeenth century would seem to indicate that the revolution in Christian dogma had an immediate bearing on the poetic act—indeed on the future course of the tradition of poetry in England. For the revolution in dogma of which I treat is no less than a revolution in our way of knowing things, time, eternity— and ourselves.

In this study, then, I am particularly concerned with the loss to the Christian symbol-maker of "the analogy of things" and "the analogy of event." After a discussion of what I call the firmament of Christian symbol (and the centrality of Eucharistic dogma in the traditional firmament), I have attempted to assess the signifi-cance for poetic symbol of the various Protestant revisions of the Eucharist. Then, by a study of the imagery of representative "low" and "high" Anglicans I hope to have demonstrated the effect of revised Eucharistic dogma on the analogical capacity of central Christian symbol in poetry.

I have not thought it desirable to plan the book as a series of studies of major seventeenth century poets. Of the major figures only Herbert and Milton receive anything like detailed considera-tion, and with Milton I am concerned only with tracing the out-lines of a new and positive firmament of symbol which begins to take shape in his work. Poets like Donne, Vaughan, and Traherne are brought to the edge of my pattern, but as they present problems both poetic and dogmatic which reach far be-yond the central concern of this book, I was unable to treat them "in the round." Crashaw serves to illustrate the numbing and narrowing effect of the revolution in dogma on even the Catholic sensibility. In a brief coda to my last chapter I try to do no more than *suggest* that the central dogmatic symbols of Christianity, abandoned for so long by poets, not only retain their vitality but now once again tempt the symbol-maker and begin to reshape the firmament within which the poetic symbol is made.

It will be noted that swarms of "little" poets (some of them quite bad poets) find their way into these pages. Every Anglican parson of the seventeenth century must have written at least one volume of verse! "Little" poetry is always little, bad poetry always bad, and it may be objected that the clichés of these little bad ones are very much like the clichés of little bad poets in any age. But I am interested here only in their *dogmatic* clichés, in the words that spell out dogma, in the semantic ghosts that haunt the ruins of recognizable ideas—clichés that are of a piece theolog-ically with the expression of the major poets of like dogmatic persuasion. The evidence of these little poets supports my thesis that changes occurring in the religious symbolism of men like Herbert and Milton are not the product of private idiosyncrasies

but reflections of a radical change occurring in the total firmament of the Christian tradition.

Incidentally, I have not tried to arrive at "full or final esti-
mates" of individual writers and individual poems but throughout the study have consciously isolated those elements of dogmatic
import which reveal a shift in the symbol-making tradition at
large. Evidence of the dissolution of the firmament of symbol
within which a poet works is not to be read as an indictment of
the individual poet's integrity or quality. Nor is it necessarily
meant to describe the poet's full and considered position on
Christian theology—or anything else. Such evidence as I present
is intended to indicate, in relation to the fundamental dogmatic
changes of the age, significant symptoms of a change in the way
that the poetic imagination works with crucial symbol. There is a
risk. An image isolated for such purposes as this may all too
easily be pushed through its own roof! The risk has to be taken.

It may also be objected that I have not sufficiently established
a "background." Here is change, presumably. But change from
what? One has to begin somewhere. I decided to limit myself to
the actual phenomenon of change, with just enough reference to
Shakespeare and Donne and the very early Milton to confirm the
existence and persistence of the analogical mode in the native
English line. Certainly it is not enough to point to Dante and
say "*There* it is!" But a reading of the First Book of the *Faerie
Queene* assures us that the mode of analogy can still in sixteenth
century England control the way in which a poet images heaven
by Cleopolis, eternity by time, the face of truth by the lifting of
a veil from the face of a woman. Still—but not for long. For
even here the analogical way of knowing is threatened by what
is known in advance, by new dogmatic formulations inconsistent
with the *habit* of symbolizing that manages for a while to survive. (My chapter "History and Poetry" might be read against
the dying echo of Spenser's First Book.)

My primary sources are indicated in the notes. Whenever
possible, I have quoted from easily accessible editions. The six-

FOREWORD

teenth and seventeenth century editions referred to are in the
possession of the Huntington library. Quotation has been kept to
the minimum. I have tried to illustrate my argument with representative examples from the major and minor poets with which
I am here concerned. Each example could be multiplied a hun-
dredfold.

It will be obvious that I owe a very large debt to the liturgical
works of the late Dom Gregory Dix, the Anglican Benedictine
monk. His monumental *Shape of the Liturgy* sharpened my
awareness of the "Anglican dilemma" and provided me with a
new approach to the poetry of the period. I should like to believe that my aesthetic conclusions are in line with his liturgical
premises. I am indebted to his enormous scholarship for such
knowledge as I have gained of the earlier liturgical tradition and
my dependence on him will be particularly evident in Chapter
Two.

I am almost equally indebted in this chapter to E. C. Messenger's *The Reformation, the Mass and the Priesthood,* especially
for its account of Luther's various revisions of traditional Eucharistic doctrine. My theological chapter is scarcely, therefore, the
fruit of "original" investigation, and Dix and Messenger were
my principal guides through the thickets of Patristic and Reformation theology. The task was to relate the evidence they
present to a problem in symbolism—and aesthetics. My sense of
the Thomist doctrine of analogy has, I trust, been cleared by
James F. Anderson's *The Bond of Being,* by Allen Tate's essays
on Dante and Poe in *The Forlorn Demon,* by Jacques Maritain's
Creative Intuition in Art and Poetry, by William F. Lynch's
essays in *Thought,* as well as by his patient and helpful com-
ments on sections of this book. L. L. Martz's work on the formal
meditation early warned me away from ground which I was
fearlessly and foolishly about to tread.

A. S. P. Woodhouse, to whom this book is affectionately dedicated, has, since the day I first met Milton in his lecture-room,
given unstintingly of his vast fund of wisdom and kindliness. I

[xi]

FOREWORD

should not wish to embarrass him by seeming to suggest that he is in any way responsible for the notions here expressed. It is a mark of his tolerance that he has, over the years, given me every possible encouragement.

I am grateful for the generous aid which I have received from many hands. Research for the present study was begun as early as 1941 under a summer travel grant from Indiana University. After the war I made a second start on the project with travel grants from the University of Manitoba and the Canadian Humanities Research Council. A Guggenheim fellowship enabled me to divide the year 1949–50 between the Widener and Huntington libraries. There I gathered material not only for part of this book but also for what, perhaps, will be a more extensive treatment of the Christian symbol in poetry. The Arts Research Committee of Queen's University has made grants for the typing of the manuscript and for travel. My wife took charge of the proofreading and the preparation of the index.

MALCOLM MACKENZIE ROSS

Kingston, Ontario
March 1954

Contents

Poetry & Dogma

The Firmament of Symbol

CHAPTER ONE

THE RESTORATION of the English monarchy in 1660 behind the façade of a ritualistic and scholarly high churchmanship ushered in the Age of Secularism. After 1660 many poets were to profess a nominal Christianity. Pope, the Deist, was to remain in communion with Rome. The King of England would still be styled "Defender of the Faith." But the centre of gravity in English culture would no longer be Christian, although persistent habits of sentiment and ethic might obscure for a while the new situation.

Now such a radical change as this from a dominantly Christian to a dominantly secular culture could not have happened overnight. And yet it appears to have happened with an unbelievable abruptness. The century which at one end saw the eclipse of the Christian tradition inaugurated, at the other, one of the most fertile movements in the whole history of English Christian poetry. Surely the vogue of "divine verse" set off by Sylvester's translation of Du Bartas could have given no hint that the time for such concerns in poetry was nearly over, indeed would not last out the lifetime of the youngest poet to publish in the first decade of the seventeenth century.

The years from Donne to Dryden—the years of the Fletchers, Herbert, Crashaw, Vaughan, Milton, and the scores of little poets sufficiently possessed by the Christian muse to build better than they knew and better than their kind has ever built since! Could these be the last years of the Christendom of the arts? The tempo of the change, this almost simultaneous flowering and withering of the Christian sensibility in poetry, is perhaps the most striking phenomenon of seventeenth century English literature. And though it may be only a phase of what, by hindsight, appears to have been a broad and leisurely pattern of change from the Christian to the secular, the intensity and self-consciousness of the movement in poetry cannot be perceived by way of any abstractive description of shifts in "the cultural background." This movement in poetry is most apparent in the life of those Christian symbols which are rooted in dogma but at the same time convey, or seek to convey, the immediate sense of existence. My study, therefore, is concerned mainly with such symbols in poetry as are intended to interpenetrate two orders of being, the divine and the natural. However, the crisis in the Christian aesthetic of the seventeenth century necessarily reflects the fragmentation and consequent deterioration of Christian dogma itself. For this is the century in which the radical Protestant revisions of dogma are digested in whole or in part by English Christian poetry. It is, of course, in Anglican poetry, hovering precariously as it must between Catholic and Protestant symbol, that one is able to sense most vividly the poignant dilemma of the Christian artist. But some scrutiny of Roman Catholic and nonconformist poetry will also be necessary for a proper understanding of the sudden declension of the Christian culture. Unavoidably, therefore, this study must be concerned with dogma, with the novel and often inconsistent colourings taken on by traditional dogma when it is put to the service of alien masters, with the loss of communicability which results to the Christian poetic symbol from tortuous internecine theological warfare and from the revision (or downright dismissal) of ancient ritual and liturgy.

I suspect that any such study should be prefaced with a statement, as clear as may be, of my critical assumptions. My belief is that the problem of the transfiguration of Christian poetic symbol in the seventeenth century can be solved neither in terms, exclusively, of the history of ideas nor by means, exclusively, of the conventional tools of the "new" criticism. Without the findings of literary history, such a study as this could not, of course, have been undertaken at all. Without some knowledge of the history of theology, the nature of the problem, its very terms, would not have existed for me. Without the lithe and pinpoint exegesis of the "new" critic as a testament, my awareness of the shape and gesture of the poetic symbol would have been far dimmer than it is.

But it may be that "new" critic and "old" scholar alike will be constrained to question the validity of the problem raised here, to say nothing of the means taken to solve it. The "new" critic in particular may object to my strategy of going outside the poetic unit to detect certain of the laws of motion which the poetry of the period must obey.

I wonder if in making a cult of our concern for the autonomous poetic unit—for the poem as a little world unto itself—we have not lost sight of vitalities which surge between poem and poem, vitalities which may indeed sustain and even determine the life of the poetic unit? For if it be true that "pressures" and "tensions" mark and make the aesthetic existence of the self-enclosed world of the single poem, is it not possible, too, that analogous pressures and tensions place this world within a larger firmament and propel it around its own proper orbit? And if this be so, can aesthetic criticism properly lower its gaze to the inspection of the static sublunary dimensions of the poem as a poem as a poem?

In assessing the relevance of central dogma for the understanding—and the full and proper aesthetic reception—of Christian poetic symbol, I do not intend to reverse the direction of Matthew Arnold and try to make religion a substitute for poetry. While such a study as this cannot rest on any gospel of pure aesthetics, it is nevertheless meant as a study in aesthetics.

Is it not by now clear that a verbalist and formalist like William Empson seriously limits his critical method when he treats of the Christian paradoxes of Donne and Herbert as though they were born of Donne and Herbert, as though they had no life before and beyond the poems in which Empson happens to find them? Professor Rosemond Tuve [1] properly rebukes the verbalistic monadism of the Empsons by opening windows to dogma and tradition, to the ancient scandalous paradoxes of Virgin Birth and Crucifixion, to the continuous conventions of iconography and typology which press not only on the poetic usage of Donne and Herbert but also on the aesthetic response of the instructed seventeenth century reader.

The scholarly corrective had to be administered. But perhaps it does not in itself close the case. If we assume that a tradition of image and symbol persists into the poetry of the seventeenth century from the very earliest Christian times, can we also assume that Herbert was read in the same way by Anglican, Catholic, and Puritan, that a typological image like Blood of the Lamb has the same force in Crashaw as in Milton, or that a twentieth century reader, with knowledge but without faith, can receive the full aesthetic impact of a seventeenth century Christian poem? Can we assume, as some do, that the specifically aesthetic effect of a poem is residual, is what is left after extraneous coverings of meaning and belief have been rotted away by time, that naked structural "tension," that "paradox" and "ambiguity" as things-in-themselves without root or roof, are presented only at this late last *sub specie eternitas,* and that therefore only now is it possible to appraise the distant poetry of Christianity in the exclusively aesthetic order?

It is my contention that the traditional Christian symbols in Anglican poets like Donne or Herbert sometimes function in contradiction to the tradition which bore them and that because of significant revisions of central Christian dogma, the actual aesthetic effect of such symbols must be searched and felt in terms of a subtle contrapuntal tension between tradition and innovation

---

[1] *A Reading of George Herbert* (Chicago, 1952), pp. 19–99. A comment on the "new" criticism as applied to Herbert with particular reference to Empson's analysis of "The Sacrifice" in *Seven Types of Ambiguity,* pp. 284 ff.

within dogma itself. It is a mistake in critical method to read the Christian paradoxes of Herbert as though he had invented them or as though he had merely inherited them. Paradox in seventeenth century Christian poetry must be felt, interpreted, and evaluated at its full height. This is not to say that we may not, with Empson, take delight in the purely structural function of paradox in poetry. Rather it is to affirm the need to swoop imaginatively from one level of symbol to another and to be present at the very instant of the incarnation of dogma in device. The aesthetic experience is the whole flight backwards and forwards through all the levels of meaning and suggestion which have been suddenly epiphanized by the stroke of paradox. If in the case of a traditional dogmatic symbol new suggestions of meaning and value occur contrary to the field of association in which the symbol has previously rested, then the aesthetic response— and the critical method—must be sensitized to the resulting tension. The tension between Catholic and Protestant dogma at the core of Anglican rhetoric must be considered as an aesthetic fact and not just as an item in the history of ideas. By dodging such considerations as extra-aesthetic our criticism is in danger of stunting its growth.

By the very nature of the poetic object we are obliged, in our reading of seventeenth century poetry, to remember that the dominant symbols before us participate in a firmament of value anterior to the poetry yet not exterior to it. We are obliged to remember that by the seventeenth century this firmament is in rapid and confused motion, and if we are wholly honest with ourselves, we are obliged to attack once again that tricky question of the agency of the belief (or nonbelief) of the critic in his total response to the poetry of belief.

The word dogma frightens us today, and we try to be rid of it. But we are concerning ourselves with Christian poetry, and Christianity is a dogmatic religion. Christianity demands of the believer a certain precision of belief. Christianity has a precise use for its own symbols—a fact which we would do well to take into account before attempting to interpret Christianity to itself with the aid of Freud and Suzanne Langer. For no matter how strongly we may be inclined to psychologize the symbols of the Christian faith, to explain them in terms of the "quest myth" and the "father image" (and thereby to explain them away), we must remember that for Christians the great symbols of revelation and dogma have ontological as well as psychological reference.

Christian poetry, insofar as it symbolizes at all, bears inevitably the stamp of dogma. This is not to confuse poetry with apologetics. The Christian poem is not a theological tract. Nor may one come to a critical judgment of a Christian poet by abstracting and counting his sound dogmatic utterances. The Christian poet is not a preacher. Nor is his end the salvation of souls. Like any artist he seeks to create beauty. His end is aesthetic and not moral. Art whether Christian, Buddhist, or Freudian is still art. The point is that a Christian artist works within a firmament of value which is a Christian firmament and not a Buddhist or a Freudian firmament. Now there are critics about who are honestly anxious to save the arts from humiliation, from subservience to the natural and social sciences, who contend that poetry must be regarded as autonomous, that it cannot be in any sense a commentary on life, that it must, therefore, dwell apart in its own verbal universe. Ultimately, such a proposition questions the ontological claim of the symbol. Clearly this is a proposition which has a direct bearing on any approach one might make to the relation of poetry and belief. At this point in the argument perhaps it is enough to say, with all emphasis, that an authentic Christian aesthetic is far removed from any notion, howsoever sophisticated, of art for art's sake. While the Christian, if he is an artist, must insist on the proper autonomy of his art, he will nevertheless assume that the autonomy proper to art is not and cannot be sustained within a vacuum. For while the end of Christian art is the beautiful and not the good, while Christian art belongs indeed to the aesthetic and not the moral order, while it seeks, essentially, to please rather than to improve, its beauty

[8]

can shine forth only so long as the firmament within which poetry moves is not disturbed. Let one star fall or leap its place and the light which this poetry gives off will flicker. And after collisions of sun and moon the light of Christian art will seem a darkness visible. It is, of course, with disturbances, with leaps and collisions in the dogmatic firmament of Christian poetry, that we are mainly concerned here. But we must seek to distinguish from all such disturbances a motion vital yet ordered in the heavens of poetry. For the firmament, if it is alive, is necessarily in motion.

I have implied that, paradoxically, the very independence of Christian art derives from the dependence of the Christian artist on dogma. To put it very simply: because the core of the Christian firmament of value is fixed and certain and because it gives off light, the Christian artist is free to go about his business of making things. No matter how dark the crevices he may wish to explore there will be light over his shoulder. He does not have to fashion his own lantern. But that the Christian artist is not enslaved, not driven to any flat conformity by his dependence on the fixed light of dogma, is evident as soon as one recollects that men as different from one another as Dante and Chaucer and Milton and Dostoevski and T. S. Eliot are Christian artists. And when one thinks of the enormous differences between mediaeval and baroque art, one is surely aware of a motion in the Christian firmament so vast that there is real difficulty in locating the fixed stars.

But, paradoxically, there is, too, a fixity in this firmament which makes possible the living motion of Christian symbol. The confusion of this ordered motion of the firmament with disruptive bursts and reforms in the violet air has bedevilled much modern criticism and may even have led men in despair out of the mighty fastnesses of dogma and ontology into the tiny oasis of pure aesthetics and psychologism. It may be well, therefore, at this point to isolate a "fixed star."

The fixed star at the centre of the Christian firmament of symbol is the dogma of the Incarnation. In this dogma, respecting as it does both the divinity of the Word and the humanity of the flesh, is contained the whole principle of the Christian aesthetic. Some of the implications of the dogma, for art as well as for life, are certainly these: Though the flesh is frail, and though nature herself has suffered the wound of sin, the Incarnation redeems the flesh and the world, laying nature and the reasonable faculty open once more to the operation of the supernatural. In other words, the Incarnation makes possible, indeed demands, the sacramental vision of reality. The flesh, the world, things, are restored to dignity because they are made valid again. Existence becomes a drama which, no matter how painful it may be, is nevertheless meaningful. And no detail in the drama is without its utterly unique reality. No thing is insignificant. There are, of course, religious idealisms which deny the validity of matter and which seek to reduce the world of things to the status of metaphor. Christianity has been invaded upon occasion by such alien idealisms. But the Christian artist, when he knows what he is about, respects his medium, respects the material fact and the historical event, respects the practical, objective limits of form. He cannot be, as Shelley was, the poet of an "unbodied joy." Nor may he seek to break through the illusion of sense experience into a realm of pure essence or even into a realm of pure art-vision, that verbal universe of the seer tricked out as a special kind of reality, sometimes even as the only reality. If he engages in such fanciful exploits, he ceases to be either a Christian or an artist. In any case he is no longer a Christian artist. For whether he defines it or not, the Christian is compelled, under the fixed star of the Incarnation, to believe in existence, in the act of existence. He is compelled to believe in the particularity, the uniqueness, the *value,* of things. Therefore, the Christian artist may not, like the Platonist and all his hybrid brood, oppose a shadow world of things to a real world of value. Rather, for the Christian artist, all things have their own separately structured, intrinsic actuality and value, while at the same time they participate proportionately in larger relationships and values which are moral and spiritual without ceasing to be actual, specific, concrete. The Word is made Flesh without ceasing to be the Word. Nor is the Flesh fleshless. Authentic Christianity does not seek to create reality by any fact-less copulation of imagination with value. Rather it discovers worlds beyond worlds even in a grain of sand—worlds that exist in a rising tier of being. Authentic Christian art celebrates the actual kinship that obtains between man and things, between subject and object.[2]

The dogma of the Incarnation is sacramental not only in its implications for the artist's concern with nature, with things, with existence, but also in its implications for the artist's concern with history, with time, with event. Nothing distinguishes the Christian aesthetic so sharply from the aesthetic of the modern myth addict than this insistence on the historical in Christian dogma. The Incarnation occurs in time. As Jean Daniélou[3] has demonstrated, pagan myth, whether classical or primitive, is inevitably cosmic rather than historical. It amounts to a kind of natural revelation, commemorating the harvest, the alternations of the seasons, and the desires and fears of man naked under natural forces. The dying corn god who is reborn in spring typifies this natural order of myth. But for the Christian, the death and Resurrection of Christ is decidedly not a cosmic myth. It is a historical event, but one which absorbs, sacramentally, the cosmic into the historical order. Thus Easter takes into its structure the rebirth of nature in spring, the ancient Jewish feast of the Passover with all its sense of the role of Providence in history, and the Resurrection of the God-man, an act which completes history by defining its end. Christianity absorbs the biological, the psychological, the cosmic myth in the completed historical symbol. And yet each level of reference now contained in the Christian structure of symbol retains its own uniqueness, its own proper truth.

[2] A penetrating statement of the analogical imperatives of Christian art is given by William F. Lynch in "Adventure in Order," *Thought* (Spring, 1951), pp. 33–49.

[3] "The Problem of Symbolism," *Thought* (September, 1950), pp. 423–440.

As early as the epic *Beowulf* one detects, however faintly and uncertainly, the specifically Christian function of historical symbol. The land is terrorized by Grendel, the Caliban-like monster who is made to show forth the dark terror of fen and sea, the natural waters of desolation which threaten primitive society. The hero, Beowulf, becomes the incarnation of the tribe in its conflict with nature. The final victory of Beowulf over the monster—the destruction at the bottom of the sea of Grendel's mother—symbolizes the absorption of the cosmic level of myth by the historical. Beowulf enters the waters of desolation. He is given up for lost. But he rises victor from the dark waters, which are converted into waters of baptism, regeneration. The poem can now concern itself with the level of history proper. The enemies of man are now avarice, envy, and pride. The struggle becomes social, moral, and fully human, not merely natural. But the awful forces of nature have not been dismissed. They have been taken up into man's nature, into the terror and hope of man's destiny.[4]

To jump from these beginnings to a poem which occurs at the very end of the main Christian development in our poetry, I think we can still see in Milton's *Samson Agonistes* the stamp of central Christian dogma. Samson, chosen by God to deliver his people, has been abandoned by God. He is at the mill with slaves, and his people groan under the yoke of the tyrant. Milton stresses the drama of Samson's moral recovery by repentance, by recognition of God's justice, by sacrificial death. When Samson comes to know himself as he is in fact, when he is willing to accept once more that dependence on God which, paradoxically, is the only source of his freedom and his strength, then he is able to pull down the pillars of the temple of the nature-god Dagon, then he is able to destroy the tyrant and liberate his people. The price is his own life. For Samson, while not precisely a Christ-type, does die the sacrificial

---

[4] I am not, of course, contending that the mythic elements of *Beowulf* were wholly conceived by Christians within the dogmatic firmament of Christianity. But the poem as we have it is susceptible to a Christian interpretation and has obviously been filtered through the Christian imagination.

and redemptive Christ-death. Samson's victory is moral and spiritual. It is also social—a victory in history. In Milton's treatment of the theme, the Cross is made to illuminate (and to bless) not only the Old Testament story but also the pain of history in Milton's day, in any day. Here, then, is a concrete drama of events in time. But time has been bisected by the Incarnation, and levels of value emerge for the life of the person, for the life of society, for the life and destiny of the race. There is no leap here into an otherworldliness. Eternity fulfills itself in time and by way of temporal thing and act. The person, the event, the tribe, participate in the full Christian symbol because they embody in their own actuality the values which they fix in symbol. They are at once themselves and other than themselves.

Beowulf and *Samson Agonistes* can both be located under the fixed star of dogma. But there is a motion evident enough here. Obviously these poems are in many respects quite dissimilar. Yet (and I think this is a matter for aesthetics as much as for theology) *Samson* is in certain fundamental respects a closer relative to *Beowulf* than to *Paradise Lost*. The motion between *Beowulf* and *Samson* is a motion *about* a fixed star. The motion between *Samson* and *Paradise Lost* is the motion of the star itself. The first kind of motion bears witness to the life of the firmament, the second to its imminent dissolution. We must not confuse these very different kinds of motion. And we must understand each thoroughly if we would dare to penetrate the crisscross energies of the seventeenth century firmament of symbol.

To consider first the necessary and ordered motion of the specifically Christian firmament: The Christian artist has worked in many very different cultural contexts. But that he created the Gothic style does not mean that Christian art is Gothic—later he created the baroque. That he mastered the art of allegorical abstraction does not mean that his medium is necessarily the abstract. Consider the luminous particularity of the actual in the poetry of

Hopkins—or of Dante, for that matter. One would have no difficulty in pointing to a continuity of dogma from Dante to Hopkins, and it is a continuity never wholly interrupted. But what of the motion which expresses itself from age to age in drastically diverse aesthetic wholes? Can differences as drastic as those which appear between mediaeval, baroque, and modern Christian poetry occur within an ordered and continuous firmament and under a fixed star?

What, for instance, are we now to think of the stylized conventions of the Ages of Faith, what is our response to those set symbols of Justice, Mercy, Hope, and Despair, and all the other allegorical daughters of God, the flesh, and the devil by means of which the artist for so long sought to perceive and to express the nature of things?

At a moment like ours when insistence on the simple, direct, sensuous, image has weakened, when the poet gropes for the relevant myth rather than for the intelligible object, we are perhaps not quite so ready as we once were to disparage the mediaeval vision. We are more careful these days not to say that Dante was great in spite of his faith. For the doctrine of progress is gone; the cult of the hard, natural rock of fact is gone; seeing is no longer believing. Truth is to be discovered, if at all, not in social statistics or in the test tube but in the scrutiny of the libidinous dream of the person and the race. Free as we are at last of nature and time and reason, is it surprising that we contrive unthinkable resurrections? Is it surprising that we conjure up, in the main, to save and instruct us not the fleshed and fashioned children of history but rather the ooze and stuff of prehistory? Is it surprising that we prefer the primitive myth stained with wish-fantasy to the theological symbol ordered by thought?

In such a temper we cannot, with any conviction, hold to a positive progressive bias against the mediaeval culture. It is even fashionable these days to be a mediaevalist, to specialize in the Middle Ages, to found academies which contain the

Summa, Chartres, the fabliaux, precisely as the geologist's box contains specimens of the pre-Cambrian. We hunt the museum piece. And if we philosophize our task, we confess that we do no more than hunt, disinterestedly, exhausted symbols, the fossils of a process of symbolization no longer living whereby man once tried to pin his shadow to the sky. We make so bold even to compare the fossil pieces with the evolved structures of living styles in art, just as we might compare the wings of the pterodactyl and the sparrow. But let no one dare accuse us of believing that the pterodactyl lives!

It would therefore seem that the great generative ideas of Christianity did their proper work, begat a St. Thomas Aquinas and a Dante, then died in the fullness of time as all man's generative ideas have died, suffocated within a shell of obsolescent rhetoric. The final hardening of a symbolic system presumably betrays the old age and predicts the imminent demise of the generative idea. But—and here we justify a scholarly interest in the corpse—*that which is symbolized is never so important as the fact that we do indeed symbolize,* as the fact that we have always shown ourselves to be symbolizing animals.

I hope that this has not been a wholly unfair caricature of at least one highly influential trend in contemporary criticism—a trend which is given complete articulation in Suzanne Langer's *Philosophy in a New Key.*[5] From the standpoint of such a book, no continuous firmament of value is possible, and no genuine ontological depth can be accorded to symbol in any of the distinct and transient firmaments in which symbol has been made to function. Thus the history of culture appears as a graveyard lined with the skeletons of abandoned firmaments. In this view the motion of culture occurs by way of drastic discontinuities. The only continuing and constant factor left to history is man's peculiar itch after meaning, his compulsion to construct symbols with which, however, he cannot for long be

[5] (Cambridge, Massachusetts, 1942.)

content. The death of the mode of Dante's poetry bespeaks the death of the Thomist firmament and of the generative ideas of a closed epoch in man's compulsive quest for meaning. And, presumably, our current myth symbols, compounded of the dredgings of Freud, Jung, Frazer, and their tribe, will petrify in turn after having nourished us for a while with illusions equivalent in psychological function to the illusions raised for a while to symbol in Thomism.

My own assumptions are very different. I believe that the evidence supports my contention that the cultural motion which shapes the differences between Dante, Crashaw, and Eliot is a motion within a single and living firmament. The ontological reach of central Christian symbol remains constant despite the surprising variety of Christian poetic rhetoric. The shift or even the downright collapse of a rhetorical tradition in symbol-making does not, as we shall see, necessarily announce a failure of dogma or the death of generative ideas. That a kind of motion destructive to the firmament does occur will soon be fully apparent. But it will also be apparent that a culture can abandon a generative idea without destroying it, without really touching it. That the motion about the fixed star is a cultural phenomenon wholly different from the motion of the star itself becomes quite evident in the reading of a study in allegory like Professor Samuel Chew's *The Four Daughters of God*.[6] The process revealed by Professor Chew's study, that of the pressure of certain common allegorical devices, mediaeval in origin, upon the temper of Renaissance poetry, illustrates for our purposes here the living motion of the Christian tradition in art, the contemporaneity at one level of two very different Christian ages despite the real discontinuity which, at another level, does indeed obtain between them.

One notes first of all an apparent surface continuity between the pictorial art of mediaeval and Elizabethan England. As Pro-

[6] (Toronto, 1947.)

fessor Chew reminds us, the Elizabethan was bred to allegory by picture. The walls of churches, shops, and taverns were still covered with representations of the Works of Mercy, the Seven Deadly Sins, and the Dance of Death. The great halls were still hung with emblematic tapestries. And there were, of course, the emblem books themselves. Yet the poetry of the High Renaissance was seldom merely ornamental, artificial, derivative. If the Elizabethans thought of their poems as "speaking pictures," at least these pictures spoke sense.

Admittedly, then, the Middle Ages provided the Renaissance artist and poet with actual and significant tissues of allegorical and symbolic reference. To this degree there is the appearance of simple formal continuity between the two ages. In striking examples from *Richard II, Henry IV, Part One,* and *The Merchant of Venice,* Professor Chew [7] is able to show how Shakespeare deepened the surface of dialogue and action by revealing, beneath the flow and floor of the specific, well-stocked, plenteous cellars of symbolic suggestion and support. Shylock, for instance, appears in the trial scene not with the scales and sword (the familiar mediaeval emblems of Justice) but with scales and knife. The suggestiveness is unmistakable. The knife, with all its associations of "cruelty and treacherous violence," is substituted for the sword with its associations of "gallantry, nobility, and stern righteousness." Surely, as Professor Chew contends, "to the Elizabethan accustomed to think in terms of symbols, the figure of Shylock may well have appeared to be a travesty of Justice." And one remembers, too, the Elizabethan dumb show, that allegory in mime deployed to uncover the intention beneath the surface of event.

Despite this use of mediaeval convention in the poetry of the High Renaissance, however, any appearance of simple continuity between past and present is, I believe, a deceptive illusion. In the cultural patterns which begin to emerge in the sixteenth

---

[7] All the quotations in this paragraph are from Professor Chew's discussion of the *Merchant of Venice* in *The Four Daughters of God,* pp. 47–48.

century and which reach their term in the seventeenth, one can detect an intriguing double motion. In the first motion the Christian idea seems to dance towards the specific, the concrete, seeking to possess it as a new dwelling is possessed. For instance, in Herbert's poetry the courtly love lyric is thus possessed and thereby transfigured into the hymn. In the late comedies of Shakespeare something of the Christian paradox of death and resurrection is expressed, not by personified abstraction and conventional allegory but in and through the fleshly images and the glancing action of particularity.

The other motion one may observe in this culture is clearly away from the concrete and the specific. Curiously enough, this motion is, for the most part, away from the Christian and towards the secular idea. For by the seventeenth century the abstract allegorical mode seems drawn towards the political and social theme. The art of Bunyan must be seen as the exception rather than the rule. Indeed, the four daughters of God are themselves put to work defending the rival ecclesiastical and political claims of the Catholic, Anglican, and Puritan parties. In illustrating topical debates, in magnifying the Virgin Queen of England, in hallowing the practices of the London merchant, the mediaeval mode of abstraction was gradually secularized and schooled for new and astonishing tasks. Soon after Milton abandoned his "Adam Unparadised" in favour of the direct, nonallegorical treatment of God and man in *Paradise Lost,* the "venerable personification" is seen to mince rejuvenated if unshriven across the stage of the Restoration theatre.

Clearly, the mode of allegorical abstraction does not enshroud the generative ideas, the deeper symbolism, of Christian poetry. Rather it comes to enshroud a secular rationalism culminating in the witty generalities of Alexander Pope—or, perhaps, in the person of Mrs. Malaprop.

Much confusion has arisen from a failure in practice to distinguish between at least two levels of the Christian symbol. The more obvious level, and that which is often taken at face value to be the whole of the symbol, is the level of rhetorical convention, now abstract, now concrete, by means of which dogma finds expression appropriate to the sensibility—and the accidents—of place and time. The other level, of course, is that of dogma itself, the conceptualization by means of symbol of what is believed to be an ultimate and unalterable truth. In the seventeenth century the Christian idea—the level of dogma—moves generally in a direction opposite to that taken by those abstract rhetorical modes which are no longer adequate for the expression of dogma. The Christian idea is thus seen to be the charitable captor of any and all the children of rhetoric. In the history of culture the Christian rhythm is always away from the sanctification of the profane to the profanation of that which is no longer sacred because no longer expedient. And this is the rhythm of the sacramental impulse.

In coming to grips with the phenomenon of the motion of Christian poetry in the seventeeth century, after taking stock of the surface lines of continuity in the tradition as a whole, one must seek to detect and delineate the process of dissociation active between the rhetorical and dogmatic levels of the Christian symbol. The process is complicated, uneven but persistent. It is a process which finally goes astray.

I have suggested that dogma is not necessarily compromised by the shift in rhetoric. The movement in expression from abstract to concrete modes can occur within the living Christian firmament and then may be regarded as a movement *about* a fixed star. Furthermore, the energies of the firmament are creative and can transfigure alien and inconvenient ingredients. In Herbert, as I have noted, the court lyric becomes a hymn. The personified essences of the morality play are converted into the illuminated existences of Elizabethan drama. Essence and existence interpenetrate in wholly new but quite proper ways in Eliot's *Four Quartets* and Fry's *A Sleep of Prisoners*.

Curiously enough, the presence of mediaeval rhetorical devices in the pious poetry of the seventeenth century sometimes indicates not a real continuity in the tradition but an uneven, unsettling pull between a rhetoric which has remained static and a dogma which has taken to turning cartwheels. We shall discover that a poet like George Herbert is pulled in opposite directions—both towards and away from the specific, the sacramental. The consequences of this double pull for Herbert's use of symbol, and indeed for the whole firmament of Christian symbol in English poetry, will, I hope, become evident. And if Milton, in his motion from the allegorical to the personalized Christian symbol, seems to stay decently within his proper firmament, it is apparent also that in his treatment of the deeper conceptual levels of traditional symbol he has chased the anciently fixed stars from their centre to the utmost pole. Beneath the play of rhetoric, beneath the surface clash of Seneca and Cicero, beneath the strenuous alteration of patristic and scholastic modes of expression, beneath the opposing claims of static and dynamic image and idiom, affecting poetry as much as piety, there is in the seventeenth century a motion in the deep dogmatic core of the Christian mind itself.

It is precisely this motion which is so difficult for the contemporary critic to comprehend, even when as a historian of ideas he is able to perceive it. For the comprehension of the dogmatic symbol one must at least be capable of a willing suspension of disbelief in dogma. If one begins by psychologizing dogma or by assuming that dogma has no aesthetic bearing, one is not prepared to read the poetry of the seventeenth century. The critic who assesses the decline of Christian poetry in this period entirely in terms of the pendulum of taste, the alliance of new science with old dialectic, the impact of social change on public symbol, is in danger of missing the inner dialectic of the Christian idea itself, an idea alive with a life of its own. For instance, the student of rhetoric may see Calvin as the direct heir of St. Thomas Aquinas. But the simple continuity observable at the level of method between the *Summa* and the *Institutes* is belied, obviously, by a radical discontinuity at the deeper level of dogma. And one must see that the primary and significant motion occurs at the deeper level.

The decline of a specifically Christian poetry in the seventeenth century demands investigation at both the rhetorical and dogmatic levels, and the interaction of these levels must also concern us. But how precisely does this interaction of the rhetorical and dogmatic levels occur? What is the effect of such a process on the motion of the culture and on the texture and integral being of single poetic wholes? These are questions which can be answered only by a practical criticism of characteristic poems. But before entering on such a task I must define certain of my terms more exactly. I have already stressed the sacramental and existential status of the authentic Christian symbol when it is fixed in its moving firmament. And I have claimed that the Christian symbol, inasmuch as it remains properly incarnational (remains a fixed star), illuminates and confirms the validity of thing and event, showing forth the participation of fact in value, of existence in essence, of time in eternity.

But here one must be careful to indicate more precisely the meaning one attaches to words like symbol and dogma. It is imperative to distinguish between the usage here and the connotation which such words have taken on in much contemporary criticism. The post-Kantian philosophy of symbolism, though bent on scanning the highest heavens of poetic vision, accords to this vision a psychological rather than ontological validity. In such thought the universe of poetry and the universe of religion are alike construed as pure emanations of the myth-making faculty. The exponents of the new symbolism trace out in art, myth, and theology itself the lofty and whimsical structures erected by feeling and wish, structures which contain within themselves, presumably, all that can be meant by words like value and reality.

The adoption of such a philosophy of value by the creative artist in our time is one thing. It may at least serve to liberate his imagination from the strait jacket of a merely historical or scientific dialectic. But it is impossible that there should be in this visionary aesthetic any genuine comprehension of the shifting and vivid particularity of a poetry which is incarnational and existential in its innermost principle and in its various and unpredictable practice. For, as we have noted, the spirit of Christian art may not abhor the womb of matter and event. Commitment to the "wish" universe of transcendental "value" puts blinkers on our proper awareness of the multidimensional reference of Christian symbol, and cannot but miss the phenomenon of motion in the Christian firmament.

Professor Martin Foss's book *Symbol and Metaphor in Human Experience* [8] illustrates the metaphysics of this current "wish" approach to symbolism. It is the author's task to differentiate the construction of art, myth, and religion from the constructions of science and thereby to reassert the validity of nonscientific spheres of knowledge. The very term symbolism has, he believes, been pilfered by scientific rationalism and should now be abandoned wholly to it. The scientific symbol rests on the relation of the part to the whole. "At the bottom of it is the idea that the part represents the whole. . . . The part is somehow the whole, identical with the whole. It is the microcosm representing the macrocosm." [9] In the interests of intelligibility and for practical ends, infinite process is reduced by this symbolic method to fixed and finite object.

On the other hand, the method of metaphor is one of expansion rather than of reduction. The comparison, the simile and the analogy (which link the known to the unknown in a comfortable pattern and which often go by the name of metaphor), properly belong to the realm of symbolic reduction. But the true metaphorical process shatters comfortable patterns and always "widens our view beyond any limit of a special practical use." [10] Seen as "a process of tension and energy manifested in

8 (Princeton, 1949.)
9 Foss, p. 13.
10 Foss, p. 56.

the process of language, not in the single word," [11] metaphor is a creative act which annihilates the fixed symbol and the familiar relation. As such, it is the lifeblood of art, myth, and religion; it is the antithesis of the scientific symbol.

Unquestionably, this distinction between symbol and metaphor does something to correct the oversimplifications of terminology characteristic of much contemporary writing on symbolism. However, Professor Foss has no intention of correcting the oversophistication of our thinking. The nonscientific sphere of knowledge which seems to be rehabilitated by Foss's semantic method amounts finally to nothing more than psychological process with no claim whatsoever to ontological root. Symbol and metaphor alike are kept clear of any genuine implication in *being*. And metaphor is preferred to symbol because it is a wholly noncommittal process of the imagination, whereas symbol is involved in statement and even belief. One must infer that while believing can be a valid metaphorical process, belief is merely symbolic and never valid in its own stated terms and claims. For though Foss protests that symbol and metaphor are inseparable in the creative process, the symbol, and particularly the religious symbol, is always for him a formidable stumbling block. Ritual is seen to petrify myth, theology hardens the arteries of mysticism, dogma is somehow alien to the "praying man." The devil himself, we are informed, was invented by theologians to "strengthen the spirit of submission to the ritual." [12] Thus religious sensibility is approved at the cost of religious sense. If we are willing to annihilate the dogmatic content of symbol, we can perhaps continue to use words like "eternity," "immortality," and even "God"—but only in connotation of a psychological activity and in the service of "metaphorical expansion."

Such metaphysics of process, in which symbolic belief and practice exist only to be annihilated in a metaphorical holocaust, or vision, must in the end deny the ontological claim of the poetic as well as the religious symbol. By this metaphysics, poetry, like

[11] Foss, p. 61.
[12] Foss, pp. 94–95.

an apple freed from its branch, is made magically to contain that tree of the knowledge of good and evil which bore it, even to contain the serpent which in evil hour proffered it. Tree and serpent live in the plucked vision but do not, cannot, exist before it or beyond it. The theological symbol is merely the raw material of poetic vision, and no more the measure of that vision than a grain of wheat is the measure of a hot cross bun. Thus the nonscientific knowledge of reality is restored, but by the annihilation of ontological possibility in the imaginative holocaust.

For the study of Christian poetry this kind of visionary aesthetic has serious disadvantages. If such an aesthetic is applied rigorously by the critic, how will he distinguish in poetry between the pressures of a sacramental and an antisacramental theology? For surely both theologies, insofar as they enter the apple at all, have been transfigured and transcended. They are no longer what they were, and what they were can have nothing to say about what they are.

Perhaps by analogy a cardinal point in the Thomist metaphysics has some relevance just here. According to St. Thomas "the principle of individuation" resides in primary matter and not in substantial form. Similarly, the "whatness" of a poem is bound up with, even determined by, the base elements of time, place, thing, event. Even the genre is thus determined. Even the culture. The matter, the medium of poetry, and of the culture, is never annihilated or transcended by vision. It is either fulfilled or not fulfilled. If there is a flaw in the sculptor's rock, vision will not heal it. It is to the deep configurations of the medium and its matter that vision must conform and in conforming create, illuminate, and communicate. And dogma is much of the matter of Christian poetry—and much of its medium as well.

Any student of religious symbolism in these latter days must defer to the work of Edwyn Bevan.[13] He has not only distinguished for us the major levels of Christian symbol but has posed with the utmost clarity the ontological problem, the claim of sym-

13 *Symbolism and Belief* (London, Macmillan, 1938). Quoted by permission of the publishers.

bol to truth. I have already suggested that we are obliged by the very nature of seventeenth century poetry to study the firmament of symbol in which Christian poetry is conceived, the fact of motion in this firmament, and the relation of belief not only to the creation of a poem but also to the complete reading of the poem. I have noted the position of at least one "fixed star" in the Christian firmament and have indicated the kind of motion which, in a con tinuous culture, affirms the life of that firmament. The other kind of motion, that which hurries towards the dissolution of the firma- ment, the motion of the fixed star itself, is, as I have suggested, a phenomenon operating at the level of belief. By an application and further development of Bevan's principles I hope to show the relevance of belief to a full and proper awareness of the aesthetic situation in the poetry of the seventeenth century. For Bevan's treatment of symbol is pertinent to this situation in a way that more recent visionary and psychologizing treatments cannot be. This is because Bevan understands symbol as the Christian symbol- makers have always understood it. He seeks to explain rather to explain away. And it is not too much to say that the total response of the critic who approaches the symbols of Christian poetry in the terms proposed by Bevan will be radically different from the re- sponse of the critic who reads in the terms proposed by Langer, Foss, or I. A. Richards. In a later chapter I shall attempt to show the effect on Milton criticism of varying shades of belief and dis- belief in the mind of the critic. Meanwhile, I can only assert that a critical method and set of assumptions useful enough in evaluat- ing the poetry of a self-conscious and sophisticated myth-maker like W. B. Yeats are not necessarily applicable to the interpretation and evaluation of the authentic, ontologically-rooted Christian symbol in Dante, Donne, or Milton.

Bevan carefully distinguishes two major types of symbol. "There are visible objects or sounds which stand for something for which we already have direct knowledge. Such symbols are not intended to give us any information about the nature of things or things symbolized but to remind us of them. . . . The other kind of symbol purports to give information about the things they symbolize, to convey knowledge of their nature which those who see or hear the symbols have not had before or have not otherwise." [14]

In the religious tradition, incense, saint-images, ritual, belong to the first class; ideas of God to the second. Bevan regards only the second class as properly symbolic and, indeed, relegates his treatment of "holy images" to a second and separate study. [15] However, in any consideration of the religious symbol as it functions in poetry no such separation of levels is admissible. Certainly in the disturbed context of seventeenth century reform it is precisely in the shifting relation of the rhetorical to the dogmatic level of symbol that the aesthetic crisis in Christian poetry is most clearly revealed.

Bevan makes a second important distinction, this time within the dogmatic symbol itself:

> There are the symbols behind which we can see and the symbols behind which we cannot see. By the symbols behind which we can see I mean those which represent an idea which we seem to discern in a way enabling us to express it in other terms more truly. (Here the symbol is *only* a symbol and is unlike the reality it suggests.) . . . The other class of symbols are those behind which we cannot see, such as many ideas we use to represent the life of God, if, as we are told, they have only analogical and not literal truth. When we speak of the love of God we know that we are speaking of something different from any love or any will we can know in man. . . . We cannot see behind the symbol . . . we cannot compare the symbol with the reality as it is more truly apprehended and see how they differ. [16]

The dissolution of a system of religious symbolism, Bevan believes, occurs when the symbol behind which we cannot see is reduced to a symbol behind which we do see, or try to see. Perhaps this reductive process is illustrated by the extreme liberal Protestant interpretation of the Resurrection. If the Resurrection is only a symbol of the persistent power of the life and teaching of Christ,

[14] Bevan, p. 11.
[15] *Holy Images* (London, 1940).
[16] Bevan, pp. 256–257.

then the Resurrection not only ceases to be fact, it also ceases to be mystery, and the symbolic truth behind which we cannot see is thereby reduced to moral picture-writing.

Traditionally, the claim of dogmatic symbol was confirmed by the doctrine of analogy. In its fullest implications this doctrine not only guaranteed the intelligibility and ontological relevance of dogma but also, inversely, it proclaimed the dignity and validity of man and creation. Distinct as the creation is from the Creator, it is never alien to Him, and the signature of God is on all things to be read by the intelligence in the sure light of analogy.

In practice the archstone of the traditional Catholic sacramental universe is the liturgy. The whole life of Christian symbol in all its reaches is enshrined and conveyed in the rite whereby eternally the Word is made Flesh. The analogical sense of Christian symbol is perpetuated by the Eucharistic insistence on the validity of the material and temporal order. In the liturgy, the eternal sacrificial act is understood to apply to man within time. Nor does the redemptive process scorn to use those simple elements which man has fashioned into bread and wine. The symbolism of the Eucharist confirms the sacramental knowledge of thing and event, assuring to both a proper analogical dignity and worth.

It is precisely this analogical esteem for things which falters in the seventeenth century. And it is by a study of the various Protestant revisions of the liturgy that one becomes aware of the motion of anciently fixed stars—and of the consequences of the motion for the life of Christian poetry.

With Bevan's distinctions in mind, I shall attempt in my next chapter to assess the bearing of the liturgy (and the liturgical revolution) on the *capacity* of Christian symbol in English poetry of the seventeenth century. For it is through the study of the liturgy that one grasps the firmament within which Christian poetry was conceived, the firmament disrupted in the seventeenth century by a collision of energies.

The Liturgy and Poetic Symbol

CHAPTER TWO

IN THE CATHOLIC LITURGY we can discern each of the levels which Bevan believes to be characteristic of religious symbol. Here are the symbols behind which we cannot see—the Real Presence, the unbloody sacrifice. Implicated in these are the symbols behind which we *can* see—the various philosophical conceptualizations of the Mass, Augustinian and Thomist, idealist and realist. Subordinate to both the dogmatic and conceptual levels of symbol, but as necessary to both as features to a face, are the rhetorical images of the ritual.

The Holy Eucharist is the central and essential rite of Catholic Christianity. It is an act of sacrifice. And it is a corporate act. Christ the high priest through the instrumentality of the priesthood of the church offers Himself to God under the species of bread and wine. The sacrifice is simultaneously one of adoration, of petition, or propitiation, of thanksgiving. It is a renewal, mystical and unbloody, of the sacrifice of the Cross. The presence of Christ on the sacrificial altar is objective and real. In the action of the Eucharist the blessed bread is broken to be shared that we, being many, may be made one body. In the words of the great Anglican liturgist Dom Gregory Dix "it is of the deepest meaning of the rite that those who take part are thereby united indissolubly with one another and with all who are Christ's because

[28]

(*hoti*) each is thereby united with Him and through Him with the Father with Whom He is One." [1]

The corporate character of the Eucharist will engage our attention later. It must first be borne in mind that the dogma of the Real Presence was accepted from the very beginning of the church and is implicit in both the symbolic and realist conceptualizations of Eucharistic theology. The dogma is grounded in the New Testament not only in the actual words of institution [2] but also in the Gospel of St. John. [3]

It is developed by patristic writers, both Latin and Greek. St. Justin Martyr affirms that "the food eucharisticised by the prayer of the word which has come from him . . . is the flesh and blood of the same incarnate Jesus." [4] St. Irenaeus believes that the earthly bread after consecration is no longer earthly but Eucharist. [5] Even more explicit is St. Cyril of Jerusalem: ". . . do not contemplate the bread and wine as bare [elements], for they are, according to the Lord's declaration, Christ's body and blood, for even though sense suggests this to thee, yet the faith establish thee . . . These things having learned, and being fully persuaded that what seems bread is not bread, even though sensible to the taste, but Christ's body, and what seems wine is not wine, even though the taste will have it so, but Christ's blood . . . strengthen thy heart." [6]

E. C. Messenger is ready to admit that "there are ambiguous phrases here and there in the writings of some of the Fathers and that, in particular, there was one group of writers in the fifth century who, in arguing against the Monophysites, used language and arguments which seem to imply the permanence of the substance of bread and wine after the consecration." [7] But Messenger

---

[1] *The Shape of the Liturgy* (London, Dacre Press, 1945), p. 1.
[2] Corinthians, xi, 27–29.
[3] vi, 49–52, 54–59, 61, 63, 64, 67.
[4] *Apology*, I, 65.
[5] *Adv. Haeres*, IV, viii, 5.
[6] *Catech.*, iv, 319–322.
[7] *The Reformation, the Mass and the Priesthood* (London, Longmans Green, 1936), I, p. 13. Quoted by permission of the publishers. The above passages from Justin Martyr, Irenaeus, and Cyril are quoted by Messenger, pp. 10–13.

has no difficulty in proving that the group, Nestorian in bias, was not in the main line of patristic thought.

Dom Gregory Dix is in full agreement with Messenger's interpretation of the patristic view of the Real Presence.

> . . . when Tertullian speaks of bread whereby Christ makes His very body to be present [*Adv. Marc.* 1.14] he uses in the word *repraesentat* ("he makes present") a term which for him and for other early Latin Christian writers makes a particular association or "overtone" which is very significant.
>
> "Repraesentatio" is the word by which Tertullian elsewhere describes that "coming" of God's kingdom for which we pray in the Lord's prayer *(de Oratione. 5.)* He uses it more than once of the second coming of our Lord to judgment, visibly and with power. The "theophanies" or manifestations of God in the Old Testament like those in the burning bush and at Sinai, are *repraesentationes.* The Son is manifested by the voice of the Father at the Transfiguration *repraesentans eum,* "declaring him"—This is My Son." The second fruition of God in the life to come by *repraesentatio et possessio* ("manifestation and possession") is contrasted with the obscure laying hold of Him by hope which is all that we can have in this world. Tertullian declares that the *repraesentatio* (physical presence) of Christ in His earthly life is what the apostles saw and were blessed in seeing. . . . [*Adv. Marc.* iv. 25.] [8]

Obviously, then, the Tertullian sense is not conveyed at all by the English word "represent." Our use of the word denies the actuality of the object. Tertullian's use affirms it. Consequently, Dix is careful to caution us against a sophisticated modern reading of such terms as symbol, figure, and antitype when applied by the Fathers to the sacrament of the Body and Blood of Christ. He notes than even Harnack, whom no one will suspect of Catholic leanings, admits the literal core of actuality in the patristic sense of the word symbol. "What we nowadays understand by a 'symbol' is a thing which is not that which it represents; at that time 'symbol' denoted a thing which in some kind of way really is what it signifies." [9]

---

[8] Dix, p. 825.
[9] Adolph Harnack, *History of Dogma* (2nd ed., 1888), I, p. 397.

The Fathers, while stopping short of systematic definition, evidently regarded the sacramental rite of the church as consisting of some external action or words constituting a sign by which an internal reality or grace was not only expressed or signified but also conferred. It was, of course, St. Augustine who made the distinction between the element, matter, or action of the sacrament, and the words used in its administration. The matter is in itself indeterminate, becoming sacramental, completing itself, only in the words of the rite. Later, the scholastics were to rationalize this distinction as one of matter and form. The telling point for our purposes is this: the efficacy and actuality of the sacraments, including the sacrament of the Holy Eucharist, were intended and maintained in the Platonic symbolist theology of the Fathers as fully if not as forcibly as in the later Aristotelian theology of the scholastics. The attempt, so frequently made since the sixteenth century, to identify the Protestant theology of the sacraments with the earlier Platonic tradition, to see the Protestant view as a simple purification of an overliteral scholasticism, springs from a misunderstanding of the nature of symbolism as such and from an inability to distinguish the dogmatic from the conceptual level of the specifically sacramental symbol. It is a misunderstanding which is far-reaching in its consequences for poetry as well as for theology. For it is a misunderstanding which, by reducing irreducible dogma to the level of speculative notion and then, by an abandonment of ritual separating even such pale notion from the flesh of fact and the flow of history, results in abstracting the faith from all possible existential experience.

From the earliest times, two conceptual traditions, the symbolic and the realist, sought to convey the one Catholic dogma of the Real Presence. In its main implications, the symbolic view, firmly established in the West by St. Augustine, was already held by Tertullian. In this view, the sign and the thing signified are indeed distinguished but, as we have noted, they are distinguished only to be united. The sign *commands* the presence—and the effect—of the thing signified. However, the difference between patristic and scholastic conceptualization of dogma is so great that real difficulties occur in any collation of dogmatic definitions. Do the following statements clash?

This is from the modern *Catholic Encyclopedia:* "The Body given to the Apostles [at the Last Supper] was the self-same body that was crucified on Good Friday; and the chalice drunk by them, the self-same blood that was shed on the Cross for our sins." [10]

And this is St. Augustine: "Christ at the Last Supper instructed His Apostles, saying, 'Understand spiritually that which I have spoked; ye are not about to eat this Body which ye see, nor are ye about to drink this Blood which these men shall shed who will crucify Me.'" [11]

Obviously there is a difference between these two statements. But it is not the difference between a literal carnalism on the one hand and a merely figurative spiritism on the other. The difference is not one of dogma at all but one of conceptualization. From the earliest times, the symbolists, shaping their concepts in the Platonic mould, sought to preserve the dogma of the Real Presence from any possibility of a crude or carnal interpretation. They did so, as we have noted, by emphasizing the distinction between the sign and the thing signified, and also by affirming the actual presence *in* the sign *of* the thing signified. The statement just quoted from St. Augustine protects the dogma of the Eucharist from any suspicion of carnalism. In effect, and in the context of St. Augustine's concepts, the statement conveys this: that the Presence of the Body and Blood of Christ in the sacrament, while Real, is veiled from the natural faculties of men and is apprehended only by the spiritual faculties, by faith. To put it more vulgarly, the natural Body of Christ is not to be licked and tasted by the natural tongues of men. The sacramental Presence, though it is the *Whole* Presence, transcends in a mystery the human powers of apprehension. St. Augustine's symbolism directs

[10] V, 575a (New York, 1909).
[11] *Enarr. in Psalmum*, XCVIII, 9.

the pious towards the contemplation of the spiritual efficacy of
the Presence and away from futile speculation as to the natural
mode of the Presence.

The actual doctrinal definition of transubstantiation was written by the Fourth Lateran Council in 1215. This doctrine was and
is a synthesis of both the symbolic and realist conceptualizations
of the Eucharist. It insists that the Body and Blood of Christ are
truly present on the altar under the appearance of bread and wine.
With the help of Aristotelian metaphysics, the schoolmen were
able to arrive at a conceptualization of dogma which seemed to
take account of all sides of the question and to affirm the actuality
of Christ's Presence without denying the symbolic mode. The
Lateran pronouncement came none too soon. Throughout the
earlier Middle Ages there had been a rash of muddled and one-
sided conceptualizations of Eucharistic dogma. The extreme symbolist view which reduced the Presence to a figure of speech was
opposed by equally heterodox realist denials of the symbolic
mode of the sacrament. Ultrarealist views underlie the popular
mediaeval superstitions about the Eucharist—visions of the Bleeding Child on the altar, or the terrifying taste of the divine-human
blood in the chalice.

The patristic Eucharist was conceived as a corporate act of
sacrifice by Christ and His church in which time was annihilated
and *through* which the eternity of the Risen Son was not only
revealed but experienced. Patristic concern was with the whole
experiential action of the Eucharist. The separation, by opposing
schools of thought in the eleventh century, of the literal from the
various allegorical levels of the symbolic whole, indicates the
growing weariness of the patristic methodology and need of a
full metaphysics to sustain the profound symbolic intentions of
the Fathers.

There can be no doubt that the scholastic development came
in answer to such a need. By the thirteenth century the pressure
of new knowledge and the growing complexity and fluidity of
society itself demanded not only a clear and distinct account of

the faith but also a comprehensive statement of its relevance to philosophy, to science, to all learning, to all experience. At the metaphysical level, the Augustinian tradition could not cope with the sudden new deluge of ideas and facts. A fresh ordering of thought was inevitable. Inevitable, also, was a reconceptualization of ancient and unalterable dogma. But it must be emphasized that the scholastic philosophy of the Eucharist no more contradicts the symbolic than it does the realist mode of describing the mystery. By using the Aristotelian distinction between *substance* and *accidents,* the Thomists were able to conceive of Christ's Presence in the sacrament as nonlocal and nonmaterial. Place, relation, quality, quantity, and all properties subject to chemical or physical analysis are *accidents*. The underlying reality to which the accidents are attached is the *substance*. The theory that the substance of the bread and wine is transformed into the substance of Christ satisfied the realist view of a true conversion of the elements; the theory that the outer accidents of the bread and wine remained (but were not as such the substance of the Natural Christ) corresponded to the symbolist insistence that outwardly the sacrament is a sign and that the sign is no mere illusion (as the ultrarealists would have it to be). The virtue of the Thomist formulation is that it avoids at once the carnal emphasis of the ultrarealists and the merely figurative symbolism of the post-Augustinians.

It must be emphasized once more that a real distinction obtains between a dogma and any conceptualization of it. St. Augustine and St. Thomas are both orthodox. The nominalist attack on Thomist metaphysics is not heretical. In itself Occam's rejection of the Aristotelian categories of substance and accidents is not in the province of heresy at all. Not yet. Even Descartes, who is forced by his philosophy to treat the accidents as sense-illusion, remains a Catholic and searches desperately for a new rationalization of a dogma which he continues to respect *as dogma*. It is only when dogma itself is questioned and denied that nominalist and Cartesian concepts can be turned effectively against the ancient belief.

I have stressed the centrality of the Real Presence in Eucharistic dogma not only because it is important in mediaeval and Reformation polemic but also because it inevitably forms the point of crisis at which the symbolic levels of dogma and concept touch. As it specifies the relation of symbol to truth, the dogma of the Real Presence controls the symbolic significance of the Eucharistic rite. The separation in the minds of the Reformers of symbol from truth-as-fact was to destroy the symbolic reach of the Eucharist by reducing it from corporate and objective act to individual subjective recollection. But it yet remains to outline here more fully the ramifications of Eucharistic symbol at the actual level of dogma itself. I am not at this point concerned with the secondary rhetorical symbols which multiplied in the late mediaeval period and which were codified by Durandus. But it is necessary to make a clear distinction between the absolute symbolism of the Mass and all such conceptualizations of the Mass as may be appropriate to a particular cultural moment. The distinction I wish to make between dogmatic and conceptual symbol can best be grasped in terms of an examination of the Mass as Sacrifice, as Corporate Act, as Communion, and as bridge between eternity and time, between mystical fulfillment and natural fact.

It is, of course, none of my purpose to recount (or to judge) the proofs from Scripture and tradition offered in support of the Catholic dogma of the Mass as true sacrifice. Very simply, the Mass in Catholic theology is the perpetual renewal, in a mystical and unbloody manner, of the one sacrifice of the Cross, which, with the balm of pain, healed the wound separating God from man, heaven from earth. Catholic dogma has never maintained that the sacrifice of the Mass added merit to the sacrifice of the Cross or rendered fresh satisfaction for the sins of the world. Rather, the Mass makes present the very Christ who had promised to be with His church always, makes present the Redeemer in His eternal act of redemption. Through the Mass the merits of the Cross are *applied*. Eternity empties itself in time.

The Mass is corporate. The Body of Christ, the church, offers itself "to become the sacrificial Body of Christ, the sacrament, in order that thereby the Church itself may become within time what in eternal reality it is before God." [12] St. Augustine and St. Thomas are wholly in accord in the belief that the sacrificial act and the fruits thereof must be understood in corporate terms.

> The city of the redeemed itself, the congregation and society of the saints, is offered as an universal sacrifice to God by the High-priest, Who offered even Himself in suffering for us in the form of a servant, that we might be the Body of so great a Head. . . . This is the sacrifice of Christians, "the many one Body in Christ," which thing also the Church celebrates in the Sacrament of the altar, familiar to the faithful, wherein it is shewn to her that in this thing which she offers she herself is also offered to God.[13]

And prior to all individual spiritual benefits and, indeed, *determining* all such benefits to souls, is, in the insistent assertion of St. Thomas, "the unity of the Mystical Body," [14] the renewed sense of the church *becoming what she is,* the single Bride of Christ.

The Eucharist is, then, at once the sacrifice of Christ and of the church. The church offers herself in union with Christ. To quote St. Augustine again: "The whole body of the redeemed, that is, the society and communion of saints, is presented to God as joint sacrifice by the High-Priest who in His passion also offered Himself for us in form of a servant that we might become members of so exalted a Head." [15]

Nature, and man's labour in partnership with nature, are offered in the oblation of the bread and wine. Here, symbols of the creation and man's creative activity upon it—the physical ground of man's life and the free exertion of his spirit—are offered and then joined to the eternal sacrifice which heals and restores the orders broken by the sin of Adam, the order of nature, the order of work. In the mystical action of the Mass, science and

[12] Dix, p. 247.
[13] *De Civ. Dei,* X, 6.
[14] Cf. Dix, pp. 247 ff.
[15] *De Civ. Dei.,* 1, 10, c, 6, 20.

society become what they are: once again man's toil is consecrated; once again the soil in which he labours can yield forsaken fruit.

In the fullest dogmatic sense, the act of communion is inseparable from sacrifice and the corporate offering. Rather than a reception of individual benefits it is a way of participation, corporately, in the life of the Holy Trinity.

Insisting that the Eucharist is ontologically joined to the mystery of the Incarnation just as the mystery of the Incarnation is joined to the Trinity, Father Scheeben finds the supernatural organism of the mysteries of Christianity to consist in this:

> . . . the mystery of the Godhead, the inner communication of the divine nature, prolongs and reproduces itself exteriorly. It is projected into the outside world so far as the Son of God assumes a created, human nature, and imparts to it, in His person and as belonging to Him, the substantial union and unity that He Himself has with His Father. Not only this one human nature, however, but the whole human race is to enter into closest union with God. To bring this union about the Son of God, made man, unites Himself to us in His humanity in the most intimate substantial fashion to form one body with us, as He Himself is One Spirit with His Father. . . . Our substantial union with the Godman is an image of the substantial union between the Son and the Father. Thus our participation in the divine nature and divine life becomes a reproduction of the fellowship in nature and life which the Son has with the Father.[16]

Such participation and union cannot, Scheeben believes, be achieved outside the Eucharistic act. By the Incarnation we are no longer adopted sons of God but are received into the onlybegotten Son as His members. In the Eucharist we are bound the more closely to Christ "for he has not only taken His flesh from our flesh but he returned to us the flesh that he assumed."[17] In the Eucharist, therefore, we have our life from God's substance.

In the highest dogmatic sense, then, the Eucharist is a unified

---

[16] Mathias Joseph Scheeben, S. J., *The Mysteries of Christianity*, trans. Cyril Vollert, S. J. (St. Louis, Herder, 1946), pp. 1188–1189.

[17] Scheeben, p. 1189.

act in which sacrifice and communion are inextricably one. Exclusive attention, in late mediaeval speculation and practice, to the notion of sacrifice is as one-sided as the later Protestant concentration on communion *apart* from sacrifice. In its fullest intention the Eucharist is clearly eschatological, lifting the whole body of the faithful out of history and into that ultimate relation with God for which man was created. And this is not in any degree an escape from history. In discovering—and experiencing—the end for which he was created (an end *beyond* history), man also discovers that he must fulfill himself *within* history. He is called eternally to redeem the time. The dogmatic theology of the Eucharist is at once mystical and practical. Time is to be fulfilled and not transcended. In this fruitful tension which dogma proclaims between eternity and time there is no support either for an idealistic otherworldliness or for a materialistic immersion in the natural and the historical processes. There is room neither for an easy utopianism nor for a stoic despair. The entry of the Mystical Body into the life of the Trinity is a reordering of nature and history in terms of the final end of creation. But the Eucharist does not melt matter into pure spirit or make angels out of men in history. The sacramental strategy is to respect, while it re-infuses, the created handiwork of God. The Word is made Flesh. The sacrament of the altar is fleshly. And from it, like ever-widening circles from the rock dropped at the centre of the dark pool, flows the sacramental principle, reclaiming place and time, but destroying nothing. Nature is consecrated and renovated by the sacramental action. And so the church, exorcising the bane of the usurper, makes over to her own spiritual uses the things of nature and time—food and drink, water and oil, salt and incense. Flowing from the Eucharist in its deepest incarnational integrity is the liturgy and ritual of the church, and all the craft of stone and sound and word. Flowing, too, from the sacrament of the altar is the active social doctrine of St. Thomas Aquinas and the contemplative spirituality of the Cistercian and the Carthusian. Opposites converge and fuse in the supernatural life endowed by an act which is at once of the flesh and of the spirit, of time and of eternity. Such, at least, is the intent.

But this has been a description of the ideal situation, the Eucharistic intention, and one might protest that such an intention is not easily realized in flesh and fact. Indeed, the realization has been and will be imperfect. It is here that one must recognize that purest dogma can be and has been distorted or at least thwarted by inept conceptualization and inappropriate ritual. The decline of the mediaeval order of faith may be traced in a growing disharmony between the dogmatic, conceptual, and rhetorical levels of Eucharistic symbol and act. In other words, one can observe in the dissolution of the Christian culture a process of dissociation between faith, thought, and art. The conditions which bred the Reformation were in gestation for centuries. However (and this is of the greatest importance for my thesis), it is not until Luther, not until dogma itself is altered, that the Christian firmament of symbol reels and rocks. As we have already noted, the firmament within which Christian poetry had moved during the Ages of Faith was compounded of nature and grace, action and contemplation, matter and spirit. The tension between opposing principles, the structural stress of this firmament, issued from the Eucharistic mystery itself, and is most fully articulated in the Thomist doctrine of analogy.

The disintegration of this firmament is characterized by a loss of tension, by a springing apart of grace and nature, action and contemplation, matter and spirit. In the period of disintegration there is evident, on the one hand, "ecclesiastical materialism," a proliferation of ritual by energies of its own without deference to dogma. On the other hand, there is evident a drift towards a disembodied mysticism which detaches itself from ritual, spurning the order of fact and thus, despite the purest intentions, wounding the heart of dogma. We must be on our guard against confusing what might be called a post-Eucharistic mysticism with the mysticism of a St. Bernard or a St. John of the Cross. Similarly, we must not confuse a post-Eucharistic ritualism with the ritualism of a St. Thomas Aquinas. Laudian ceremonialism, for instance, must not be equated with a fully Catholic sacramentalism. In any comparison of Catholic and Anglican ritual, the dogmatic core of Eucharistic symbol must be seen in relation to the shifting and conflicting levels of concept and rhetoric.

Certainly, the conceptual squabble worsened in the late Middle Ages, and philosophy did little to cure popular superstition or to make its own conceptualizations of dogma transparent to the gaze of the mind. And in the same period, ritual, by a merely fanciful process of elaboration, began to obscure the inner dogmatic intention of the Mass as with a shroud. It is perhaps inevitable that liturgy, fashioned by its very nature to the popular sensibility, will undergo cultural change and development and take on what seems to be a life of its own, a purely rhetorical being. W. H. Frere is our best guide to what happens at the rhetorical level of Eucharistic symbol.

> The broad general outlines of the history of ceremonial controversy have something to teach by way of caution and patience. Disturbances of this class seem to recur in cycles, and one phase of them follows upon another in a more or less regular sequence. The full cycle may be expressed by these divisions: first comes a period of experiment or innovation; after this has continued for some time, as the controversy attendant upon it dies down, there follows a period of consolidation and settlement; finally comes a period of quiet, tending to stagnation and formalism, before the cycle begins to recur. This general description is not uniformly accurate: a cycle may be interrupted or partial, or the periods may co-exist or overlap: but history gives continual instances of such an alteration in some such form and sequence.[18]

Frere observes such a cycle as this in the Pauline church. Another begins in the Carolingian period with the introduction of Roman ceremonial to the Frankish Empire. An era of experiment followed, until in the twelfth century there began a long age of quiet inevitably tending to stagnation and formalism. The

---

[18] *Principles of Religious Ceremonial* (A. R. Mowbray, London, and Morehouse-Gorham, New York, 1928), p. 3.

Reformation brought this cycle to a close and inaugurated a new cycle.

> The sixteenth century in England exhibits in rapid succession the familiar trio: innovation in no small degree and with no little controversy, followed by partial settlement under Archbishop Parker in the early part of Elizabeth's reign, and a brief period of comparative quiet under Archbishop Whitgift at the end of the century and the reign. With the new century the cycle began afresh: part was full of experiment and innovation; bitter controversy followed until the crisis came of the Laudian era and the Great Rebellion; settlement was not reached till the Restoration, and then followed the Hanoverian torpor.[19]

It would be possible, I believe, to trace similar cycles in the nineteenth century Anglo-Catholic revival and in the modern liturgical movement of the Roman Catholic Church. Without doubt the formal rhetoric of the liturgy undergoes changes which appear in cyclical patterns. And the greatest threat to the inner dogmatic symbol usually appears at the end of the cycle, at the stage of formalism and torpor. However, two significant qualifications must be made to this theory of the inevitable cycle. First, the cycles observed by Frere are seldom if ever self-contained or conclusive. There is continuity of one kind or another between them. Between the Pauline and Carolingian cycles there is clearly a continuity of dogma. There is also a discernible continuity of form, although the later cycle is marked by an overwhelming elaboration of the formal and rhetorical element. Similarly there is doctrinal continuity between the Parker and Laudian phases of the Anglican cycle, with a characteristic elaboration of the rhetorical element in the later phase.

However (and this is a decisive point), there is a revolutionary leap between the Catholic and the Reformation cycles, and this leap occurs at the level of dogmatic symbol. Contrast the rapid motion of the two Reformation cycles outlined by Frere with the slow assimilative gait of the mediaeval cycle. The explanation of the difference in tempo is obvious. The motion of the mediaeval

---

[19] Frere, pp. 1–5.

cycle is always restrained by the compulsions of orthodoxy. The Pauline dogma and rhetoric are absorbed and developed. But the relative stability of Eucharistic theology throughout the mediaeval period helps to freeze rhetorical convention, just as it protects even advanced nominalist speculation from final heresy.

But why the lightning movement of the second group of cycles? It is to be explained by the nature of the Reformation inheritance from the mediaeval cycle. The Reformation did not seek to absorb the mediaeval movement in the way that the Carolingian cycle had absorbed the Pauline. Rather it sought to repudiate the mediaeval past and to return, in varying degrees, to primitive or, at the very least, to patristic practice. There is in this Reformation movement no genuine stability of dogma but an uncertain vacillation between Lutheran, Calvinist, and Zwinglian opinion. The quick pace of this cycle is therefore not the result of a natural development in concept and rhetoric but of an artificial effort to adjust, in all haste, recent innovations in dogma to such fragments of ancient ritual as could be hurriedly disinfected of the popish taint. The reappearance of altar and crucifix in the Laudian cathedral is by no means a reversion to popery. Nevertheless, the liturgical past is not easily dismissed wholesale. And Christian poetry in the Caroline period is plainly marked by the confused contention of traditional and novel images, beliefs, and ideas.

Such continuity as does exist between the mediaeval cycle and the hurried and confused liturgical cycles of the Reformation period is merely fragmentary. The difference obtaining between these cycles is the difference between two firmaments: one, no matter how clouded it may have become, still with the single, fixed sun at its centre; the other a flashing medley of light and dark in which every star becomes a sun, until the centre can no longer be located.

Is this brilliant chaos the consequence of a simple purification of mediaeval errors in worship and dogma? One doubts it. But one may not doubt that there did occur a deterioration of symbol within the mediaeval cycle itself. Is the Protestant revision of the liturgy perhaps a further stage in the breakdown of the Catholic cultural pattern?

It is true that the dogmatic core of the Mass was always threatened by inadequate and inconsistent conceptualization as well as by the persistent aesthetic tendency to play the game of rhetoric for its own sake. Whatever the purist may say, style is seldom for long the servant of content. It would seem that the tendency of style to achieve its own autonomy is one of the sure marks of decadence. And the elaboration of Eucharistic rhetoric in the High Middle Ages, though splendid, ingenious, and exuberant, is nonetheless decadent. This process of elaboration occurs in two main ways: in the actual ceremony of the Mass itself and in the symbolic interpretation of the form and surface of the rite. Particularly in the country of the Franks, Germans, and Celts, the Mass was soon decked out with a sumptuousness foreign to the Roman usage. "The ceremonial element of the liturgy flourished, borrowing from imperial courts the marks of homage customary in the Orient or in a feudal system. . . . From the Orient came the fondness for multiple incensation, which in Rome had been reserved for the entry of the Pope and for the reading of the gospel. . . . The reading of the gospel also developed into an elaborate processional rite in which incensation, lights and acclamations combined to make the carrying of the sacred books a triumphant cortege leading to the major ambo." [20]

The elaboration of the ceremony meant inevitably a reduction of the role of the laity in the ritual action. More and more the action of the Mass became the action of the celebrant only. Thus the essential corporateness of the Mass in practice, if not in theory, was lost to view. Finally, such a decline in practice could not but threaten dogma itself. And almost immediately the concept (as distinct from the ultimate dogma) of the Mass was affected by this decadent movement at the rhetorical level of symbol. In-

[20] Paul Doncoeur, S. J., "Lessons in Eucharistic History," *Orate Fratres* (June, 1949), pp. 351–362. The entire article is relevant to my point.

creasingly, as the participation of the laity in the action of the Mass diminished, the priestly act of consecration was understood to be the essence of the rite. Here we can detect a fascinating process of interaction between the rhetorical and conceptual levels of Eucharistic symbol. The mediaeval debate over the doctrine of transubstantiation had focused attention on the actual moment of consecration. At the same time rhetorical expansion had reduced the role of the laity in the overt practice of the rite. Thus by a conjunction of conceptual and rhetorical pressures the layman had little more to do than "hear Mass" and see "the Host."

Dogma is not unaffected by this development at the rhetorical and conceptual levels of Eucharistic symbol. In the twelfth century theologians emphasized the presence of "the total Christ" in the consecrated wafer. Now such a dogmatic development, taken by itself, is orthodox enough. Nor can there be found anything contrary to the proper dogmatic implications of the Catholic Eucharist in the devotional consequences of such an emphasis— the Elevation of the Host, the exposition of the Blessed Sacrament, the procession of Corpus Christi. Indeed, these rich ramifications of the Eucharist carried the benediction of the sacramental Christ into every nook and cranny of mediaeval life, and it might even be argued with considerable force that the loss of lay participation in the Mass was offset by this projection of the sacramental life into the very streets and fields. For if the formal rite of the thirteenth century is less corporate in practice than the liturgy demanded, surely the popular life of the age was more thoroughly imbued with a corporate sacramentalism than the life of any age before or since.

In all fairness, too, it must be recognized that this decline in the corporate action of the Mass was neither as rapid nor as complete as modern commentators like Dom Gregory Dix would have us believe. To begin with, the liturgy itself, no matter what practical abuses may have occurred, articulated in fixed accents the real participation of the whole body of the faithful, living and dead. Nevertheless, we have sufficient evidence to be sure that religious individualism did not originate with the Reformation. Certainly by the late Middle Ages lay devotion had been in some measure detached from the corporate and objective action of the Mass and had turned towards an interior piety, towards a subjective kind of contemplation. Ceremonialism had apparently bred its opposite: a predominantly nonritualistic cult of interior devotion.

But it is surprising to find the Reformers counterattacked for their emphasis on the corporate nature of the Eucharist. It is an anomaly so startling that it gives us pause before leaping to Dom Gregory Dix's view that the individualism and subjectivity of Protestant worship are the natural outgrowth of late mediaeval theory and practice. We cannot have it both ways. Protestantism can scarcely be at one and the same time the innocent victim of a late mediaeval individualism and the champion of a properly corporate worship. We soon recollect that Cranmer's theology is utterly subjective and individualist and that he sought greater intelligibility for the rite, not in the interests of corporate participation in the Sacrifice of the Mass but in the interest of a clear and forthright destruction of the very possibility of corporate sacrifice and communion. The dogmatic issue is obscured for a while by the bitter sixteenth century debate over usage, over rhetoric. In a period of great unrest, at the very moment of exhaustion in the great liturgical cycle of the Middle Ages, at the point, too, in the life of ideas when Catholic dogma was almost wholly unprotected by the shield of metaphysics, it is not strange that the movement of reform failed to distinguish clearly between the dogmatic, conceptual, and rhetorical levels of Eucharistic symbol. Nor is it strange that excited attacks levelled against the overrefined surfaces of rhetoric and concept should blunder through to the citadel of dogma itself.

Paradoxically enough, Luther, who began his opposition to the Church with a proper indignation against sacramental and practical abuses, was quite willing to retain much of the sensuous rhetoric of the Catholic Mass. On the face of it, he seems less Protestant than Calvin in his restatement of Eucharistic dogma. Yet, beyond question, his doctrine of "justification by faith alone" is the decisive concept of the Reform and is, in particular, wholly destructive of traditional Eucharistic dogma and the sacramentalism that flows from it. The Lutheran doctrine of justification, conceived originally as a corrective to what had become a mechanical reliance on good works, cuts out the heart of the Catholic theology. It denies the efficacy of human reason and abolishes the Catholic view of sanctification, the view that man, bending his own will to the compulsion of grace, is indeed sainted. For Luther, of course, original sin is total in its effect. Man's sin is incurable. Even his good works are no more than blasphemous presumption. Only the act of faith, the belief in God's mercy and the redemptive sacrifice of Christ, can save him from damnation. The sinner in being saved does not become holy. He remains as corrupt as Adam. Christ's righteousness does not begin to live within him. It is merely imputed to him, and God, for the sake of His Son's sacrifice and pain, winks, presumably, at the ugly reality.

This transaction is felt in the heart of the believer. It is an utterly subjective phenomenon. As Dom Gregory Dix points out, the Catholic view of the church was destroyed at one stroke by the exclusively emotional and interior nature of this novel doctrine. "The idea of The Church was reduced to the only one compatible with Protestantism—it was regarded chiefly as the divinely founded society for continually proclaiming the history of redemption as it happened long ago in Judaea, and so challenging every individual to make the personal act of faith which alone serves." [21]

Obviously, this view opposes the Catholic dogma of the church as the Mystical Body of Christ, as the extension in time of the Incarnation. The church becomes a mere organization, retained as an expedient. The sacraments, the living arteries of the Mysti-

[21] *The Question of Anglican Orders* (London, 1944), pp. 23–24.

cal Body, could have no final or necessary claim to validity in the Protestant system. Sacraments are retained as mere tokens of an economy of salvation which operates only in the deep interior of the individual belief. The *ex opere operato* efficacy—and integrity—of the Mass thus becomes wholly inconceivable. In effect, the sacraments are to become little more than relatively useful stimuli to the emotions of faith.

By the very fact that it can exist only within its own feeling for itself, this new religious individualism constitutes far more than a denial of particular Catholic dogmas; it effectively denies the possibility of any dogma as a symbol "behind which we cannot see." It denies the possibility of dogmatic objectivity. It not only annihilates the Catholic Eucharistic symbols; it ensures that no religious symbol can have more than a personal psychological force or reference.

We may justly complain that late mediaeval speculation on the nature of the Eucharist injured the popular understanding of dogma and therefore contributed indirectly to the strange distortions of dogma in the theology of the Reformers. But we must remember that the Catholic tradition, though it allowed wide freedom of speculation, always maintained a sharp distinction between dogma and pious opinion. One of the tasks of the Council of Trent was to restate dogma as dogma, and in such a fashion as to underscore its autonomy and its independence of changing fashions in speculation. But the subjective individualism of the Reform could scarcely pretend to any distinction between dogma and opinion. It is instructive to observe how Luther's own conceptualization of the Eucharist hopped from one level of opinion to another as the import of his doctrine of justification took hold of him. In 1523 he brought out a new Latin Mass, the *Formula Missae et Communionis*. His main concern at this time was to eliminate from the liturgy anything suggesting the sacrificial character of the Mass. However, he retained an emphasis on the reality of Christ's Presence on the altar. When Zwingli attacked the formula as a concession to Catholic superstition,

Luther replied with his "doctrine of Christ's Ubiquity." As Christ is everywhere, he is already in the bread and wine, already in the soul of the believer. The function of the Eucharistic act is therefore not to effect a real change in the elements but to deepen in the believer an awareness of Christ's Presence. Such an argument defends the Real Presence by abolishing it. And, logically, it abolishes the Eucharist except as a stimulant to individual perception. Gone, of course, is the analogical awareness of the simultaneous Presence of the Mystical, the Historical, and the Glorified Body of Christ. Gone is the corporate sense of participation in the redemptive act. There is left a simple univocal sense of an almost pantheistic Christ, to be apprehended only by religious feeling.

In the Augsburg Confession of 1530, Luther affirmed the Real Presence of Christ under the species of bread and wine. By 1540 he is asserting that Christ is not present *under* the bread and wine but is *exhibited together with* the bread and wine. The word exhibited is sufficiently vague to allow the Zwinglian interpretation of a token Presence. It should be noted, too, that the revised Confession of 1540 specifically repudiates the Mass as sacrifice other than as the sacrifice of praise and thanksgiving.

The Lutheran revision struck at the very possibility of objective Eucharistic dogma; it specifically eliminated the Catholic dogma of sacrifice, reduced the liturgy to the status of a pious stimulus, and shattered the ancient eschatological reach of the Mass. Christ's death happened a long way off a long time ago. It is to be remembered. It cannot be experienced. Eternity cannot puncture time.

And a strange phenomenon has taken place, one with vast implications for poetry, particularly for Anglican poetry. As we have noted, Luther's key doctrine of justification undermined the whole sacramental tradition. But Luther retains not only the gestures of the sacramental system but also much of the sacramental rhetoric of Catholicism. Unlike Calvin, Luther sees no blasphemy in the sacred use of pictures and statues. Ceremonial is permis-

[48]

sible. There is no harm in exploiting the five senses of the praying man. Let there be incense! And Luther can talk of the Real Presence in what seems to be Catholic language, although his meaning is far from Catholic.

Obviously, the retention by Luther of ceremonial and some of the formal rhetoric of the sacraments must not be interpreted in a Catholic sense. Luther permits sensuous worship as a stimulus to feeling, as a lure appropriate to the fallen nature of the heirs of Adam. But this retention of the Catholic surface, of the rhetorical symbol detached from dogma, confuses and complicates the new Protestant firmament and, particularly in Anglican usage, blurs all proper distinction between dogma, concept, and rhetoric.

In general, Anglicanism followed Luther in his contention that any rite or symbol is permissible that is not specifically condemned by Scripture. But from the earliest days of the Elizabethan settlement, Calvinist and Zwinglian objections to the use of sensuous ceremony arose within the Anglican communion. Image-breakers repudiated with violence all the "badges of popery." We shall observe within Anglicanism, at all the levels of symbol, a strange and uneasy tension between Catholic sacramentalism, Lutheran pseudo-sacramentalism, and thoroughgoing Puritan antisacramentalism. It is therefore necessary to assess briefly the Calvinist and Zwinglian contributions to this difficult new Protestant firmament of symbol.

Zwingli completed the destruction of the Catholic firmament of symbol. In his thought, symbol and fact are fully and finally put apart.

> The body and blood of Christ are nothing else than the word of faith, namely that His body which died for us and His blood which was shed for us on the Cross, redeemed us.[22]

> In the Holy Eucharist the real body of Christ is present by the contemplation of faith. Thus it is, those who give thanks to the Lord for the benefit conferred on us in His Son, recognize

[22] *Opus Articulorum*, Art. xviii. *Opera* (1581), i, 37.

[49]

that He took real flesh, that in it He really suffered, that He
really washed away our sins by His blood, so that everything done
by Christ becomes as it were present to them by the contemplation
of faith.[23]

"The real body of Christ is present," but only by "the contemplation of faith." The memory of the real is substituted for the real
as such. Psychological act replaces ontological fact. Yet the old
Catholic words are still used. Here, surely, is an instance of the decline of symbol into metaphor, of the unfleshing of the word.
Here we look behind a symbol behind which we cannot look, and
we see exactly what we want to see.

How elusive the word now is! Luther, to our confusion, retains
the sacramental symbol shorn of its sacramental reference. Zwingli,
too Puritan by far to suffer the sweet smoke of a pagan popery,
keeps to the language of the Eucharist even as it dissolves on his
tongue. The verbal universe of seventeenth century Christian
poetry is therefore unimaginably treacherous, nor is it afforded
any real stability by Calvin's attempt to find a middle ground between Luther and Zwingli. Unsympathetic alike to Zwingli's abstract rationalization and to the distant suggestions of carnalism in
Luther's revised Mass, Calvin advances a compromise doctrine.
The Presence of Christ is Real indeed, but in a wholly spiritual
manner. Christ is in heaven, not under or attached to the species
of bread and wine, but he does confer graces upon the communicant by way of the sacramental tokens of His Presence.

They are greatly deceived who suppose there is no presence of
Christ in the Supper unless it is placed in the bread. For by such
an idea they leave nothing to the secret operations of the Spirit
which unites Christ Himself to us. Christ does not seem to them
to be present unless He descends to us, as if we did not equally
possess His presence if He draws us up to Himself. . . . Rather
is Christ to be adored spiritually in the glory of heaven than this
so dangerous way of adoration devised, full of a gross and carnal
idea of God. . . . What is idolatry if it not be to worship the gifts
instead of the Giver.[24]

[23] Zwingli, ii, 541.
[24] *Instit. IV*, xvii, 35–36, col. 1038–1040.

Not only does Calvin make this drastic separation of the sign from the thing signified, allowing Christ a Presence *in absentia,* but also, and inevitably, he denies the Catholic idea of sacrifice. The whole of the Eucharist for him is Holy Communion. The faithful receive Christ spiritually. "He has given us a table at which to feast, not an altar on which to offer a sacrifice. He has not consecrated priests to sacrifice, but ministers to distribute the sacred banquet." [25]

It is Calvin who first stresses the idea, pervasive in Anglican theology, that the Eucharist insofar as it can be called a sacrifice, is a sacrifice of praise and thanksgiving and therefore can have nothing to do with a "renewal" of Calvary, or with the efficacious remission of sins. The word sacrifice in Calvinist theology is drained of its biblical and traditional content. Sacrifice in Calvin is as nonsacrificial as Presence, in Zwingli, is absent. The semantic difficulties mount. It will soon be no simple matter to write a simple Christian poem—or to read it.

Further, English churchmen, and poets, susceptible to the influence of both Luther and Calvin, found themselves in a curious predicament. Whereas Luther permitted, even encouraged, sensuous forms of worship, Calvin inculcated an absolute liturgical puritanism. For Calvin, no form of worship can be acceptable that is not specifically authorized by Scripture. Man is corrupt; his works cannot be pleasing to God. Therefore, ritual not prescribed by the Bible is positively sinful. For churchmen, and poets, heedful of both masters, the choice had to be between a thoroughgoing rejection of ancient liturgical and ritualistic symbol and a carefully selective use of such bits and pieces of traditional symbol as can be disinfected of germinal Catholic implication. Not only, then, are the meaning and suggestiveness of Christian symbol made uncertain for everyone who deals in it, but also the sure line of communication begins to waver and "public truth" in all the

[25] *Instit.* IV, xviii, 12, col. 1059. For an account of the Eucharistic ideas of Luther, Zwingli, and Calvin see B. J. Kidd, *Documents Illustrative of the Continental Reform* (Oxford, 1911). Translations here as given in Messenger.

high matters of the faith threatens to become merely a collection of private truths, each couched in a public language but each signifying something quite different to Lutherans, Calvinists, Zwinglians.[26]

The tension between an absolute Puritanism, with its own abstract frame of reference, and a Lutheran pseudo-sacramentalism, with its Catholic surface and Protestant core, will particularly plague the Anglican compromise. For the desperate voyagers of the middle way must seek to reconcile Luther, Calvin, Zwingli, St. Augustine, and even St. Thomas Aquinas!

Before coming fully to grips with the English situation, it will be necessary to consider still another doctrinal contribution of the Reform. How is the corporateness of Christian life and worship affected by Protestant teaching? What becomes of the Mystical Body of Catholic faith and practice?

> It may be said that he [Calvin] rediscovered the sense of the Church as the New Israel, the people of God. This doctrine is unmistakably reflected in his theory of worship. It produced both the deep sense of homage and reverence before God emphasized in his service by the reading of the Decalogue and by the confession of faith that was made by the believers as a solidarity in Christ. It is seen no less in the deep and spontaneous gratitude that bursts forth in the psalms sung by the congregation. And it is this doctrine as well as that of the communions as a "sigillum verbi" that makes Calvin emphasize the unity of the ante-communion with the Communion. The Communion is . . . no mere appendage to a preaching service; it is the service of the faithful where God seals His promise to the elect. The doctrine of Election with its reflection in the corporate nature of the Calvinist cultus contrasts with individualism that characterizes the Lutheran service.[27]

Here is a highly significant point and one which further demonstrates the complex and often contradictory nature of Protestant-

[26] For an illuminating discussion of "Calvin and the Arts," see the article by Leslie P. Spelman, *Journal of Aesthetics and Art Criticism* (March, 1948), pp. 246–252.

[27] Horton Davies, *The Worship of the English Puritans* (London, Dacre Press, 1948), p. 20. Davies gives a clear account of the difference between Lutheran and Calvinist influences on English worship.

ism. Luther, while retaining some of the surfaces of Catholic sacramentalism, is the pure Protestant individualist. His Eucharistic cult is wholly individualistic and subjective. Calvin, the absolute Puritan, bases his Eucharistic rite not, as Luther does, on interior subjective experience, but on the exterior, wholly objective, and authoritative biblical text. And, curiously enough, it is in the thoroughly nonsacramental Calvinist phase of the Reformation that the emphasis on corporate worship is recovered. It is, however, a corporate worship shorn of sacramentalism. Calvin deliberately reduces the sacramental symbols to bare figures. For instance, he retains the rite of confirmation but only as means of catechizing children. Later Puritans were to drop the rite altogether as an inconvenient vestige of popery. Marriage and burial lose their sacramental character entirely and so become mere civil ceremonies. Whereas Catholicism, through its sacraments, had sought to extend the redemptive Eucharistic power into the natural and social orders, Calvin, by reducing the sacraments to baptism and communion (and by de-sacramentalizing even these), prepared for an abdication of the rule of the spiritual life over matter, time, and place, thus inviting the complete secularization of human thought and practice.

And Calvin's emphasis on corporate worship is by no means inconsistent with his drastic antisacramentalism. He preaches the corporateness of a tiny elect predestined to salvation, saved from a world which cannot be saved. Calvin's City of God, unlike St. Augustine's, is rigidly exclusive, seal-tight. The Catholic Church is in the world but not of it. Calvin's church, as such, is not really in the world at all. Its members, erect and stiff as Prussian Guards, stand at attention in the Hand of God, high and dry above a shipwrecked humanity.

Our semantic problem deepens. The elect of Calvin form One Body. And the strongest sense of corporate Christianity in seventeenth century England is to be found in the language of the revolutionary Puritans. Indeed, by contrast with the corporate tone of Puritans on the march, the Catholic poetry of a Crashaw will seem utterly individualistic and subjective. And just such a contrast will provide us with insight into the bewildering, restless firmament of Christian symbol in seventeenth century poetry.

In the main, then, the firmament within which seventeenth century Christian poetry is conceived, is determined by the conflicting revolutions in Eucharistic dogma precipitated by Luther, Zwingli, and Calvin. Such a generalization awaits, of course, the support of chapters to come. Meanwhile, it is proper to keep in mind certain consequences of the sixteenth century revolution in Eucharistic dogma, consequences in idea and attitude which leave their mark on the firmament of poetry: The sacramental efficacy of the Eucharist is now at least in doubt. The corporate nature of Christian life and worship is either denied or forced to find a new and non-Eucharistic rationalization. The language of crucial Christian symbol is either reduced to mere metaphor or made uncertain and treacherous by the confused and vacillating relationship now obtaining between dogma, concept, and rhetoric.

The influence of each of the main dogmatic tenets of the continental Reform will be observed in English Christian poetry of the seventeenth century. And it will be seen that as a result of the multiple dogmatic pressures that converge in the period, the firmament of poetic symbol from the early years of Elizabeth to the settlement of William and Mary is characterized by incredible confusion and continuous motion. For this reason it may be dangerous to isolate a single poet or a single poem of the period for final interpretation and judgment. But we shall find that the outright abandonment of Eucharistic sacramentalism moves poetry in a relatively straight line towards an inevitably secular destination. Anglican poetry, rooted in sacramentalism, but tinged also with the pseudo-sacramentalism of Luther and the antisacramentalism of Calvin and Zwingli, moves by zigzags, detours, and returns, and presents us with a difficult but fascinating problem in aesthetics. It is to Anglican poetry, and to the conflicting dogmatic and social pressures put upon it, that we must go first—and last— for a vision of the new firmament of Christian poetry taking shape in the seventeenth century.

The Anglican Dilemma

CHAPTER THREE

THERE CAN BE no doubt that Archbishop Cranmer, cautiously while Henry still lived and recklessly after the boy Edward took the throne, sought by all means to abolish forever in England the Catholic system of sacramentalism. It is also the case that Cranmer's private intentions were not necessarily the intentions of the Church of England. It would be unfair to ignore the persistence of a Catholic party in the Establishment and to put a Protestant label on the whole of Tudor and Stuart churchmanship. And it is simply mistaken to regard the Anglican situation of the time as a miraculous *via media,* a pure golden thread of patristic (and reasonable) doctrine and practice without knot or snarl, unspotted either by the rich purple of Rome or by the thin milk-white of Geneva. This myth of a gentle Anglican middle way, comforting as it may be to those who must read back a sweet and tidy reasonableness into a precarious and turbulent past, has done much to damage our understanding of seventeenth century poetry. The Anglican firmament is neither wholly Protestant nor wholly Catholic, and the opposing theological and practical tensions are never truly resolved. Indeed, the Anglican firmament becomes a whirling jumble of every conceivable dogmatic stress. Under the influence of the double talk of continental reform, the language of symbol, as one might expect, vacillates uncontrollably between Catholic and Zwinglian extremes, missing none of the intervening notes of the scale. And it was Cranmer who, by his

[55]

skillful reshaping of the Eucharistic liturgy, bequeathed to Anglican poetry a semantic problem that is perhaps insoluble.

We need not pause for long over the question of Cranmer's attitude to Catholic sacramentalism in general and to the Catholic Mass in particular. He has the clearest of minds and sees at a glance the dependence of the entire sacramental system on the Mass. Never for a moment is he confused about the fundamental nature of Catholic dogma.

> What availeth it to take away beads, pardons, pilgrimages and such other popery, so long as the two chief roots remain unpulled up. . . . The rest is but branches and leaves . . . but the very body of the tree or rather the roots of the weeds, is the popish doctrine of transubstantiation, of the real presence of Christ's Flesh and Blood in the sacrament of the altar (as they call it) and of the sacrifice and oblation of Christ made by the priest for the salvation of the quick and the dead.[1]

We are thus reminded that image-smashing, the conversion of altar into communion table, even the desecration of church windows, originates not with Puritan partisans but with Anglican churchmen of Cranmer's cast of mind. A denial of the Real Presence and the Real Sacrifice is inevitably a denial of the whole Eucharistic grip on reality and therefore a repudiation of the sanctification of natural things, therefore, too, an assault on the analogical validity of the poetic symbol.

That Cranmer subverts the inner dogmatic core of Eucharistic symbol is indisputable:

> The eating of Christ's Flesh and drinking of His Blood is not to be understood simply and plainly as the words do properly signify, that we do eat and drink Him with our mouths; but it is a figurative speech spiritually to be understood, that we must deeply print and fruitfully believe in our hearts, that His Flesh was crucified and His Blood shed for our redemption. And this our belief in Him is to eat His Flesh and drink His Blood, although they be not here present with us, but ascended into heaven. As our forefathers before Christ's time did likewise eat His Flesh and drink His Blood, which was so far from them that it was not yet born.[2]

[1] *Defence. Works,* ed. Jenkyns (London, 1533), II, p. 289.
[2] Cranmer, p. 381.

As Dom Gregory Dix puts it: "whenever Cranmer speaks of spiritually eating the Body and drinking the Blood of Christ we must understand that he means by this 'thinking with faith that Christ died for my sins on Calvary,' and nothing else but this." [3] And Dix is surely right in calling Cranmer's Eucharistic thinking Zwinglian.

It is interesting to note that Cranmer attacks the doctrine of transubstantiation on purely nominalist grounds. He argues that *substance* and *accidents* are inseparable. Transubstantiation, by making the outward part of the sacrament an illusion, "involves a deception of the senses" and overthrows the nature of a sacrament. The Catholic nominalist, unable to accept the Aristotelian rationalization of dogma, looks for a new metaphysical superstructure. But in Cranmer the distinction between dogma and concept is lost. And in the same stroke the rhetorical level of symbol is confused and disembowelled. Body and Blood, Real Presence, Sacrifice, stray like ghosts through a strange new firmament of symbol.

Sacraments are still named by their ancient names in rites which defy the sacramental principle. The Eucharistic action, for instance, is obviously reduced by Cranmer to sheer psychological process. To quote Dix again: "It would appear . . . that the sacrifice and oblation in the Eucharist consists for Cranmer in the emotions and ideas of those present at the Eucharist, and not in anything appertaining to the rite itself." [4] The objective *ex opere operato* reference of the act is gone. Things and words are no longer what they seem.

It is pointless for our purposes here to press home from either the Catholic or the Protestant side a tidy partisan estimate of the orthodoxy or otherwise of the Anglican liturgy in its final Restoration form. A strong case can be made either way. Even Newman for a while was able to find a Catholic sense in the liturgy, indeed in the Thirty-Nine Articles. The question of whether or not

[3] *The Shape of the Liturgy* (London, Dacre Press, 1945), p. 649.
[4] Dix, p. 655.

Catholicism can exist outside the Roman communion is, in any event, beyond the scope of this study. It is sufficient to show here that Cranmer's revision of the liturgy (and subsequent Anglican attempts at counterrevision) deprived the symbolism of the Eucharist of security if not of validity, at each of its levels. In the rapid and bewildering intellectual and social motion of the age, this lack of security prevented Anglicanism from speaking with a single and certain voice. Dogma, concept, and rhetoric became hopelessly intertangled and confused with one another.

What, then, in brief, are the immediate consequences for liturgical symbol of Cranmer's reform, and to what extent does the Stuart counterrevision restore to the liturgy a valid sacramental reference?

Dix's summary of Cranmer's second (1552) revision of the Mass is succinct, accurate, and telling.

> What remains of the old four-action shape? (1) There is no offertory in bread and wine at all; it has been deliberately discarded. (2) Whether the "eucharistic prayer" remains is not easy to say. The notion of "consecration" has been deliberately watered down to that of "setting apart to holy use." . . . (3) But what of the *eucharista,* that "thanking" which is the apostolic nucleus of the prayer, and the solemn concluding doxology, the glorifying of the name of God? Of the first there remains a clear trace in the preface. But only during four weeks of the year, when a proper preface is provided, is it in any sense an *anamnesis* of the Person and work of Christ as in the primitive rites. . . . And the doxology, that "blessing of the Name" . . . has similarly been removed from the prayer to beyond the communion. The fraction, ordered in 1549, has disappeared in 1552, apparently because Bucer warned Cranmer that it was an opportunity for superstition. (4) There remains the communion, which Cranmer himself insists is only a "token act"—"Take and eat in remembrance that Christ died for thee." [5]

Obviously, the Eucharistic action which Cranmer proposes is in effect as well as in intention utterly subjective and individualistic. There is no corporate act of Sacrifice in which the Mystical Body

[5] Dix, pp. 670–671.

participates with the historical and the risen Christ. There is merely a pious memory of the distant act on Calvary and an individual reception of the tokens of grace. The Eucharist is no longer a sacrifice but the celebration of the memory of a sacrifice. Praise and thanksgiving are offered, the souls and bodies of the communicants are offered, but Christ in union with His church is not.

This is the rite that puts its stamp on the Christian poetry of the Tudor, Jacobean, and Caroline periods. For despite the Laudian recovery of ceremonialism in the reign of Charles I, it is not until the Restoration that an attempt is made to undo Cranmer's mutilation of the liturgy. In the *Revised Prayer Book* of 1662 the offertory and the fraction are both, in some degree, restored. But the emphasis on a sacrificial oblation of the elements remains uncertain. In the words of Dix: "By directing that the bread and wine were to be placed upon the altar immediately after the alms and before the prayer was said" the revised rubric "made it possible to understand these words and 'oblation' as referring to the Eucharistic bread and wine." [6]

Possible, one notes—not certain. The rite at this and at every other crucial point could still be taken in a Protestant as well as in a Catholic sense. It is significant, too, that the dogma of the Real Presence, like the dogma of sacrifice, is allowed to remain ambiguous. For if the Stuarts were able to rid the rite of Cranmer's Zwinglianism, they did not necessarily go beyond Lutheran and Calvinist formulae in order to do so. Dix does not seem quite to realize how revealing is this admission: "Overall's statement that 'the Body and Blood of Christ are verily and indeed taken and received by the faithful in the Lord's Supper' was added to the Catechism of 1604 on the petition of the Puritans themselves and was nowhere challenged." [7]

The Calvinists shared the "high" churchmen's dislike of Cranmer's crude Zwinglianism. They insisted, therefore, on a doctrine of a Presence *spiritually* Real. The rhetorical level of the ancient

[6] Dix, p. 694.
[7] Dix, p. 676.

symbol is thus retained. But the dogmatic core has been drastically altered, at least in the Calvinist intention. There is nothing to prevent a thoroughgoing Protestant reading of the 1662 rite. For despite the statement, at several crucial points, that the Body and Blood of Christ are "verily and indeed taken and eaten in the Sacrament" (words which by 1662 are susceptible to a Calvinist if not to a Zwinglian reading), the words of administration are unchanged from Cranmer's second prayer book: "Take and eat this in remembrance that Christ died for thee, and feed on him in thy heart by faith, with thinksgiving."—"Drink this in remembrance that Christ's blood was shed for thee, and be thankful."

Such words wholly contradict the Catholic view of the Real Presence of Christ on the altar, just as they deny implicitly the corporate sacrificial action of the Mass. Therefore, despite the elimination of Cranmer's more blatant Zwinglian innovations (as abhorrent to the Calvinists as to the "high" churchmen), the prayer book of 1662 in its main symbolic structure and intent is ambiguous and even opportunist. Like the *Thirty-Nine Articles,* it achieves not so much a settled compromise as a condition of permanent vacillation. Neither friend nor foe has ever been quite able to take hold of it. Thus it evades the most difficult dogmatic tests by a flickering energy all its own.

In the interest of specifically poetic symbol one must here observe rather carefully certain of the main developments in Anglican attitudes to the Eucharist after Cranmer and before the final prayer book revision of 1662. To begin with, it is, I think, mistaken to see in the Anglican development anything like a consistent return to the symbolic conceptualization of Eucharistic dogma characteristic of St. Augustine and the patristic tradition generally. Most Anglicans, like St. Augustine, and in conscious difference with the Aristotelian realists, do indeed distinguish between the verbal or ritual sign and the thing signified. But whereas the Fathers refuse to separate in fact what they have distinguished by definition, the Anglicans of the seventeenth century, instructed as much by Calvin as by Plato, generally understand nothing more than a convenient metaphorical relationship to obtain between the sign and that which it signifies. Thus Jewel: ". . . three things herein we must consider; first, that we put a difference between the sign and the thing signified. Secondly, that we seek Christ above in heaven. . . . Thirdly, that the Body of Christ is to be eaten by faith only, and none otherwise." [8]

This is the spiritual Presence of Calvinism. The separation of the sign from the thing signified, of the sacrament from the Body and Blood, is here as unequivocal as language can make it. This is highly sophisticated Reformation thinking. It is not Augustinian, patristic, primitive, Pauline. It is utter innovation, in effect separating heaven and earth, past and present, spirit and flesh, and leaving to the ancient symbolic words a purely psychological function.

The most influential of the Elizabethan divines was, of course, Richard Hooker, and in his *Ecclesiastical Polity* he seeks to still the controversy over the dogma of the Real Presence with the notion of the "instrumentality" of the sacrament. That alone which is material in the Eucharist, he asserts,[9] is "the real *participation* of Christ . . ." by means of this sacrament. But Hooker will have nothing to do with a Catholic *ex opere operato* view of the sacrament. In common with the "central" churchmen who follow him, he insists that Christ's Presence is not finally to be found in the sacrament itself but in the soul of the communicant who has received the sacrament worthily. The Presence of Christ is thus a purely subjective one and is conceived only in terms of the psychological activity of the individual recipient. Similarly, there is no place in Hooker's thought for the Catholic dogma of sacrifice.

Yet, in striking counterpoint to the dominant Calvinism of Jewel and Hooker (as to the Zwinglianism of Cranmer) there is the Eucharistic thought of Catholic-minded Anglicans like Andrewes, Forbes, Thorndike, and Montague. Although they are bound to reject the Catholic conceptualization of dogma, in par-

[8] *A Reply unto Mr. Harding's Answer. Works,* ed. Parker Society (Cambridge, 1845), I, p. 949.
[9] Ed. Keble (Oxford, 1888), II, p. 352.

ticular the doctrine of transubstantiation, they hold that there is no ultimate dogmatic difference between Rome and Canterbury on the point of the Real Presence. Unquestionably, however, this constitutes a minority report in seventeenth century England and does not represent the settled mind of the church (there is no settled mind). Indeed, the language of symbol had become so ambiguous and slippery that it is difficult for us to calculate with any certainty in just what sense a writer like Andrewes was generally understood. True, the Laudian revival of ceremony, coupled with "high" church condemnation of Calvinist predestination, drew the cry of "popery" from Puritans both within and without the Anglican communion. But nothing illustrates so vividly the process of fragmentation of sacramental symbol in the period as Laud's "high" churchmanship and the general response to it.

Actually, in his Eucharistic doctrine, Laud is scarcely more Catholic than Hooker. He asserts the purely spiritual Presence of Christ in the sacrament, and he denies the sacrificial action of the Mass. Laud's famous debate [10] with the Jesuit Fisher reveals fully his essential Protestantism. Throughout the debate he uses the term Protestant to describe himself and to align his own doctrinal views with those of the continental reformers other than Zwingli. He gives full approval to Calvin's notion of the Real Presence. "For the Calvinists, at least they which follow Calvin himself, do not only believe that the true and real Body of Christ is received in the Eucharist, but that it is there and that we partake of it, *vere et realiter,* which are Calvin's own words." [11] Calvinists believe no such thing. Here in the very citadel of seventeenth century "high" churchmanship is to be found the most thorough confusion imaginable in the reading and writing of symbol. As one would expect from this, Laud's doctrine of Eucharistic sacrifice is wholly and typically Protestant.

What, then, of Laud's Catholic-looking ceremonialism? Cere-

[10] *A Relation of the Conference between Wm. Laud and Mr. Fisher. Works* (Oxford, 1849), II, pp. xl, 440.
[11] Laud, p. 326.

mony is not, of course, necessarily sacramental in intention or effect. Luther permits such ritual as is not proscribed by Scripture. Laud's concern with ritual is not, however, merely permissive in the Lutheran sense. To a large extent, he is impelled in his ritualistic reforms by a practical desire for order and decency in church worship. Not only had there been in the seventeenth century a marked falling off in church attendance, occasional outbursts of vandalism at the expense of windows and statues and public crosses, there had also come about everywhere a distressing slackness in the manner of worship. Laud was convinced that external order guaranteed the security as well as the decency of the Establishment. But that ceremonialism was for Laud nothing more than a practical expedient, that it had for him no genuine sacramental or Catholic relevance, is clear enough from these words: "And scarce anything hath hurt religion more in these broken times than an opinion in too many men that because Rome has thrust some unnecessary and many superstitious ceremonies on the Church, therefore the Reformation must have none at all. . . . Ceremonies are the hedges that fence the substance of religion from all the indignities which profaneness and sacrilege too commonly put upon it." [12]

Here is the complete and wholly explicit separation of the rhetorical level of a sacramental symbolism from any living embrace with dogma. Only the fanatical, witch-hunting Puritan could see under Laud's garbled rhetorical usages the hideous, lurking, dogmatic spectres of sacrifice and transubstantiation. When we remember that the Puritan would have none of the ring in marriage or the cross in baptism for fear that these might seem to suggest powers *ex opere operato*, we can measure not only the extent of Calvinist superstition in the time but also the confusion which had come to prevail in the use and in the reception of thousand-year-old symbols. The paradox is that the rhetorical signs and gestures of the ancient symbolism continued to suggest actual dogmatic

[12] Laud, from the dedication to the King of his *Conference with Fisher*, p. xvi.

values to the Puritans long after the Anglicans had put them to merely ornamental or expedient use. The ghosts of sacramentalism continued to haunt the superstitious Puritan mind long after they had been carefully exorcised by Anglican reasonableness. The Puritan, then as now, attributes a far greater degree of sacramental suggestion to the vestigial Catholic rhetoric of Anglicanism than does the Anglican himself. We shall find that the decisive movement of the period at the level of poetry is the movement of traditional Christian symbol from the centre to the periphery of expression and experience, a movement, in other words from sacrament to ornament, the declension of symbol into metaphor. This is a movement which, at the level of poetic expression, accompanies the distortion and eventual destruction of central Eucharistic dogma.

Little Gidding, often taken to be the closest approximation in seventeenth century Anglicanism to the devotional life of the Counter Reformation, helps us to understand how misleading the rhetorical surfaces of religious activity can be. To the Puritan, suspicious of every formal reminder of Catholic worship, Little Gidding was the "Arminian nunnery." Here, as faithfully as in a Benedictine monastery, were kept the watches of the night. Alms were distributed to the neighboring poor. The Ferrar family led a highly ritualized life of formal devotion and good works.

No one will dispute the fact that Little Gidding gives off the purest light of the century in England. But it is quite another thing to conclude that this light is evidence of a Counter Reformation sensibility. On the face of it, Herbert's literary and spiritual friendship, Crashaw's direct and personal comradeship with Ferrar, might seem to link, subtly but surely, the *via media* with Tridentine spirituality. The way from Bemerton to Loretto seems to lie through Little Gidding. And yet there was nothing in the devotional life of the Ferrars to offend the most zealous Calvinist. The spirituality of Little Gidding is intrinsically different from the spirituality of Trent. It is informed by a profound and unmistakably dogmatic Protestantism. We must not be misled by the superstitions of seventeenth century Puritans who were unable to distinguish between the ornamental and the sacramental. Actually, the entire devotional life of Little Gidding was scriptural and not in the least sacramental. The daily and nightly round of offices and watches, the regularized reading of psalms and gospels and pious legend all aimed at devotion by way of edification. It will be remembered that the Protestant emphasis on edification, usually in the shape of sermonizing, had been made in deliberate opposition to the sacramental religion of "good works." It is highly significant that Ferrar himself did not complete holy orders, never going beyond his ordination as deacon. There was no resident priest at Little Gidding, and it was deemed sufficient to celebrate the Eucharist on one Sunday of every month through the offices of a visiting priest. Just as striking, and consistent with a forthright anti-Catholicism, is the fact that in the chapel of Little Gidding "the Lord's Table" was placed not altar-wise, but east and west. This in itself is convincing evidence of Ferrar's Protestant anti-sacrificial view of the Eucharist. And the chapel at Little Gidding is a characteristically Anglican phenomenon. Here is, beyond question, a devotionalism of beauty and depth expressing itself through fragments of a Catholic imagery the cross, a statue or two, holy pictures—but carefully isolating these images from the Eucharistic sacramentalism which had created them and which alone justified them.

A writer who certainly cannot be accused of any lack of sympathy for Little Gidding makes my point with clarity and force.

This worship . . . was essentially biblical rather than sacramental; and it is difficult that it was not, to that extent, narrowed and improverished. A firmer framework of sacramental doctrine and practice would perhaps have lent to their way of life a certain warmth, even a certain ease and lightness which would have greatly enriched it. The recovery of a full and balanced sacramental life was one of the principal achievements of the Counter-Reformation . . . it seems clear that the English reformers entirely failed to arrive at a balanced sacramental teaching. There had been a serious dislocation; and no more striking instance could be cited than the fact that the weekly celebration of the Eucharist had fallen into complete disuse.[13]

Ferrar's unsacramental devotion, though it redeems by its zeal the wavering indifference of seventeenth century Anglicanism, nevertheless shows the blight which had come from the distortions and evasions and corrections and countercorrections of Eucharistic dogma. The fact that, between them, Laud's ceremonialism and Ferrar's unsacramental devotionalism should loom before the Puritan as a return of the Beast is some indication of the treacherous state into which religious rhetoric fell when it fell away from orthodox dogma. We must not, therefore, read the Catholic surfaces of Anglican poetry at face value. We must be on the look not only for the tension between Catholic surface and Protestant core but also for the rapidly changing relation between dogmatic intention and rhetorical convention in this disintegrating firmament of the Christian symbol.

The Anglican problem is more complicated than any other in the period, because of the retention by Anglicans not only of much Catholic rhetoric but also, in varying degrees, of certain traditional dogmatic beliefs. One cannot *assume* in a seventeenth century Anglican poem that a Catholic image is merely ornamental and without a function appropriate to fixed dogma. Nor can one assume the opposite. Indeed, single poems may contain clashing Catholic and Protestant biases. But Anglicanism is in motion throughout the period, and the motion is by and large away from any fixity of dogma. The drift towards private judgment is easily discernible. We have noted that even the Catholic-looking Laud can align himself in principle with the independent (and irreconcilable) thinkers of the continental reform. In Ussher, Field, Bramhall, and Jeremy Taylor one finds explicit tolerance of the most divergent theological opinions. Taylor places "the liberty of proph-

[13] A. L. Maycock, *Nicholas Ferrar of Little Gidding* (London, Sheldon Press, 1938), p. 219. I am deeply endebted to Maycock's analysis.

esying" above the authority of all creeds and councils. And in Taylor's Eucharistic thought there is apparent a gradual drift from an initial "high" view of the sacrament to a position scarcely more Catholic than Cranmer's.[14] The loss of central dogmatic faith opens the way to toleration, by indifference, of contradictory dogmas of every sort. There is soon to be no fixed sun at the centre of an ordered motion of the firmament. By its comprehension of the many diverse theological tendencies of the time, Anglicanism comes to display in the poetry of its children the full crisis in the Christian aesthetic.

If we are able to dismiss from our minds the illusion of a neat and quiet *via media,* if we are able to recognize the tortured compulsive motion of Anglicanism, we may have to regard Milton's Protestantism and Crashaw's Catholicism not as belonging to utterly separate poetic firmaments but as expressing, with a final clarity, the opposite horns of the Anglican dilemma, indeed of the Christian dilemma, in an age of disintegration. And we may be forced to conclude that while the *via media* is an ideal never realized in fact with any stability, the extreme developments away from this ideal, whether Catholic or Protestant, fail equally and alike in confirming a new firmament of Christian value and symbol able to absorb and yet to subdue the new secular presumptions of the seventeenth century.

Before dealing specifically with the aesthetic crisis as it appears in the work of major Anglican poets, it will be well to scrutinize generally the structure and the stresses of the Anglican firmament. The task at this point is to note the process of separation between surface and core, between rhetoric and dogma, as it operates in the fluctuating firmament of Anglican symbol. One has no difficulty in finding a surface of rhetorical continuity between the

[14] For a clear account of the development of Taylor's Eucharistic thought, see C. W. Dugmore, *Eucharistic Doctrine in England from Hooker to Waterland* (London, 1941), pp. 93–188.

symbols of Anglican poetry and the traditional iconography of Catholicism. But one also discovers that the conceptual and dogmatic reference of crucial symbols has been altered drastically, and this alteration has consequences for even the simplest poetic image. Actually, the plight of language within the Anglican firmament appears in two phases. In general, the poetry of what we would now call "the low church party" displays an uninterrupted decline of the analogical symbol into simple metaphor. In the poetry of the Catholic-minded Anglicans a countermovement occurs, and the rhetorical and dogmatic levels of symbol strain towards each other, touch, but never finally fuse. I shall discuss first this drift towards the unfleshing of the word, a phenomenon most apparent in early and aggressively Protestant-Anglican verse, but, as we shall note in subsequent chapters, one which exerts a decisive pressure on the Anglican firmament as a whole.

A useful index of the Protestant sensibility of earlier Anglican poetry is Farr's anthology of Elizabethan devotional verse.[15] It was the editor's stated aim to present pieces which might be considered as "an illustration of some of the results which the English Reformation produced on the literature of the age and in the minds of the people at large." [16] Quite obviously, these "results" are in the deepest sense anti-Catholic. And when one remembers that Farr includes excerpts not only from major poets like Spenser, Drayton, Daniel, and Breton but also from the work of over one hundred obscure or unknown poets, one takes confidence in one's impression that the effect of dogmatic revision on Anglican poetic symbol has been overwhelming.

The Elizabethan age is certainly not the great age of the specifically Christian poet. Many of the pieces presented by Farr are little more than perfunctory rhymings of Scripture. For our purposes, the most striking thing about the anthology is the consistency of the Protestant bias, and the clear bearing of this bias on

---

[15] *Select Poetry Chiefly Devotional of the Reign of Queen Elizabeth.* Collected and edited for the Parker Society by Edward Farr (2 vols., Cambridge, 1845).
[16] Farr, Preface.

the means of expression. In particular, one notes a repeated insistence on the doctrine of justification by faith alone, and the consequent concern with the interior psychology of justification. Sacramental symbol and image disappear in favour of psychological and moral abstraction. Biblical paraphrase and the habit, not yet lost, of illustrating dogma with concrete incidents from the life of Christ prevent this tendency towards abstraction from becoming absolute. However, the concreteness of image thus preserved is secondhand, illustrative—seldom immediate, inventive, properly sacramental.

The interior psychological concern with justification by faith apart from works links everywhere and inevitably with the denial, often wholly explicit, of the sacrificial aspect of the Eucharist in anything like the Catholic sense. The sacrifice of praise and thanksgiving is stressed as central and sufficient to the Eucharistic intention. Sacramental language is never more than broadly metaphorical. As will soon be apparent, analogical symbol is driven out of a firmament which consistently reduces the anciently concrete image of Eucharistic tradition to merely verbal shadow.

Two short verses from George Whetstone's *The Rock of Regard* illustrate the way in which the Lutheran doctrine of justification dissolves for poetry the objective, analogical symbolism of Eucharistic sacrifice.

> A contrite heart is the sweet sacrifice
> That Thou dost seek, ere we our favour win;
> The which, dear God, with sighs and weeping eyes
> I offer up in recompense of sin
>
> Attending still when trial of my faith
> Shall tread down death, and Satan force to reel;
> And boldly say, Till latter gasp of breath
> My soul, through faith, the joys of heaven doth feel.[17]

One would not suggest, of course, that the broken and contrite heart is irrelevant to the sacrificial sense of the Eucharist, or that

[17] In Farr, I, p. 340.

faith may never heal the agony of repentance. One notes, however, that repentance here is not a condition of penance, that the trial of faith is not at all involved in act and object. The sacramental Eucharistic sanctification of *things* never intrudes on this kind of interior Lutheran *angst*. More precisely, the word sacrifice has been thinned to convey little more than a personal sense of remorse. A kind of psychological crucifixion is the wage one pays for the act of sin. Sacrifice is a metaphor here, not a symbol. In effect, the pain of remorse is compared to the distant pain of Christ on the Cross. But such pain is not caught up in the objective, immediate, but perpetual act of the altar.

Whetstone's poem is quite characteristic of the psychologism which begins now to dominate Protestant poetry. The slain Christ makes metaphor for tortured, separate souls. A quite new firmament of value and reference takes its shifting and chameleon structures from the whirling aggregate of private wishes and terrors and comforts. In the language of poetry one observes a widening cleavage between idea and fact, between the conceptual and rhetorical levels of expression.

In Barnaby Barnes' sequence *A Divine Century of Spiritual Sonnets* one can see clearly the characteristic Protestant cluster of justification, a subjective individualism, the abrupt separation of the interior emotional religious centre from the corruptible but irrelevant flesh, the inevitable deterioration of Eucharistic symbol into illustrative metaphor. In "Sonnet XIV" the soul seeks in the wounds of Christ a solace that would seem possible only by a denial of the physical order.

> O Benign Father! let my suits ascend
> And please they gracious eares,
> Even as those sweet perfumes
>   as incense went
> From our forefathers' altars; who
>   didst lend
> Thy nostrils to that myrrh which
>   they did send
> Even as I now crave thine eares to
>   be lent.

My soul, my soul, is wholly bent
To do thy condign service, and
    amend;
To fly for refuge to thy wounded
    breast,
To suck the balm of my salvation thence;
In sweet repose to take eternal rest,
As thy child folded in thine arms'
    defence;
But then my flesh methought by Satan fired
Said my proud sinful soul in vain aspired.[18]

This is not just the ancient tension of spirit and flesh implicit
in all Christian theology after St. Paul. This is, rather, the dilemma
of a subjective, unsacramental Protestantism which seeks in private
prayer a return equivalent to the spiritual benefits of the sacrifice
of the altar. This is an offering of the prayers of the Mass without offering Mass. May these prayers be received as the incense,
symbolic of sacrificial prayers, was once and long ago received.
There is, of course, no hint of union with the Mystical Body in a
sacrificial act. The poet yearns, by an exercise of prayer and by a
disembodiment of himself, to drink salvation, spiritually, by faith
alone, from the ghostly stream of Christ's redemptive mercy. He
cannot offer Christ; he cannot join himself with the sacramental
Body. His flesh, which has no place in the redemptive process,
challenges the aspiration of the soul. Flesh is an obstacle to atonement; Christ's bleeding Flesh can be nothing more here than a
metaphor of the divine compassion. Sacramental images of altar,
incense, and wounds are reduced to arbitrary and external counters
for an utterly interior experience which finally shatters itself on
the alien and evil physical existence. The poet's hope cannot rest
in any reconciliation of spirit and flesh, in any sacramental and
corporate renewal within the Mystical Body. Atonement through
the ancient act of sacrifice is an impossible feat for the isolated and
utterly passive soul.

The same kind of Lutheran anguish is to be found in Henry

---

[18] In Farr, I, p. 441.

Lok, who expresses in simple direct statement the only kind of
hope possible to this kind of religious sensibility.

> . . . I see now no release
> Unless my Saviour dear this burden take
> And faith a ship of safety for me make.[19]

Man cannot give. He can only receive, and through an act of
divine condescension which he can in no degree himself merit.
Clearly, sacramentalism is wholly alien to such a theology. It is
therefore instructive to observe in the language of a poet like Lok
the deployment of traditional sacramental images to ends which
are clearly antisacramental and unsymbolic. "Sonnet XC" is a fine
illustration of how Eucharistic symbol in this new dogmatic context is first reduced to metaphor and is finally discarded outright.
This process of reduction is characteristic of the dissolution in
early "low" Anglican poetry of the ancient firmament of symbol.

> One sweet and savory bread of wholesome kind
> Which in thy word thou offer'st store to me.
> To feed upon the flesh doth loathing find
> And leaves to lean, O Lord, alone on thee:
> The leaven of the Pharisees will be
> The surfeit of my soul, and death in fine
> Which, coveting to taste forbidden tree
> To carnal rules and reasons doth incline.
> So lavishly my lusts do taste the wine
> Which sourest grapes of sin fills in my cup
> That lo, my teeth now set on edge, I pine
> Not able wholesome food to swallow up,
> Unless thou mind my taste, and heart dost frame
> To love thy laws and praise thy holy name.[20]

Note that there are two breads and two wines here. Neither
sort is Eucharistic. The life of the unregenerate flesh is imaged
metaphorically in "the leaven of the Pharisees" and "the sourest
grapes of sin." The bare elements, then, of the sacrament of the
altar are used by Lok as signs of the sin of lust, of the carnal

---

[19] "Sonnet LXXXI," *First Century of Sonnets.* In Farr, I, p. 140.
[20] In Farr, I, p. 141.

life. They are not to be offered, consecrated in a sacramental action. They degrade. These elements, the ancient signs of nature and of man's creative action upon it, are here submerged in sensual evil.

The other bread, "the sweet and savory bread" of redemption, is offered to man only in "the Word," the Word *unfleshed*. Man's salvation is to be sought only in a change of heart and a change of taste—a loathing for the bread of the flesh, a longing for the bread of the unfleshed spirit. The effect of the poem rests on a paradoxical annihilation of the Eucharistic symbols, proceeding by way of a dissociation of the Word and the Flesh and thence to a flat repudiation of the sacramental honouring of created things. Presumably the Incarnation is now to be reversed. In consequence, the state of evil is properly suggested in terms of the physical appetites and functions, by a positive and direct reference to eating and drinking. But the bread of heaven, the unfleshed Word, is suggested negatively and by a subtle indirection. The tooth which touches this bread is, one supposes, lodged in the heart! But not, of course, the heart that lusts after the flesh, the heart of muscle and blood beating hot under the ribs of death.

And in Lok, as in other poets of the Protestant-Anglican side, the sacrificial images of the Eucharist are abstracted cleanly from any sense of objective and corporate action. In "Sonnet III," Lok prays for an increase of faith,

> . . . that plenty I may find
> Of sacrifices pleasing in Thy sight
> Of faith and love which are Thy soul's delight.[21]

Within the frame of this purely subjective view of the Eucharistic act it is not surprising to find the old images of the Mass appearing with subtly altered value. Observe, for an instance of this, the wine-water symbolism of "Sonnet XLV."

> If thou vouchsafest Lord of Thy goodness rare
> To sanctifie with holy presence Thine

---

[21] *Poems by Henry Lok, Gentleman. Miscellanies of the Fuller Worthies Library*, ed. Grosart (London, 1871), II, pp. 97–456.

The Cana marriage where Thou didst not spare
First miracle of water turned to wine;
Then be Thou present at this wedding mine
Which 'twixt Thy Church and me by faith is meant:
To see the want in me Thy eyes incline
—Whose wine of grace by wanton youth is spent—
But—being touched with view thereof—repent
And crave that water of Earth's heartless well
May issue forth from heart with sorrow rent,
And turned to wine, may so with grace excel
That all that see and taste this change in me
May grant this work, of Thee alone to be.[22]

For Lok, the transubstantiation of water into wine at Cana is a happier image of the redemptive process than is the sacrificial wine of Christ's blood. For the Fathers, the wine of Cana is, of course, a type of the blood which, mixed with water, is to flow from Christ's side. In Lok's poem all such typological reference is lost. Lok opposes the wine of grace to the waters of desolation, to worldliness and carnality in the abstract. He prays that as Christ once at a wedding changed actual water into actual wine, may the power of Christ, at this spiritual wedding of the soul to the church, change the poet's worldliness into a godliness so manifest that all can "see and taste" it. The use of "taste" in such a context is some measure of the abstract process of reduction to which Lok has subjected the physical image. There is no analogical participation of image in idea anywhere in the poem. The image becomes the shadow cast by the idea.

And that the symbol of the Body and Blood has been deliberately abstracted and reduced by Lok in clear and conscious opposition to Catholic tradition is obvious in these lines from "Sonnet XII":

A Nazarite I am, who do forsake
The delicacies of the World's delight,
Whose thirst thy purest fountains still shall slake
With faith and truth, the which with sin shall fight;
I will not taste the wine of Satan's slight
Which doth confound all reason and all sense.[23]

22 Lok, *Poems.*
23 Lok, *Poems.*

The fountain pouring forth its invisible metaphorical fluids "faith and truth" is contrasted with that benighted Catholic illusion, "Satan's slight" [sleight], the Objective Presence, which Lok, faithful to the nominalistic theology of Cranmer, believes to be a mockery of "all reason and all sense." In the antisacramental imagery of Lok and his kind, wine is never Blood. It is never even the wine one tastes on the tongue and feels along the pulse.

Lok will serve to illustrate the outright dismissal of Eucharistic symbol by the Protestant Anglicans of the Elizabethan age. A more subtle process than this is the reduction of Eucharistic symbol to metaphor not by a direct assault on dogma but by the perfunctory juxtaposition of traditional symbol with the merest metaphor, and in such a way as to destroy all genuine symbolic possibility by association. The process whereby the Blood of the Lamb is eventually to become the bloodless commonplace of the evangelical hymn is already discernible in these lines by Thomas Gressop:

Here is the *spring* where waters flowe
To quench oure heat of sin;
Here is the *tree* where truth doth grow
To lead our lives therein.

Here is the *judge* that stints the strife
When man's devices fail;
Here is the *bread* that feeds the life
That death cannot assail.

The tidings of salvation dear
Comes to our ears from hence;
The *fortress* of our faith is here
The *shield* of our defence.[24]

Images which still retain traditional symbolic possibility are used without conscious distortion—"spring," "tree," "bread." And while the poem is meant as a eulogy of Scripture, of the written

[24] In Farr, II, p. 469. Gressop's stanzas, untitled, were printed in the 1578 folio edition of the Geneva translation of the Bible.

Word (it first appeared as a prefix to the 1578 edition of the Geneva Bible), one concedes readily that praise of Scripture is not necessarily a denial of sacramentalism. But in this poem the multiplication of images succeeds in dissociating each separate image from a properly sacramental frame of reference. The "bread" is made little more than the equivalent of "the shield" and "the fortress." Thus the merely metaphorical character of the rhetoric is fixed, held short, by this act of equivalence. The "bread" stands for the written word only; it cannot *be* the living Word. It is not the Word, but the word that *tells* of the Word. Without the need of a direct attack on the traditional Catholic firmament in which these images had been nourished and raised into symbol, Gressop parades his images as so many semantic ghosts which blur into one another. And not only has the symbolic possibility of the "bread" been rubbed thin against the flat wall of the "fortress," but also the wholly arbitrary and artificially literary way in which such images have been made equivalent robs them of any real reference to things; they are now no more able to suggest the sensuous immediacy of things than does "June" when rhymed with "spoon." Indeed, we see here symbol reduced below the level of metaphor to cliché. Deprived of its dogmatic, typological, and objective reference, the traditional language of Christianity is being made into a set of bloodless verbal counters.

For a traditional rhetoric used apart from, and even in contradiction to, the dogma which bore it and nourished it tends quickly to wither away. A poem by Thomas Turke will permit us to observe in small space and with no straining of the eye a process which thus far in this study has been presented in scattered fragments interpreted deductively. This poem is later than anything in the Farr anthology, but it will serve to sum up the Protestant-Anglican view of the Mass as it came down into Caroline poetry. We must note how completely rhetoric has been separated from dogma until the ancient images appear as the furthest husks of a de-Catholicized language of symbol.

Priests make their Maker Christ ye must not doubt;
They eat, drink, box Him up, and bear about.
Substance of things they turn: nor is this all;
For both the signs must hold in several.
He's whole ith' bread, whole ith' cuppe
They eat Him whole: whole they sup;

     .   .   .

The bread and wine themselves are gone.
Shows of them tarry still, but substance none.

     .   .   .

And as the whale did Jonas, so they eat
Him up alive, body and soul, as meat.
As men eat oysters, so on Him they feed;
Whole and alive, and raw and yet not bleed
This cookery, void of humanity,
Is held in Rome for sound divinity.[25]

Here, of course, is the flat nominalism of Cranmer's attack on transubstantiation. And one notes, too, a cynical parody on Catholic typology. As the whale swallows Jonah, so the Catholic swallows Christ. But "as men eat oysters, so on Him they feed." The typological symbol is cleverly dissolved in this ludicrous equivalence.

Even more striking is Turke's clear and deliberate relegation of the Presence of Christ to the historical past.

We read of Christ twice made: and that is all
Of woman and under Law . . .

     .   .   .

Is't not enough for Him, and for us all
That He was once born, and once under thrall
But that he must yet, day by day
By you be made and offered, as you say? [26]

This denial in the present of the Presence of Christ shatters, inevitably, the analogical grip of the Eucharistic symbol. The

[25] *The Holy Eucharist and the Popish Breaden God*. Ed. A. B. Grosart, *Fuller Worthies Library*, (London, 1872) III, pp. 1–44. The poem was first published in 1625.
[26] *The Holy Eucharist.*

process of descent from symbol to metaphor will now be wholly obvious.

> Yet more; this God ye seem so to adore
> Ye basely prostitute to knave and whore;
> Teaching that the wicked His flesh may eat,
> Whereas Christ Jesus is to such no meat.
> For He, that eats His flesh and drinks His Blood
> Shall live, and therefore sure he must be good.
> Yea he that eats Christ's flesh in Christ doth dwell
>
> . . .
>
> He must be of Christ's flesh that eats His flesh:
> And only those with it He does refresh.[27]

The rejection of the efficacy of the sacrament *ex opere operato* is clearly intended to be a rejection of the actuality of Christ's Presence in the sacrament. One must already live in Christ spiritually in order to receive the spiritual benefits of Holy Communion. In terms of symbol, "the visible signs of an invisible grace" are indeed no more than signs. Grace operates in the area of these signs (the ritual act of communion) but only touches those who are already in the state of grace. The eating of the Flesh and the drinking of the Blood is a purely metaphorical exercise. Christ who was once on earth is now in heaven. Our communion with Him is an utterly spiritual act done to the accompaniment of certain conventionalized physical gestures.

It is naked sense perception which forbids, in the Mass, a sensuous mode for the divine act of condescension.

> I pray you show then, why we should not trust
> Our senses here, as if they were accurst,
> Sith that in other precepts of the Lord
> They stand us in great stead to keep His word.[28]

Carried far enough, this kind of nominalistic empiricism could demolish the faith entire. It almost did. The sensuous life is made to retire to its own domain. Bread can be no more than bread,

[27] *The Holy Eucharist.*
[28] *The Holy Eucharist.*

no more than the accidental illustration of an Idea that cannot be illustrated.

Turke, of course, argues that Christ Himself spoke metaphorically and not symbolically when he said "This is my Body."

> And ye may plainly see what IS means there
> To put IS for SIGNIFIES is not rare
> As he soon may see, that to see does care.

Therefore any renewal of the Sacrifice of Christ is a hoax.

> Yet confess we that a representation
> Is in the sacrament of His oblation
> Who once did offer up Himself for sin
> But since that hath never offered been.[29]

In short, Holy Communion is a purely spiritual exercise possible only for those already spiritually possessed by Christ—an exercise in which bread and wine are signs suggesting the comfortable words of the indwelling Christ. The communicant becomes more conscious of a state of grace which is already his. But he does not act, he does not give, he does not share. Traditional metaphors help to sharpen his individual and interior perception of his own high spiritual state.

And yet the ancient words are used.

> To say that men prepared do eat His flesh
> And drink His blood, their souls for to refresh
> Even His very flesh and His very blood
> May well be said, if it be well understood.[30]

"Well understood" to have no conceivable reference to the objective, sacrificial Presence of Christ on the altar.

Thus the word is unsettled just as the Word is unfleshed. The firmament is in dissolution. The Catholic fusion of word with thing, of the symbol with that which is symbolized, has been systematically destroyed. The great social and political crisis of

[29] *The Holy Eucharist.*
[30] *The Holy Eucharist.*

the Caroline age will put the new Reformation dogma to the severest test and will present the Christian poet with ultimate problems in the use of symbol. Milton, for instance, seeks to find in his theology the principle which can restore order to the chaos of raw nature and brute event. It may seem far-fetched to assume any connection between Milton's desperate theodicy and the plight of symbol in minor Tudor and Jacobean religious verse. And yet this descent which we have observed of symbol to metaphor to cliché is not the consequence of a problem in personal style. It is, rather, evidence of a radical transformation in the Christian apprehension of reality, evidence of a shift in value so drastic that it must finally force a re-formation of value, a new kind of firmament. For these little Tudor versifiers out of Cranmer and Whitgift, and Jewel are not only engaged negatively in the destruction of the Catholic firmament of symbol. They are also laying the cornerstone of the firmament of Milton. This will soon be apparent. But it would be well now to look at one characteristic "low" Anglican poem of authentic power to see, in terms of more serious creative activity in the earlier period, how this deterioration of the firmament actually affects the shaping power of the artist.

Giles Fletcher's *Christ's Victory and Triumph* is an important "Milton source"—a poem opening into the Miltonic firmament. It is a fine illustration of just how the Anglican dilemma in aesthetics dramatizes and determines the precarious and volatile character of the new Protestant firmament.

Fletcher seeks to depict the redemptive action of Christ in language and symbol at once traditional in colour and wholly appropriate to Reformation and Renaissance sensibility. Technically, he employs the highly abstract allegorical devices of mediaeval art, the startling paradox of orthodox and traditional Christian expression, and the voluptuous surfaces of Renaissance naturalism. The art of the Catholic Counter Reformation is to bring into a proper totality precisely these levels of value and device, and at first glance Fletcher may seem to be one of those

[80]

who managed to conserve the soul of the Gothic in the exciting new body of the baroque.

The very first stanza of the poem illustrates Fletcher's mastery of what might be called organic Christian paradox.

> The birth of Him that no beginning knewe
> Yet gives beginning to all that are borne;
> And how the Infinite farre greater grewe
> By growing lesse, and how the rising morne
> That shot from heav'n, did backe to heav'n retourne;
>   The obsequies of Him that could not die,
>   And death of life, end of Eternitie;
> How worthily he died that died unworthily.[31]

This type of paradox is not, of course, the invention of the metaphysical school. From Origen to Chesterton, paradox has been the fittest flesh of a gospel which was and is "foolishness to the Greeks." Paradox is the only mode in which the intellect is able to grasp at all the fact of the cohabitation of finite and infinite. Christian paradox may be called the intellectual shadow of Eucharistic theology, an act of transubstantiation going on in the verbal marrow of wit.

Without doubt Fletcher has an almost patristic flair for the language of paradox. However, his poem consists of three main stylistic layers: the paradoxical, the allegorical, the sensuous. Not only do these layers remain separate, fail to cohere in an artistic totality: they annihilate each other. In brief, the proper dogmatic implications of Fletcher's paradox are contradicted by the conceptualizations of his allegory and made wholly irrelevant to the final layer of sensuous rhetoric.

In the first book, Christ is already on earth while Justice and Mercy contend in heaven for the fate of man. The Father is the abstract of a vacillating, will-less old man whose mind must be made up for him. Christ is absent from the debate and has no part in the decision which permits the act of Redemption. The paradoxical mesh of the infinite-finite Christ gives way to a

---

[31] *Christ's Victory and Triumph* was first published in 1610.

merely logical clash of abstracts. Remember that this contention of Justice and Mercy occurs in the presence of a bewildered Father and in the absence of a purposeless Son. And nothing is done *poetically* to make Justice and Mercy symbolize the distinct but single Persons within the Godhead. Indeed, by putting Christ quite out of heaven, any possibility of such symbolization is destroyed—and with it all the central and orthodox dogmatic assumptions of the paradoxical layer of the poem. What one had read as dogma now seems to have been the merest rhetoric, the conventional language of dogma with none of the intention. The holidaying Christ of the allegory is not of the same family as the patristic Christ of the opening stanzas.

The main concern of the first book seems to be in giving to the mediaeval abstractions of Justice and Mercy a kind of Renaissance concreteness. To the extent to which this is achieved the possibility of imagining them as types of Father and Son is destroyed. They become rounded and independent beings. Note, for example, this eulogy of the beauty of Mercy:

> Upon her breast Delight doth softly sleepe
> And of Eternal Ioy is brought abed
> Those snowie mountelets, through which doe creepe
> The milky rivers, that as inly bred
> In siluer cisternes, and themselves do shed
>   To wearie trauailers, in heat of day
>   To quench their fierie thirst, and to allay
> With dropping nectar floods, the furie of their way.[32]

Such a description, with its note of Renaissance voluptuousness, destroys the very function of the mediaeval figure which, because of its abstract, featureless face, could be made to mirror the features of the Divine. The analogical possibility of the mediaeval device is thus lost. The figured idea cannot here look out suddenly with the very eyes of Christ—or Mary. This face wears its own distinctive flesh and is lightened by a look exclusively its own. And just as Mercy is figured as wholly separate

[32] *Christ's Victory,* I, st. 50.

from the bewildered Father and the exiled Son, so both God and Christ are made to seem less than they are. Levels of value and expression—the dogmatic, the conceptual, the rhetorical—proper to a Christian art and to each other have somehow lost coherence, lost their ancient analogical relevance one to the other.

It is of the greatest significance for the aesthetic effect of the poem as a whole that the conceptualized allegory of the first book deprives Christ of his function as mediator. He has no part in planning the economy of Redemption. He is away. It is decided for Christ that He will be sacrificed. He is indeed the victim, but no longer the Priest Who offers Himself as victim. Without His knowledge He is offered. He *does* consent. But the old liturgical idea of the ultimate priestly act is gone, and the fine dogmatic paradox of the opening stanzas is wholly nullified. One notes, too, that Mercy, after pleading for Man, offers herself as victim along with the Son (Who does not yet know what is in store for Him). If Mercy had been properly delineated (one cannot forget her "snowie mountelets"), an analogical identification of Mercy and Christ might here have been possible. But in this stanza, and in this conceptual context, Christ is clearly a second choice for the sacrificial function. Nor does He know that there has been a choice at all. Mercy here pleads with the Father.

> Who shall Thy temple incense anymore?
> Or at thy altar crowne the sacrifice?
> Or strewe with idle flow'rs the hallow'd flore?
> Or what should prayer deck with hearbs and spice
> The vialls, breathing orisons of price?
> If all must paie that which all cannot paie?
> O first begin with mee, and Mercie slaie,
> And Thy thrice honour'd Sonne, that now beneath doth stray.[33]

"Stray" gives a just account of the Son's position at this moment in the poem. However, soon giving way to Christ as victim, Mercy sings her tribute to the eventual role of the slain lamb on earth.

[33] *Christ's Victory*, I, st. 74.

He is a path, if any be misled;
He is a robe, if any naked bee;
If any chance to hunger, He is bread;
If any be a bondman, He is free.[34]

At the conceptual level of the allegory, Christ is deprived of His plenary sacrificial reality. At the level of rhetoric, Christ is deprived of His plenary sacramental reality. He is no more present on the altar than He was present in the allegorical heaven of Redemption. As in the Gressop poem, the sacramental symbol of "bread" is thinned by association with secondary metaphors—"path," "robe." Symbols which bespeak the simultaneous reality and presence of the historical, the mystical, and the sacramental Christ (i.e., symbols of analogical weight and reach) give place to images of Christ, sometimes brilliant, personal, intense, often compounded of a fulsome Renaissance sensuousness and immediacy, but images, nonetheless, never properly symbols, because of the strange displacement which has now made movement impossible from the rhetorical to the conceptual to the dogmatic levels of religious experience and value.

The Christ of the second book, Christ on earth, is the lovely boy of the Renaissance.

> His cheekes as snowie apples, sop't in wine,
> Had their red roses quencht with lilies white
> And like to garden strawberries did shine,
> Wash't in a bowl of milk, or rose-buds bright
> Unbosoming their breasts against the light:
>   Here loue-sicke soules did eat, thear drinke, and made
>   Sweet-smelling posies, that could neuer fade—
> But worldly eyes Him thought more like some liuing shade.[35]

It is, of course, "loue-sicke *soules*" that "did eat, thear drinke" . . . In his notes to the poem, Fletcher tells us that we "feast our hearts" on the Eucharistic Christ. This is the purest Cranmer, and the cleanest possible separation of spiritual from physical

---

[34] *Christ's Victory*, I, st. 77.
[35] *Christ's Victory*, II, st. 11.

communion. The appetizing physical beauty of Christ becomes a metaphor for the spiritual nourishment of communion. Indeed, the metaphor is made with such sensuous texture that any thought of an eating and drinking that is not the soul's would be utterly repugnant.

However, Fletcher is not a Gressop or a Lok. He is a poet. In him, as surely as in them (for the process is negatively the same), the analogical participation of the sensuous in the divine has ceased. But if symbol is thus reduced to metaphor, there is no further descent into cliché. Fletcher's exploits the sensuous level of rhetoric with a Renaissance heat, either adoring physical beauty for its own sake or employing it as objective correlative of spiritual beauty. But the separation of spirit and flesh is real, even if one can still be made to suggest or stand for the other. It is one thing for the Word to be made Flesh, quite another for the Word to be mimicked by the flesh, however prettily. Nor is the task of finding a correlative *in* the object *for* the subject anything like the task of discovering *in being itself* the analogical participation of each of its levels in the other. What we have come to think of as the Cartesian dualism of subject and object, of value and fact, is already in birth here. The mighty domain of the sensuous life is being forced into the menial service of the idea. No wonder that it ultimately revolts and constitutes its own self-sufficient empire!

The second book must remind us of an Elizabethan dumb show. The victory of Christ on earth is illustrated rather than dramatized. Christ does not act. He is silent and still and lovely. He is exhibited to confound the world, the flesh, and the devil. He was absent during His victory on heaven. He is passive and alone during His victory on earth. The perspective of motion, of the journey of the Christian in union with Christ, is thus denied. The idea of Christ is manipulated for diverse ethical and spiritual ends; as an *idea,* Christ is even adored. But He is here the Word illustrated by the flesh and no longer the Word made Flesh. As we will note later, Milton's Christ is the Christ of

Fletcher. And Milton's vast structures of sound and sight will be seen as the imposing substitute for a shattered liturgy, a massive objective correlative for an interior predicament. For Milton, like Fletcher, is forced to be an illustrator.

Fletcher's poem is a dogmatic ruin. With the loss, dogmatically, of sacrifice, Real Presence, and the corporate action of the members in the Mystical Body of Christ, there appears another kind of objective correlative, another kind of illustration—this time at the level of history rather than at the level of things. In the fourth book, the victory over death is illustrated by the victories of England over enemies at home and abroad. The corporate unity of the Mystical Body is thus made into a metaphor for English solidarity under the crown. And, presumably, only England can provide a proper illustration of the consequences for history of Christ's resurrection.

> And if great things by smaller may be ghuest,
> So, in the midst of Neptune's angrie tide
> Our Briton Island, like the weedie nest
> Of true halcyon, on the waues doth ride,
> And softly sayling, skorne's the water's pride:
>   While all the rest, drown'd on the continent
>   And tost in bloodie waues, their wounds lament
> And stand, to see our peace, as struck with wonderment.[36]

The English state and the English throne are the first true fruits of the Resurrection and the continuing mirror of Christ's triumph. This eulogy of James snaps the last thread of analogical possibility in Fletcher's use of rhetoric:

> Dear prince! thy subject's ioy, hope of their heirs,
> Picture of Peace. . . .
>
>   .   .   .
>
> Within thy sacred brest, that at thy birth
> Brought her with thee from Heav'n to dwell on earth
> Making our earth a Heav'n and paradise of mirth.[37]

[36] *Christ's Victory*, IV, st. 21.
[37] *Christ's Victory*, IV, st. 24.

Just as the loss of analogy, consequent upon the destruction of Eucharistic dogma, divorced the sensuous from the divine and even tempted it towards a life proper to itself alone, so the loss of analogy reduced the Christian idea of corporateness to the accidental level of the political—and the local. The new national state comes to be not so much an illustration of the Mystical Body as a parody on it. And this is a phenomenon which occurs at the very heart of the new and anti-Eucharistic firmament of symbol. It must be studied separately and at some length.

History and Poetry: The Decline of the Historical Concrete

CHAPTER FOUR

THAT THE FIRMAMENT of value within which Christian poetry was conceived had undergone drastic change by the mid-seventeenth century becomes quite clear from a study of what might be called "the historical concrete" in the poetry of this period. The term "historical concrete" is used here not only to mark an awareness in poetry of the actual historical and social event, but also, and chiefly, to suggest an awareness in poetry of the movement and pattern of events as a kind of incarnation, or true analogue, of the eternal engagement of God and man as it shapes itself in the startling sculptures of time.

It is obvious that in Dante there is analogical kinship between the personal-moral, the personal-historical, and the personal-divine life of the soul in its ascent to the Beatific Vision. The ascent is simultaneously moral, historical and corporate, and spiritual. Indeed, the spiritual ascent is incarnated in the moral and historical texture, just as the Beatific Vision is incarnated in the radiant episode of Beatrice.

It is perhaps less obvious, but none the less true, that in Shakespeare the historical serves not just as vehicle but as true analogue of the spiritual strife of Lear, Macbeth, Hamlet. Certainly the event in time, as Shakespeare treats it, is no mere parable made, as in the *Mirrour for Magistrates,* to point up a moral cliché. Moralizing art of this lesser breed is merely univocal. The magistrates as they appear in this mirror are no more than ticketed specimens of the vices and virtues. But Shakespeare's characters are free, their action is willed, their destiny is fixed only at the point where Providence and perversity collide. In Shakespeare the destruction of the tragic hero is far more than a moral demonstration (although, inescapably, it is that too). The fine point of a tragedy like *Hamlet* is an epiphany in which the historical structure is suddenly illuminated in its height and in its depth, in its matter and in its form. The full formal dimension of the Shakespearean tragedy is apprehended in an act of analogical awareness. The shape of the actual event in time swings into focus with the beckoning shape of the potential, revealing to vision that which had been obscured in actualization by the perversion of human will. The event in time which in itself was futile or obscene is raised to dignity by a climactic moment of participation in the engagement of human and providential will. Shakespearean tragedy is never a closed transaction between immoral man and the moral order of the universe. Within the structure of the tragedy there is a window (in *Hamlet* the window is Fortinbras) through which the illumination of the final tragic insight streams out towards proper fulfillments, fresh actualizations, genuine redemptions.

I would not and need not argue that Shakespeare's analogical sense of history is as secure as Dante's. And Shakespeare is not all of a piece. No doubt one can detect points of infection both in the early and late plays through which seep slowly the diseases of Erastianism and pessimism. But in the main the great tragedies, if in varying degrees, express an awareness of the fecundity and the validity of history impossible to the genius of the Greeks, possible only to the Christian-sacramental knowledge of time as the appointed vessel of fulfillments.

It is precisely this kind of awareness which is lost in the specifically Christian poetry of the early to middle seventeenth century. And never was there a time more needy in its bones for the Christian analogical knowledge of itself. Instead there is everywhere evident a raw nervous exposure to the accidents of time. The decline and disarray of human affairs at the end of the Elizabethan era seemed for Godfrey Goodman,[1] in *The Fall of Man, or the Corruption of Nature,* to prove a deterioration in the great macrocosm itself. The whole creation can be seen to travail and heard to groan—but without issue. There is a heavy Lutheran pessimism in Goodman's unrelieved vision of the radical corruption of nature by man's original (and seemingly incorrigible) sin. The relation here of microcosm to macrocosm is that of a simple one-to-one correspondence. This is a nerveless, fatalistic univocity of history and the universe—the flat antithesis of the analogical dynamism of Shakespearean tragedy.

Significantly, George Hakewill's famous rebuttal of Goodman, *An Apologie for the Power and Providence of God,*[2] achieves its optimism by deriding and discarding the link between microcosm and macrocosm and, in effect, separating history from the universe. In spite of Hakewill's conventional (and unquestionably sincere) acknowledgment of the sovereignty of God in the affairs of men, the historical process in the final implications of Hakewill's thesis is self-redemptive—just as in its final implications Hakewill's theology is deist rather than theist. Such implications become explicit in the thought of the eighteenth century.

---

[1] For a full account of the Goodman-Hakewill controversy and its consequences, see Victor Harris, *All Coherence Gone* (University of Chicago Press, 1949). An odd circumstance should be observed here. Goodman's *The Fall of Man* appeared in 1616. By the 1620's Goodman was being accused of holding Roman Catholic views of the Real Presence. Certainly Goodman died in the Catholic faith. It would be instructive to trace in his later work the effect of a full developed Catholic theology on Goodman's understanding of nature and history. Meanwhile it is sufficient to note that while mediaeval and modern Catholics have indeed held to opinions as dark (and as univocal) as those expressed in *The Fall of Man,* such opinions do not and cannot proceed from Catholic Eucharistic dogma. In seventeenth century England the widespread philosophy of despair and withdrawal is clearly not Catholic in inspiration.

[2] See note 1.

For our purpose it is enough to note that whereas in Goodman the relation of history to the universe is seen as univocal, in Hakewill the relation is clearly equivocal. The analogical understanding of the unity in proportion of natural, historical, and divine is beyond the reach of this kind of optimism and this kind of pessimism. In Goodman the divine stands outside nature and time, preparing fires of judgment equally and simultaneously for both. In Hakewill, while the Scriptural prophecy of the final destruction of things is never denied, the catastrophe is pushed ahead indefinitely in time, leaving in view and to hand the self-sufficient universe and a self-redemptive history.

This contrast has been labored here because it provides something of the contemporary frame of reference necessary for any examination of the loss of "the historical concrete" in Christian poetry of the period. Without doubt, the time from the death of Elizabeth to the restoration of the Stuarts is a time of excursions and alarums and bursts in the violet air. Machiavelli had made of practical statecraft an end in itself, free of ethical and spiritual compulsion. In philosophy, concern for the process of nature displaces the proper metaphysical concern for value. Meanwhile, the revival of neo-Platonism in the period goes in an opposite direction, threatening to spiritualize man out of all recognition. A wholly nonsacramental mysticism develops as a vessel for the life of the spirit set free from world, flesh, and time. No wonder that society falls victim to the Machiavellians and that knowledge is finally captured by the materialists. There were no defences left against these marauders. What are the consequences? Instead of the total universe of traditional Christianity there emerge in the seventeenth century many separate universes, each with its own god and its own law—the political universe, the scientific universe, the sensuous universe, the spiritual universe. For many Christians, grace seems now to operate apart from nature, faith has no regard for works, the invisible church confounds and confutes the church visible. In the psychology of Descartes, man is no longer a unity of soul and body but, as

Jacques Maritain has said, "an angel in a machine." It was not long before man came to be regarded either as all angel or all machine. In recent literature, Virginia Woolf, with her concentration on the psychological interior, illustrates the "angelism" which grew out of the abandonment of the sacramental universe. And the naturalistic novel of Arnold Bennett, which Miss Woolf so much disliked, simply represents the other half—the machine which the angel had discarded.

If by the end of the seventeenth century man seems to have been wrenched apart from nature, from God, even from himself, is it just to place the onus solely or chiefly on the disturbing social and intellectual energies released by the Renaissance? True, the traditional structure of Christian thought and practice was beset in the sixteenth and seventeenth centuries by what seemed to be alien forces. But were these forces really alien? Was the new science in itself alien? Was the rapid motion of society necessarily in defiance of the Christian social order? Was the new individualism intrinsically un-Christian? Or did these impulses become alien to Christianity because Christianity failed to comprehend them, failed to sacramentalize them?

The contention here and throughout this study is that while revolutions in natural science and in political theory and practice may indeed connive as material, and perhaps as efficient, cause of the Christian poet's radical sense of displacement in time, it is nevertheless the case that the final cause of this displacement, of this predicament in the poetry—as in the lives—of Christians, must be sought, insofar as the poetry is Christian, at the level of Christian dogma. The salvo of ideas and events was surely no deadlier in the time of Milton than it was in the time of St. Augustine or than it is in the time of T. S. Eliot. The Christian response to any possible phalanx of natural, historical, and intellectual assaults, insofar as the response is and remains Christian, will be determined not on the "outside," not in the milieu, but in the deep root-structure of the Christian mind and heart. Furthermore, any separation of heart and mind, any reliance on Christian sensibility at the expense of what might be called the dogmatic intelligence, will necessarily bring about either a compromise in the Christian response, an accommodation to the very circumstances and proposals which seem to threaten the specifically Christian grip on time, place, and value —or else the reliance on pure sensibility will coax the Christian out of time and place in a disembodied hunt for value, essence. It might be noted, for instance, that Godfrey Goodman, in effect, washes his hands of history and of any practical responsibility within history. Hakewill's rationalistic optimism makes alliance with history, which is conceived of, ultimately, as a self-moved, self-contained entity without ontological reference. Hakewill accommodates his thought to the new rationalism; Goodman abandons history outright. In neither writer, significantly enough, is there any reference to that central dogmatic act of Christian worship which confirms both the fecundity and the validity of history, thereby admonishing the faithful against the extremes of accommodation and withdrawal, of complacency and despair. It will be apparent that the rejection (and the revision) of traditional Eucharistic dogma had enormous consequences for the shape and direction of Christian culture.

In the pages which follow I shall treat the problem of "the historical concrete" as it appears and disappears in the work of representative Anglican, Puritan, and Catholic poets of the earlier seventeenth century. However, at this point it is necessary to state the problem more exactly than I have done thus far, to suggest some of its ramifications for the aesthetic life of symbol, and to indicate the bearing of Eucharistic theology on this process of deterioration in the analogical sense of history. In the present pages I am confining the discussion to Protestant poetry. The difficulties confronting the Roman Catholic poet of the period are complex and of a different kind and will be dealt with separately.

One soon discovers that there are marked differences between the poetic-historical symbols of Catholic and Protestant-minded

Anglicans. It is not surprising that there should be a difference
between the historical symbols of churchmen (of whatever alti-
tude) and nonchurchmen. Nor would one expect to find conformity within dissent. Calvinist, Quaker, and Digger do not
share the same historical bias. Yet the diversity of symbolization
and bias is not so slippery as one might expect. When one moves
from the more Catholic Anglicans leftward, one encounters a
strikingly proportionate series of rationalizations concocted of apt
accommodations between fragments of Christian doctrine and
the various aspirations of particular social groups or classes. For
example, Calvin's terrifying distortion of the Pauline doctrine of
predestination is further distorted by English Calvinists to fit
their immediate revolutionary needs. In Calvinism (whether English or continental) the ancient Christian sense of corporateness,
of unity in the Mystical Body, has been sharpened into a sword
to attain and to maintain the narrow class-exclusiveness of the
self-elect. At the extreme left the persecuted Digger transforms
the predestination of the person into a predestination of the
sinless social order. Neither Calvinist nor Digger loses "the
historical concrete." All unawares both are lost *in* it, and in precisely the same manner, the way of accommodation and rationalization. Clearly, the analogical sense of history as both fecund
and valid vanishes in any such univocal monism, whether the
order predestined is individualist or communist in its dye.

There is also the way of withdrawal, the abandonment of "the
historical concrete." Consider as symptom in the poetry of the
time the persistent nostalgia for the Golden Age, the lost Garden.
There is Vaughan's retreat into the childhood garden and away
from the world of miser, spendthrift, courtier, and statesman.
There is the golden garden of Traherne with its visionary fulfillment of promises lost to time but not, perhaps, alien to eternity. The golden childhood garden of these poets does not, like
Spenser's Garden of Adonis, bear the seed of the future. The
poignant sadness which lies like a shadow under each bright
image in the poetry of Vaughan is not, as in Dante, born of the

purgatorial spasm of time itself, but rather comes from the certainty that the glories of the hidden garden are locked forever against flesh and time. Even the joy which runs in the visionary universe of Traherne is a joy in transcendence, in the solipsistic construction of a world without history, in defiance of history. For the garden of Vaughan and Traherne, unlike the Garden of Genesis, is a way out, not a way in. The child in Vaughan and Traherne is clad eternally in swaddling clothes. He will never grow to confound and instruct the doctors in the temple. He will never enter that darker garden of the sleepless agony. Though he is given the innocence of the dove, he cannot be entrusted with the wisdom of the serpent.

One is tempted to attribute the abandonment of time in these poets to a simple revulsion against the victory in time of the "barbarian" revolution. Professor Victor Harris, in his valuable study *All Coherence Gone*,[3] has traced the mark of Godfrey Goodman's type of historical pessimism through the work of such writers as Raleigh, Donne, Davies of Hereford, Heywood, Alexander, Wither, Herbert, Vaughan, and Milton. This double sense of decay in nature and in history is obviously not confined to the moment of royalist defeat. Nor is there any question here of the direct influence of Goodman's book, which merely articulates a general malaise. However, the phenomenon, while in evidence throughout the first half of the seventeenth century, seems to be most poignant in the poetry of Vaughan and Traherne, at the moment when no reconstruction of kingly myth, and therefore of earthly hope, appears to be possible. But there is one great exception to any simple thesis that the abandonment of history is nothing more than a royalist rationalization of disappointment and defeat. In Milton's *Paradise Lost* the abandonment of history is utterly specific.

The Archangel Michael, in the final books of the poem, displays to Adam the consequences of his sin. The history of the

[3] (University of Chicago Press, 1949.)

[95]

world is unrolled before Adam's eyes. After the long agony of pre-Christian history has passed before him, Adam cries out with joy at the entry of Christ into time. But his joy is short-lived. For Adam discovers that after the brief apostolic age the leaven of the Word is lost. Worldliness infects the church. Even the Reformation does not reform, and the world wags on "to good malignant, to bad men benign," until the last days of history when Christ comes again, not to inaugurate the Millennium but "to dissolve Satan and his perverted world." Note that it *is* Satan's world. History is doomed. It contains no creative possibilities, no real fecundity, because it has no validity. It has become, in fact, the image of Satan. Christ will return to the world from outside it. Therefore the Archangel instructs Adam, and presumably the sons of Adam, to seek and cultivate the interior garden, "the paradise within." Salvation for man is made conditional on the absolute withdrawal from history.

No doubt Vaughan and Traherne in their retreat have in mind the victory of the Cromwellian revolution. And Milton has in mind the subsequent defeat of the revolution. But for royalist and republican alike the final cause of the retreat into the timeless garden lies deeper than the immediate political event.

This is not the place for a careful analysis of the Eucharistic theology of each of these poets. Obviously Milton's rejection of Catholic dogma is more thoroughgoing than Vaughan's. But it will be observed in the poetry of Anglicans, as well as in the poetry of an avowed antisacramentalist like Milton, that time is never understood to be in any way *contained* by the Presence of Christ. In prayer book, as well as in Presbyterian and sectarian theology, the sacrifice of Christ is understood as pinned to a receding point in time. Now if the sacrifice is confined to a moment within history, it cannot be conceived of as encompassing history, nor can history, in any degree, fulfill an event from which history must ever move further away.

Milton's Christ can no more stretch and renew Himself forward in time than can Vaughan's child, stunted eternally like

Peter Pan, fit his little limbs along the High Cross. As I have already noted, the Christ of *Paradise Lost* returns to the world from outside it and only at the tail-end of time. The doctrine of Christ's sacramental Presence in history has, of course, been rejected in all the new Eucharistic theologies, as clearly and unmistakably by Cranmer (and by Anglicans as diverse as Jeremy Taylor and Laud) as by Luther, Calvin, and Zwingli. True, the Presence of Christ to faith and by faith is assured to them who "feed on Him in their hearts." And God's direct intervention in history through portent and miracle seems credible to Christians as various in doctrine as Donne and Milton. But such belief, though it may accompany, is by no means identical with, the ancient Eucharistic dogma of the actual Presence of Christ on the altar joining historical man to Himself in the unbloody renewal of the sacrifice of the Cross, an act at once annihilating time and freshening it, reordering it. In Catholic belief, the Mass provides corporate entry into the life of Christ, through repentance, at the point of sacrifice. The faithful, therefore, in their proper order, participate in the redemptive economy, which is confined to no one place, no one time, but spread throughout creation from before it and beyond it. And it is from the Catholic dogma of the Eucharist that the analogical sense of history takes large sustenance.

For Christ, while judging from beyond it, is not only present to history but is engaged in incorporating historical man into His Presence. In the Eucharist not only does man, the historical creature, enter the Body of Christ as member, but also he brings forward with him the very tissues of the natural order as he has acted upon them and thereby raised them to the historical order. In the Eucharist the cosmic enters the historical, the natural level of experience passes into the human and thence into the divine. The liturgical action catches up the things of nature humanized in the form of the bread and wine of man's social labour. And the human community, historical and concrete, is lifted to communion in the Body of Christ.

In Catholic theology the historical Christ of Galilee, the Christ
who sits at the right hand of the Father in Heaven, the sacramental Christ of the altar, the Christ of the Mystical Body are,
analogously and actually, one Christ. Perpetuating His Mystical
Body in time by the sacramental renewal of Calvary, Christ joins
to Himself not only historical man, but also the works of man
and therefore the concrete historical event. This is not to say that
Christ is identical with history, becomes history, but rather that
the Incarnation extends itself within history, perpetually reordering it, reshaping its broken structures, never abandoning history,
but redeeming it.

It is inevitable that in any such paradoxical view of an eternal
Presence in history there should also be an intuition of an eternal
present, of a level of being in which persons and events, no matter how separated they may be by time, can nevertheless participate. For if time is the vessel of fulfillments, nothing of it is lost.
Nor can it be conceived of either as a mere recession from a
vanishing golden point, or as a simple linear progression towards its own intrinsic completion. Perhaps it is in what Erich
Auerbach calls the *figura* that one sees most clearly how the
Christian analogical sense of time holds on to events and persons.

In his article, "Adventure in Order," William F. Lynch sum-
marizes Auerbach's claim for the *figura*. "Altogether essential to
the *figura* is the inward historical reality of the two events or
persons that are related: 'one of them not only means itself, but
also the other; the other, on the contrary, encloses or fulfills the
first.'—'Both lie as real events or forms inside time.' Yet there
is also a sense in which both are open to a third future image
which 'though still incomplete as event is already completely fulfilled in God and has been so in His Providence from all eternity.'
Thus this new history remains everywhere real and open, as
complete and incomplete as the heart would have it." [4]

[4] *Thought* (Spring, 1951), p. 46. Erich Auerbach's *Mimesis: The Representation of Reality in Western Literature,* trans. from the German by Willard R. Trask
(Princeton University Press, 1953), expands and further applies ideas first put
forward in the essay "Figura," *Arch. Roman.,* XXII, p. 436.

In a *figura,* Isaac is the type of Christ; the sacrifice of Christ "encloses or fulfills" the sacrifice of Isaac. The fulfillment of sacrifice, already realized in God's design, is that very fulfillment towards which history is borne by the sacramental Presence of Christ in His church. Therefore, as Father Lynch is at pains to point out, *figura* cannot be translated into our word "figurative" with its merely illustrative connotations. In the *figura Christi:* "Adam, Joseph, David . . . are full of their own historical reality, and, on their own analogical planes of being, are already doing the work of Christ. Nevertheless, both their meaning and actuality are deepened by their Christic relation. What a corruption of the actual order of things it would be to make them pure univocal relations of Christ and no more. For one thing it is hard to imagine God dying for a bundle of metaphors and illustrations." [5]

There can be little doubt that the analogical worth of the *figura* is sustained by the Eucharistic assumption of the Presence of Christ throughout history, sacrificially redeeming history, and drawing time before and time after into a design eternally present. Outside traditional Eucharistic theology, *figura* is lost entirely or reduced to "a bundle of metaphors." In Milton, Noah's ark cannot be a type of the church because for Milton the visible church, if not anti-Christ, is, at the very least, Christless. And, significantly, the "forerunners" of Christ in the vision of history vouchsafed to Adam by the Archangel are not Christ types. They are not sacrificed in history but are miraculously extricated from it. Indeed, these saints of the Old Testament, like the saints scattered sparsely through the aftertimes, are really moral signposts let down for a spell in the desert of history—a desert through which the Blood of Christ can never seep.

Milton is a thoroughgoing Protestant, and he rejects the rhetoric as well as the dogma of Eucharistic Catholicism. With the Anglican poets the situation is often more difficult to get at.

[5] Lynch, p. 46

Professor Rosemond Tuve [6] has demonstrated a clear continuity between many of the images in Herbert's poetry and the iconographical usage of mediaeval Catholicism. Within the limits she has set herself, Miss Tuve's demonstration is wholly convincing. But it would be misleading for us to assume that a continuity of rhetorical symbol necessarily implies a like continuity at the level of dogmatic symbol. Actually, it is the peculiar tension which comes to exist between the traditional rhetorical surface of image and the novel or ambiguous core of dogmatic symbol that characterizes the precarious firmament of Anglican poetry in the seventeenth century. In reading a poet like Herbert we must do more than consider the iconographical and typological traditions which shape his Eucharistic rhetoric. It is one thing, for instance, to recognize that the Wine-Press and Joseph's Coat are both traditional Eucharistic symbols and types of Christ's sacrifice. It is quite another thing to assume that Herbert's understanding of this sacrifice is as consistent dogmatically as it is rhetorically, certainly, with the mediaeval tradition. And obviously the life of Herbert's poetry cannot be known or felt apart from a proper perception of its entire organic structure and texture. Any tension that may operate in a poem between rhetorical convention and dogmatic conviction is of the first importance for one's reading of that poem and for one's aesthetic response to it.

This is a hint to the kind of difficulty which is presented by the seventeenth century Anglican poets who still wear their Catholic vestments. It is possible for such poets to retain the traditional rhetoric as ornament without retaining it as function. For instance, Joseph's Coat would be a rhetorical ornament without genuine analogical function in any context in which the sacrifice of Christ is thought of as historically static, fixed in time, a single event illustrated by an earlier event.

What can one say of the typology of George Gascoigne's Elizabethan poem, "Good Morrow"?

[6] *A Reading of George Herbert* (Chicago, 1952).

The Rainbowe bending in the skie
Bedeckt with sundrye hues
Is like the seat of God on high
And seems to tell these news:

That as thereby he promised
To drown the world no more
So by the blood which Christ hath shed
He will our health restore.[7]

The "rainbow" covenant may properly typify the New Testament of Christ's Blood. The cup of the Eucharist is the fulfillment
of God's first promise of mercy to man. The antitype can "enclose
or fulfill" the type. But is just such an enclosure effected in this
poem? The actual rainbow before the poet's eyes reminds him of
the real, yet typical rainbow of the covenant. This actual sixteenth
century rainbow "seems to tell" that whereas God signified once
by a rainbow that he would "drown the world no more," so by
another sign (traditionally associated with the first), the sign of the
shed Blood, God makes still another promise, the restoration of
"our health"—atonement. Now is there a dynamic, analogical
unity of the images "rainbow" and "blood"? Or does Gascoigne
merely retain a pattern of association, a univocal metaphorical relation, between the two? And is the blood, in Gascoigne's meaning, shed once and for all from a Body crucified to a single point
in time, or is it possible also to understand it as shed, analogously,
by the Lamb slain from before the beginning of time? More precisely, the question one must raise about all such Catholic-looking
imagery is this: Does the New Testament antitype "fulfill" the Old
Testament type by arresting it at the historical moment of Crucifixion (and thereby reducing to a metaphor of the new covenant
in Christ), or are both type and antitype "open to a third future
image" in which Calvary bisects time by perpetual Eucharistic renewal? Without searching beyond the poem for Gascoigne's intentions does not one infer that just as the rainbow now in the heav-

[7] In *Select Poetry Chiefly Devotional of the Reign of Queen Elizabeth*, ed. Edward Farr (2 vols, Cambridge, 1845), I, p. 37.

ens recalls that prophetic rainbow which once, and only once, appeared, so the wine of the communion cup suggests, illustrates, the promise of the blood which, long ago, was shed once and for all?

The contention here is that typological symbolism which assumes a fulfillment in the historical but not in the sacramental Christ loses analogical validity and is reduced to the status of metaphorical adornment. A full analysis of the pressure exerted by this kind of foreshortened *figura* within the work of major Anglican poets like Herbert must be reserved for separate treatment. My concern here has been to indicate broadly and in terms of "the historical concrete" the kind of change which is being effected in the firmament of Christian symbol and to relate this change to the drastic Protestant revision of Eucharistic theology.

It is easy enough to detect the anti-Eucharistic sense of Christ's departure from history in the following lines from Christopher Lever's formal meditation, "A Crucifix." To be entombed in the heart is not to be alive in history.

> Now (holy Joseph) help me to inter
> This sacred corse; my heart's a fitting place
> Wherein thou maist His sepulchre prepare.[8]

Indeed, Lever's poem, which is clearly influenced by Catholic manuals like *The Spiritual Exercises* of St. Ignatius, is an interesting example of how Catholic devotional rhetoric put to the service of Protestant Eucharistic dogma can be a trap for the unwary modern reader. In "The Crucifix," Lever attempts a "composition" of time and place in the Ignatian tradition of formal meditation.

> My soul conceits a very Christ before
> Spreading His sacred body on the tree.
> Methinks His very torments I doe see.[9]

The poet then pauses over the bleeding feet, side, and heart of

[8] In *Fuller Worthies Library*, ed. A. B. Grosart (London, 1872), III, p. 660.
[9] In Grosart, III, p. 642.

Christ with a devotion that at first seems to suggest Southwell and Crashaw. But note how Christ's death is applied:

Now give me breath (O sacred breathing spirit!)
With faithful affectation to apply
This death, this Christ, this competence of merit
Unto my soul. . . .[10]

Not only does this clearly imply an individualist reception of the merits of the Cross by faith alone (with, of course, no participation in Eucharistic sacrifice), but these wounds and this death are to be drained of their proper actuality.

The speare hath made a passage to thy heart,
The entrance then is open; let me in
To see the merit that hath vanquished sin.[11]

Lever has not sought, as the Ignatian must seek, to realize in the imagination a Presence which in fact already is; he seeks to re-create in the imagination a Presence which once was. But with no grasp of the analogical unity of historical, mystical, and sacramental Christ, Lever falls into simple moralism, abstracting even the wounds of the historical Christ. The past itself—the actual event of Calvary—blurs, losing its own concreteness as event, and is spiritualized into nourishment for pious speculation and resolve.

In such poetry the loss of "the historical concrete" is obvious, and the connection between this loss and the loss of traditional Eucharistic theology is equally obvious. And there should be little difficulty in seeing how a theological drift of this kind prepares for the "extricationism" of poets like Vaughan and Traherne and the Milton of *Paradise Lost*.

But if Milton's pessimistic account of history (as abandoned by a Christ who returns to it only for the burning) is anti-Eucharistic, the optimistic antithesis of such an account is equally anti-Eucharistic. For the redemptive action of Christ is not completed by time,

[10] In Grosart, III, p. 651.
[11] In Grosart, III, p. 654.

although it operates in time and through time. It does not come to rest in Charlemagne—or in Charles I. It is not an Erastian process aiming at the exaltation of particular kings or peoples. Christ did not offer Himself first and always for His Englishmen. Nor is His sacrifice fulfilled in "the historical concrete" by the return of Arthur or by the defeat of the Armada. Any such nationalistic millenarianism is quite contrary to the implications for history of Catholic Eucharistic theology. Indeed, the illusion of historicism hints at the tension which will always exist between the Two Cities, between the action of Christ in history and the pretentious resistance of historical man. The dogma of the Eucharist does not guarantee the temporal perfection of "the historical concrete." In the Catholic view, the church itself, the Bride of Christ, the visible extension in time of the Incarnation, is ever and inevitably infected by sin. There is always tension between the sacramental holiness of the church and the historical sin of the church, just as there is always tension between the Presence of Christ in history and the denial of Christ by history. But if in this situation there is no ground for complacency, neither is there ground for despair. The redemptive process is never arrested.

What Karl Rahner says of the sinful church applies, in general, to the Eucharistic hope for sinful history: "When the Church suffers from sin she achieves redemption from her guilt, for she suffers her guilt in Christ Crucified, because sin, since it is not in the secret recesses of the heart but in the world and thus also in the Church, remains sin. . . . But sin at the same time is also the consequence of sin (because it is the embodiment of the secret malice of the heart), and being absorbed as such by the Church, gives her the possibility of atoning for it and conquering it." [12]

Similarly, in the fully Eucharistic view, the failures of history do not dam up the redemptive possibilities of history, do not undermine the condition of history as analogue of the engagement of human and divine will, suffered with patient purpose by Divine Love. Infinite lapses are countered by infinite restorations, reorder-

[12] "The Church of Sinners," *Cross Currents* (Spring, 1951), p. 65.

ings, infinite illuminations and epiphanies. For while history is left free, it is never left to itself.

The danger inherent in any anti-Eucharistic view of history is that success in any given historical circumstance is finally as fatal to it as failure. Christianity, in short, endangers itself as much by the optimistic accommodation to history as by the pessimistic withdrawal from it. Certainly it would not do for us to mistake an optimistic acceptance of history, bred and nourished by a happy chance of events, for an analogical perception of history, bred and nourished by Eucharistic dogma. An optimism of the former kind is perishable because it cannot be weaned from the mother that bore it. A mere change of circumstances may convert it quickly into its opposite.

How, then, does one square the sure promise which the young Milton of the revolutionary prose saw unfurling itself in time with the epitaph on history written into *Paradise Lost*? Is there any real change in Milton's philosophy of history? Does the later pessimism reveal any sudden new dogmatic principle in Milton's thought? Or has his sense of history from the beginning been precarious? Did not the young Milton seek to complete his *figura* of historical purpose in the England of Cromwell, just as Spenser had sought to complete his *figura* in the glory of Elizabeth? It must be remembered that Spenser in his view of the Eucharist and the Romish "cup of abomination" is scarcely less Protestant than Milton.[13] For Spenser, England's greatness is fulfilled by the Virgin Queen. In the myth of the return of Arthur, one is aware

---

[13] Virgil K. Whitaker in his recent monograph, *The Religious Basis of Spenser's Thought* (Stanford University Press, 1950), emphasizes the conservative elements in Spenser's Anglicanism. But, as Whitaker concedes, "in Spenser's reference to the Holy Communion there is no suggestion of the Catholic doctrines of transubstantiation or of the Mass as a sacrificial rite. . . ." (p. 52). Spenser would appear to hold the central Anglican view of the Real Presence. This dismissal of the doctrine of sacrifice is, of course, crucial. An emphasis on communion to the exclusion of the sacrificial act of Christ in and with His Mystical Body is in effect a dismissal of the corporate *historical* Presence in favor of a view of the Presence as a spirit received *individually* and "in the heart." In such a view the efficacy of the sacrament is not denied (as it is denied by extreme Protestantism). But the historical reference of the sacrament is severely limited. While the sacrament, thus conceived, may touch history, it cannot encompass the historical.

of a striking secular parallel to the Christian *figura*. Elizabeth "encloses or fulfills" the promise of Arthur, and though at one level of the allegory Arthur indeed symbolizes divine grace, it is quite clear that Spenser understands spiritual fulfillment as possible only by way of a nationalistic fulfillment and in terms of a theology which is at once Erastian and anti-Eucharistic. Because, and only because, the Golden Age has seemed to return with the defeat of Rome and the rule of this latter-day English Virgin, history teems with possibilities and the Garden of Adonis assures the fecundity of time.

And for a while Milton can share Spenser's confidence in the natural order and look with hope to the horizons of time. But only so long as the greatness of England (confirmed by the sign of the broken Armada) can be identified with partisan political and religious aspirations. For Milton, the Reformation, like the Commonwealth, had seemed the direct univocal consequence of a divine act. Therefore, the eventual defeat of the good old cause could signify nothing less than the direct abandonment of history by God. History is thus a series of signs from on high. The return of Charles finally cancels out the return of Arthur. God has changed His mind.

In much the same way the cynical despair of Cowley's Golden Age is tails to the heads of Spenser's Erastian coin. To the Cavalier the victory of Cromwell makes Spenser's world a faerie world indeed. And the new Iron Age, closed on itself like a gate, prepares to rust.

Underlying all the moods and manners of Protestant religious poetry in this period, then, one can detect the loss of the analogical sense and, ultimately, the loss of the Eucharistic knowledge of history. In the manic-depressive vacillation between Spenserian optimism and Cavalier despair, between the revolutionary assertiveness of *Areopagitica* and the reactionary dismissal of history in *Paradise Lost,* there can be found a unifying principle, although a negative one. New principles and values with a positive force will be seen to emerge as the old firmament of Christian symbol falls apart. History refuses to be abandoned. But it is a very different firmament which now takes shape and which will henceforth shape the direction of English poetry.

Amidst the chaos of doctrine and under the pressure of events, the historical and social symbols of seventeenth century Anglican poetry break clear of their traditional frame of reference and develop in different, even antithetical, directions. The first is the way of accommodation to the actual historical event, to the new Erastian situation. The second is the way of withdrawal and the abandonment of the historical concrete. This splintering, within the Anglican tradition itself, of the historical and social symbol is symptomatic of the plight of poetry in the age. The firmament of symbol for Puritan and Catholic, as well as for Anglican, is rapidly dissolving and reshaping itself. Neither Milton nor Crashaw really escapes the pressures, whether political or doctrinal, to which Anglicanism is forced to bend. A somewhat more specific appraisal of these pressures as they touch upon the life of symbol must therefore now be given.

We must address ourselves to the intense nationalism newly abroad in the land. And we inevitably ask such questions as these. To what degree, in the popular imagination of the age, does the royal supremacy usurp the place of the displaced papal supremacy? To what degree does the Catholic corporate sense, bred by membership in the Mystical Body, now reduce itself to the merely patriotic sense of membership in the body politic? What, precisely, is the effect on central religious symbol of this complex new English mesh of secular and sacred impulses?

Neither theological nor social history is irrelevant to our problem, and before examining the historical level of symbol in Anglican poetry itself, it may be well to inspect the actual historical situation as it appears to a Catholic theologian like Newman and to a "disinterested" historian like J. W. Allen. Both writers, from very different viewpoints, are concerned with the relationship between church and state which develops in a peculiarly English way in the seventeenth century. And both writers say things which have a bearing on our interpretation of seventeenth century poetry and on our knowledge of the firmament within which this poetry was perforce conceived.

Newman, in noting the ineffectuality of the Non-Jurors after their break with the monarchy, draws this conclusion about the glittering period of seventeenth century Anglican churchmanship:

> How great and mysterious are the doctrines which they [Laud, Andrewes, Taylor, etc.] teach. And how proudly they appeal to primitive times, and claim the Ancient Fathers! . . . Look on, my brethren, to the Non-Jurors, and you will see what these Anglican divines were worth. There you will see that it was simply their position, their temporal possessions, their civil dignities, as standing round a king's throne, or seated in his great council, which made them what they were. Their genius, learning, faith, whatever it was, would have had no power to stand by themselves. These qualities had no substance, for, as we see, when the State abandoned them, they shrank at once and collapsed and ceased to be. . . . The High Church died out . . . for it had neither dogma to rest upon, nor object to present.[14]

Is this overstatement? Certainly it is an oversimplification. In all fairness one must be prepared to make or admit a real distinction between Anglicans like Andrewes and Taylor. The more Catholic-minded Anglicans of the time do not regard the king as pope, do not equate the Mystical Body with the body politic. The purely Erastian view of the church was never, in theory at least, held by high churchmen. And J. W. Allen argues on the basis of solid evidence that the notion of the Divine Right of Kings as the antithesis of parliamentary sovereignty was never seriously maintained by Anglican thinkers until the Civil War threatened the monarchy with extinction. Throughout the Tudor rule and until the climactic years of the revolution a very real kind of popular sovereignty was generally assumed. "The King of England was

[14] *Certain Difficulties Felt by Anglicans in Catholic Teaching* (London, 1870), I, pp. 223–224.

indeed frequently said to make law but lawyers and divines alike agreed that he could make it only 'in Parliament' or that he made it only at the request or with the assent of the Houses." [15]

Allen is equally persuasive in his contention, "that in the quite literal sense of the term, the reformation of the English Church began not with Henry VIII or Elizabeth but with the reign of James I. The Tudor sovereigns had freed England from Rome and nationalized this Church by means of a doctrine of Royal Supremacy in ecclesiastical causes. But they had almost wrecked the Church in doing so. The reconstituted church of Elizabeth was constructed and governed with a view to the avoidance of actual friction and without regard to logical coherence and real unity." [16]

One is compelled to add that at this stage the question of authority was also unsettled. There can be no doubt that in the absence of clear definition of dogma, and in the presence of Catholic and sectarian challenges both doctrinal and political in character, the Tudor church leaned heavily on the prestige and strength of the monarchy. Elizabeth was in fact Head of the Church. But by the time of James I the clergy felt more able to assert its proper authority. Allen notes that in the political writings of the Jacobean divines there can be traced "a movement away from Elizabethan Erastianism and towards a new and an older conception of the Church. Very distinctly there appears a tendency to conceive of the Church as a society radically distinct from the State, even though included within it; a society standing on its own separate base and properly and rightly governed by the clergy. The development of that view was part of the general movement of thought among the clergy in the reign of James." [17]

Certainly one may observe in the ecclesiastical theorizing of the period a growing acceptance of the apostolic origin of the episco-

[15] *English Political Thought, 1603–1660* (London, Methuen, 1938), I, pp. 100–101.
[16] Allen, p. 119.
[17] Allen, p. 129.

pacy; and with this new sense of the integrity of the church, there is, inevitably, a clear insistence on the right of the clergy to define doctrine, fix ritual, and administer clerical discipline. While it is conceded that it is the function of the crown to sanction and enforce the positive laws determined by the church, it is generally held that the crown may not initiate or veto such laws. Now in all this there can be seen some recovery of the sense of continuity with the Catholic past. Similarly, the renewed emphasis on ceremony and liturgical decency in the Laudian era would seem at first glance to illustrate a revival of Catholicity in the Church of England.

In the light of these recoveries and renewals in Anglican thought and practice, Newman's blast against the seventeenth century divines appears to be quite wide of the mark. But is it? Allen describes the theorizing of Anglican divines in those years which had seemed so propitious for the Establishment between the accession of James and the heyday of Laud. But Allen admits the Erastianism of the Tudor church and also of those frantic Caroline churchmen who clutch at the doctrine of the Divine Right of Kings at the moment when their king is on the edge of having no rights at all. For it was only while "the going was good" that the church felt able to contemplate aloud the recovery of its integrity and its self-respect. In the reign of James, the church began to rise from the cringing posture before the throne adopted for it by Cranmer and the Elizabethan bishops. And something like a genuine Catholic theory of the inviolability of the church did then begin to emerge. As we will note, the fruit of this recovery of a decently religious sense of the church is to be found in the poetry of Anglicans like George Herbert. But, alas, this fruit ripens out of the sun and over the wall—and just as the axe bites at root and branch. By a perverse paradox, the renewed Catholic sense of the church's integrity will shape, in the best Anglican poetry of the age, a symbolism of withdrawal from history and from the life of the English state. And in this symbolism of withdrawal the ancient corporate sense of membership in the Mystical Body will have no place at all. It will be noted, too, that Anglican poetry which is not touched by this yearning for spiritual integrity vacillates between an almost blasphemous Erastianism and a thoroughly cynical secularism.

Furthermore, it will be apparent that popular feeling for the crown is unaffected by abstract ecclesiastical argument. Welling up from the inchoate Catholicism of age-old devotional habits, a need for warm, firm, and visible symbol overwhelms in the popular imagination all the neat dialectical distinctions and reservations made by the ecclesiastical theorist. In the popular imagination, deep in the myth-making faculty of the masses, the king for a while is pope as well as monarch. The king for whom Anglicans, after Cranmer, pray is surely set above all others in the land. The prayer is not that he may always and sedulously consult the will of parliament (and convocation), but that he may incline his will to God's will, that he "knowing whose minister he is may above all things seek the honour and glory of God"; and that "we (duly considering whose authority he hath) may faithfully serve, honour and humbly obey him." Prayers for the king (and his kin) occupy a much larger place in the Anglican service than do prayers for the Pope (and his intentions) in the Catholic rite. And there can be no gainsaying the fact that in all the prescribed Anglican services, prayers for bishops and clergy are relatively scant and decidedly secondary. The crown is almost the focal symbol in Anglican devotion. This emphasis has never been altered, although by the reign of William and Mary it had become incongruous to the point of the ludicrous. Sober clerical reflection on the antonomous rights of the church apart from the crown at no time affected deeply the myth-making faculty of Englishmen. From the beginning, it is the crown which, both at the religious and secular levels, symbolizes for the Anglican his sense of membership in the City of God as in the city of men. Indeed, under the peculiar circumstances of the English Reformation the crown is the only compelling symbol of man's participation through time in the eternal. And at first, despite Erastian theologizing and antisacramental dogmatizing, the crown symbol is capable of a properly analogical reach. Paradoxically, then, a Catholic quality remains to the historical symbol in the Erastian Tudor period of anti-Catholic churchmanship. This quality is lost by the time the Jacobean divines are attempting, self-consciously, to recover a Catholic sense of the church. And Catholic corporateness is wholly rejected in the poetry of Catholic-minded Anglicans like Herbert!

The fate of the crown as religious symbol is diverting in itself. And it displays clearly the process whereby the analogical grip on history was loosened and lost. To understand the process we must be prepared to recognize that imaginatively the analogical sense of time was not at first seriously impaired by the break with Rome. As we shall see, the genius of Hooker saved for a while the ancient patterns of symbol and response. But before Hooker there had been Henry VIII—and Cranmer. And after Hooker— the deluge.

The Crown as Religious Symbol

CHAPTER FIVE

IN THE POETRY of the English Renaissance, the Crown is a dominant culture symbol. It is compounded of fancy and fact, born of delight and necessity, at once the creation of vision and event. This culture symbol is brought to ruin not by any lapse of the individual poetic imagination, not by a lonely fault of vision, but by the eventful dislocation of a total organism of thought, feeling, and act. We are to be concerned here, then, with the laws that govern the life and death of a culture symbol.

In the imagery of Shakespeare the crown is always something more than a sign of stately power and magnificence. And it is never identified in any simple fashion with the head that wears it. Richard II is acutely aware that his person fails the great symbol of the crown. Henry V is moulded by the symbol. He grows into it and wears it well—but it is greater than he is; his own greatness is a kind of participation in the virtues conveyed and held by the symbol. And these virtues are as much inward as outward, as much corporate as personal, as much spiritual and religious as political and national. We might remember, too, that in the first book of Spenser's *Faerie Queene,* King Arthur, though he does represent the reborn energies of England, is meant also to represent nothing less than the downward sweep of the grace of God.

That the royalist symbol in Shakespeare transcends the merely courtly and does manage to reach beyond the personal glorification of monarchs—even of Elizabeth herself—is surely witness to something more than Shakespeare's artistic integrity and power. It is an indication that Elizabeth was, for a while, greater than Elizabeth, that the monarchy did, for a while, seem to suggest and sustain values vaster than monarchy. For a while, the crown was able to stand duty as religious as well as political symbol. But not for long. By the end of the reign of Elizabeth, the secularizing process was already far advanced. And the religious layering of the crown symbol was soon to undergo distortion.

I am mainly concerned in this chapter with the fantastic fate of the religious level of suggestion in the crown symbol, with the drift to what can only be called "Emperor-worship" once the spiritual and political implications of the symbol are made to tumble over one another. This shift in the symbolic nature and function of the crown cannot be understood at all without a glance, however brief, at the substance of the symbol as it came to be compounded in the earlier English Renaissance.

We shall attempt in a moment to assess Hooker's uncanny understanding of the popular need for a symbol at once corporate and analogical in its capacity. The final implications for symbol inherent in the peculiar—and immediate—history of the English crown did not at first, for a variety of reasons, impair the imaginative and religious function of the crown as Hooker saw it and as Shakespeare realized it. But the implications were there. They were to emerge in the firmament of Anglican poetry because they were at the very marrow of Anglicanism, because the early history of Anglicanism is an aspect of the history of the English crown.

In itself and by itself, Henry's denial of the papal authority was not necessarily a denial of Catholic tradition. Throughout the Middle Ages there had been notable struggles between the spiritual and temporal powers. Nor was there anything really novel in Henry's affirmation of a national autonomy which was to be spiritual as well as temporal. Catholic kings of Spain had gone as far. And a French king had once held a Pope captive. The novelty of the English situation lies not in the jurisdictional dispute as such but in the startling Henrican definition of the *nature* of a national church!

> The unity of these holy churches, in sundry places assembled, standeth not by knowledging of one governor in earth over all churches. . . . This Church of England, and other known particular churches, in which Christ's name is truly honoured, called on, and professed in faith and baptism, be members of the whole Catholic Church . . . and so every Christian man ought to honour, give credence and to follow the particular church of that region so ordered (as afore) wherein he is born or inhabited. . . . Likewise, so they be by Christ's commandment, bound to honor and obey, next unto Himself, Christian kings and princes which be the head governors under Him in the particular churches.[1]

The church, therefore, is no longer to be understood as the Mystical Body of Christ visible in a single form. The unity of the church is now properly invisible. Visible churches may be as many as there are political states, and "princes to govern." And that the invisible church does not transcend political and cultural divisions by any deep-lying unity of doctrine is quite apparent from the incredible confusion of doctrine which obtains between and within political states. The ancient sense of the Mystical Body of Christ as visibly and historically one is shattered beyond repair, now in theory, eventually in fact and in symbol. For the invisible unity of a church divided by geographical and political accident and by wholly diverse and incompatible doctrines is a unity that mocked the reach of the analogical mind. Indeed, no possibility of analogy is left between the visible and the invisible, between the city of men and the City of God.

But there are princes to govern—a pope on duty for every fragment of the church visible. Elizabeth is to be more prudent than Henry in this matter of the royal supremacy. And as we have noted, the Jacobean divines are to claim more and more power for the church as such. Yet, surely, the Jacobean and Caroline divines could claim an ecclesiastical autonomy only by a convenient lapse of memory. Historically, practically, finally, did not the Anglo-

---

[1] *King's Book* (State Papers, 1543), pp. 244–248.

Catholic objection to Roman authority rest on the royal claim to plenary power within the realm of England? And if one concedes to the crown all coercive power (as the Jacobean divines unhesitatingly did), ought not one to be ready to admit that the church's defence against Catholicism and Puritanism alike depends utterly on this coercive power?

It must also be recognized that within the doctrinal bedlam of the whole Stuart period, any notion of the church thinking and acting as an autonomous, self-instructed organism is sheer delusion. A striking passage in a treatise by the Reverend Alexander Ross, a chaplain to Charles I, gives us a vivid picture of the religious situation in Caroline England and reveals both the confusion and the impotence of church and sects.

> Some reject scripture, others admit no other writings but scripture. Some say the devils shall be saved . . . others that there are no devils at all . . . Some will have all things in common, some not. Some will have Christ a body only in Heaven, some everywhere, some in the Bread, others with the Bread, others about the Bread, others under the Bread, and others that Christ's Body is the Bread or the Bread His Body. And others again that this Body is transformed into his Divinity. Some will have the Eucharist administered in both kinds, some in one, some not at all. . . . Some will make Christ two Persons, some give him but one Nature and one Will. . . . The main causes of these distractions are pride, self-love, ambition, contempt of Church and Scripture, the Humour of Contradiction, the Spirit of Faction, the Desire of Innovation . . . the Want or contempt of Authority, Discipline, and order in the Church. . . . Therefore wise Governors were forced to authorize Bishops, Moderators or Superintendents (call them what you will) for regulating, curbing and punishing such luxurious wits as disturbed the peace of the Church and consequently the State. . . .[2]

One notes, of course, the thoroughly un-Catholic conception of the bishop (or superintendent, "call him what you will"). The Catholic sense of the apostolic church is by no means universal in the Stuart period. More significant is the assumption that wise

[2] *Pansebeia: or a view of all religions in the world* . . . (London, 1658), pp. 239–240.

governors (the upraised secular arm) command the bishops to enforce such uniformity in doctrine as will ensure the peace of the realm. In this regard it is well to remember that the most widely divergent doctrinal views were admissible within the Anglican communion, were indeed encouraged by the adroitly ambiguous Thirty-Nine Articles. Thus a man like Thomas Turke, presumably, is orthodox. Lancelot Andrewes is also orthodox. Now this is only possible in a situation in which orthodoxy means little more than a consent to be godly and quietly governed, a consent to be loyal. What really is the yardstick with which to measure heresy? Decent order. That kind of uniformity which is the note of quiet. Men who differ as widely in their views as Turke and Andrewes are held together only by institutionalism, only by church polity, and not by the dogma of the church. And if both men have faith in the church, which one can be said to have the faith of the church? What is that faith? Leaving aside the scandalous extremes of the time, is there a sober doctrine of any importance held outside the church which cannot, quietly and safely, be held within it? Cannot an Anglican believe in a Calvinist predestination, in a Lutheran justification, in a Zwinglian Eucharist—or in one or all of the alternative Catholic doctrines? Finally, when the battle comes, is it not obvious that what really divides the Calvinist churchman from the Calvinist non-churchman is loyalty to the throne? The Puritan royalist remains within the church, the Puritan antiroyalist rides against Rupert.

Objectively, then, the crown as an enduring symbol of the "historical concrete," of the living participation of the body politic in the Mystical Body, is doomed from the start. With Henry, at the moment of schism, the crown is the sum symbol of the fragmentation of Christendom, a fragmentation marked and defined by political expedience. The crown is the sign of the divided visible order. The church is entirely of the invisible order, and no sign here below is ripe to be its symbol. Time and eternity are put apart. And if, from the moment of schism, the crown is properly the sign of a fragmented Christendom, it is to become, in the end, the sign of a divided and embattled England. For, as the passage from Alexander Ross nicely illustrates, this invisible unity of the Protestant Church is signified to mortals only by endless dispute and the proliferation of the most fantastic doctrinal inventions. The Prince must govern. Who else can? Where else but in the crown is there *authority*? For whatever motive, doctrinal, political, economic, one chooses one's side. And the religious as well as the political authority of the crown is questioned with the sword.

It may even be said that once the authority of the crown was questioned with any sharpness, the status of the crown as symbol was quickly lost. But when Shakespeare writes, the final implications of Henrican royalism have not yet pricked the imagination; Lovelace—and Herbert—are still beyond the horizon. Paradoxically, the very realities which were ultimately to doom the crown as symbol operated at first to make it wholly susceptible to the reach of the analogical imagination. The essentially divisive character of the national-Protestant crown was for a while obscured—at the level of rationalization by the genius of Hooker, and at a far deeper level by ancient habit, by a need both spiritual and political, and by a sudden, brief, but heady and glorious patriotism. For it would seem that in the wake of Cranmer's liturgical and doctrinal revolution only the throne stood like a rock above the torn waters. With the drastic revision of ancient Eucharistic theology and with the isolation of England from a Christendom conceived of as universal and supranational, only the crown could give visible and practical symbolization to the deep psychological needs and habits of a people reared in the corporate sensibility of Catholicism. Deeply engrained habits of thought and feeling are never uprooted overnight by the heave and tug of lawmakers. Indeed, the strategy of Hooker's great book *The Ecclesiastical Polity* derives from a recognition of just this fact. Hooker's formula, "Every Englishman a churchman, every churchman an Englishman," is aimed at transferring corporate loyalties from the mediaeval focus in the church universal to a new and urgent focus in the church national. Hooker perceived with astonishing clarity that without the imaginative lift of a unifying symbol, the ecclesiastical body and the body politic alike would fall to pieces. The threat of an extreme Protestant individualism could be checked only by providing the popular imagination with a symbol able to evoke, simultaneously, the new and athletic national ambitions of England and the older deep-lying compulsions of the religious sense born from the fact of membership in the church universal and the Mystical Body of Christ. Hooker's *Ecclesiastical Polity,* with its brilliant fusion of spiritual and secular impulses in the single symbol of the crown, is therefore the indispensable primer for any study of royalist symbol in English Renaissance poetry. And, of course, events conspire to give to the crown symbol a force which could scarcely have been imparted by Hooker's ingenious myth-making alone. After the defeat of the Armada, national pride is such that only the Puritan or Catholic extremist can resist it. Buoyed up in the imagination by the cleverly contrived myth of the return of Arthur and in fact by strength of arm and gold in the purse, the crown as symbol of unified state and church would seem quite able to survive without further benefit of clergy. However, Hooker's achievement in symbol-making is a precarious one. The transfer of loyalties from a body universal and visible to one national and invisible may have been for churchmen a costly affair after all. For if the English church is now to be properly invisible, the state is to become increasingly and triumphantly visible. In poetry, at any rate, the visible has a knack of getting the best of the invisible, and it should not be surprising that the colour of royalist symbol in Anglican poetry is increasingly secular rather than religious. By the last years of Elizabeth's reign, Hooker's ideal of the unified church-state is threatened by the fact of economic and social division. By the reign of Charles I the crown is no longer the symbol of a tight, island "Christendom-in-little." It is the badge of an embattled party. And if the legerdemain of Hooker did seem able for a while to shrink Christendom to the size of an island (or rather half an island), there was surely no magic capable of shrinking it still further into a royal retinue of bishops and knights scurrying for the drawbridge. Indeed, the note of delusion already present in the Elizabethan treatment of the crown as quasi-religious symbol is not fully explicit until the political predicament of Charles reveals the aesthetic predicament of Anglican poets who continued, at an unpropitious moment, to chant the prayer book notion of the crown as God-set above and over the affairs of all sorts and conditions of men. And, as we shall see in a moment, the Cavalier trick of paying tribute to God in the person of Caesar is quite as unfortunate for poetry as it is for piety.

Despite the successful use in Shakespeare of the crown as symbol of virtues inward as well as outward, spiritual as well as political, the popular drift away from this usage is discernible even while Shakespeare writes. Already a short-circuiting of religious emotion can be seen in certain forms taken by the veneration of Elizabeth. If in Shakespeare the crown is never wholly identified with the head that wears it, in countless Elizabethan poems one encounters the thoroughly personalized icon of Elizabeth the Virgin Queen. Elizabeth is substituted for Mary. It may have been fortunate that the accident of Elizabeth's virginity allowed some of the substance of ancient devotional habits to be secularized without at first compromising that deeper corporate need which created, and was re-created by, the symbol of the crown.

The Virgin cult in Elizabethan poetry has been described and documented by Professor Elkin Wilson. The phenomenon is a neat illustration of the growing confusion of religious and secular impulses—and of the way in which the declension of the religious level of royalist symbol actually occurred.

There can be no doubt that centuries of Catholic devotion lie behind the ardour of the cult now devoted to the Virgin Queen of England:

> In Elizabeth's England a very ancient conviction still had a standing hallowed from the darkest antiquity. That the virgin way of life is somehow the more blessed one . . . was a belief that a dominant church had favoured for centuries. Now came a

mere English princess who persisted in exalting her virginity when official allegiance to the church had been severed, and when hostility to it was increasingly synonymous with love of country and devotion to its queen. Human devotion changes more slowly than its objects shift. From 1558 the virgin queen was the object of a love not dissimilar in quality from that which for centuries had warmed English hearts that looked to the Virgin Queen of heaven for all grace.[3]

Implicit in this statement of Wilson's is the belief that a symbol cannot be understood or described solely in terms of the symbolic object or image. The great culture symbols are born of needs and confirmed by habit. "Human devotion changes more slowly than its objects shift"—and the devotional psychology of Mariolatry persists well after the name of Mary conjures up for many only a vision of Protestant martyrs and the bonfires of Smithfield. In Dowland's *Song-book* one actually finds the cry "Viva Eliza" sub-stituted for the traditional "Ave Maria." [4]

It is not merely that the Queen of England begins to replace the Queen of Heaven in popular devotion. The implications for sym-bol are more subtle and more profound than any such simple substitution would at first seem to suggest. It must be remem-bered that the poetic cult of Elizabeth the Virgin parallels other cults of purely secular reference. The whole of classical literature is winnowed by Elizabethan poets in search of emblematic flat-teries for the royal patroness. Thus Elizabeth is hymned not only as "Eliza the Virgin" but as "Cynthia, Lady of the Sea," "Laura, Lady of the Sonnet," "Elisa, Queen of Shepherds," and so on. The quasi-religious veneration of virginity loses its original colour (and certainly all its properly symbolic possibilities) as it blends into this chorus of literary compliment. In such a context of fashionable flattery all that finally clings to the Virgin allusion is the notion of the Queen as protectress and dispenser of gifts, a notion abstracted from the cult of Mary and applied (appropri-ately enough) to the practical offices of the earthly ruler. But it is

[3] *England's Elisa* (Cambridge, Harvard University Press, 1939), p. 215.
[4] Quoted by Wilson, p. 206.

not just that the religious colouring of the Virgin allusion is dimmed by secularizing abstraction and by shoulder-rubbing with conceited literary allusions of a specifically non-Christian kind. The very possibility of symbolic "lift" is lost in the process of personalizing the queen. As we have already noted, the crown in Shakespeare's symbolization of it remained to a degree impersonal, thereby serving as focus for deeply corporate intuitions of universal value. For the crown was properly symbolic inasmuch and for as long as it was able to gather up the temporal into the eternal, was able to coax flights of angels to bear aloft the upraised banners of mortality.

The personalization of the royalist symbol de-symbolizes it. Clearly, the representation of Elizabeth as Eliza or Cynthia or Laura aims, in each instance, at the celebration, first, of a personal quality and, then, of a public office or function of the Queen. One recalls that "Mariolatry" is traditionally and essentially an act of participation by the church militant in the life of the Mystical Body. It therefore represents a commingling of past, present, and future, of earth and heaven. Whatever one's theological bias, one must perforce admit that the transcendent symbolic potential of the old Mary cult is roofed over and squattened by this new English cult, which, rather than offering and raising the temporal order to the divine, depresses a soaring form of worship to the merest political and personal idolatry.

On the one hand, then, the tendency to personalize the crown in Elizabeth, to idolize Elizabeth both as person and as ruler, reaches towards an eventual deification of the state, towards a political mystique. And this tendency, by drawing off something of the ancient devotional sense proper to the Mary cult, results in extreme cases in a forthright substitution of the Queen of England for the Queen of Heaven. On the other hand, the deeply laid corporate sense, mediaeval in origin, which Hooker had so aptly exploited and which Shakespeare had so magnificently expressed in and through the politico-religious symbol of the crown, can scarcely withstand the divisive social crisis of the Stuart period.

THE CROWN AS RELIGIOUS SYMBOL

Verbal skirmishes between court and city mark the dying years of the Elizabethan era and foreshadow the deep internal conflict which is to ripen throughout the reign of James and reach fruition in the reign of Charles. On the secular side of its reference, the unifying symbol of the crown cracks under the pressure of social and economic forces. And on its religious side the symbol was foreshortened by the rapid advance of a self-conscious and articulate Puritanism which threatened increasingly to break out of the Establishment into its own independent institutional forms. The Hooker formula of "Every Englishman an Anglican" fell into obsolescence as England took its way from the tomb of Elizabeth to the scaffold at Whitehall.

And despite the early personal popularity of James I and Prince Henry, a new and quite un-Elizabethan conception of royalism began to emerge in the theatre. "The king in Beaumont and Fletcher's *Maid's Tragedy* is a dissolute wretch but above and beyond moral criticism simply because he is a king. In the same writers' *A King and No King,* the heroic monarch ardently desires to commit incest. Fletcher's *Loyal Subject* is a servile creature who submits to endless indignities at the hands of a king, and for his patience is rewarded finally by the royal favour. It is as if the court dramatists deliberately sought to defy citizen morality with degenerate and wastrel kings. Shakespeare's ideal monarch had divinity in him. Beaumont and Fletcher wrote in self-conscious defiance of the city and the moral code. Their work represents the advancing disintegration of the corporate, moral and religious reference of the crown symbol." [5]

The more pious Anglican poet of the Stuart period avoids these theatrical excesses. Nor will he seek in patriotic zeal a secular outlet for his perplexed religious emotions. He will seek, rather, to reconcile the prayer book conception of the crown with a decent sense of personal religious devotion. But, as we shall see, he gets himself into a thicket of difficulties. Is it to be wondered that as

[5] Malcolm M. Ross, *Milton's Royalism* (Ithaca, Cornell University Press, 1943), p. 30.

corporate Christianity deteriorates not only does religious sensibility become more individualistic, but also the crown, insofar as it
is still used at all to convey religious implication, is individualized,
fashioned, and fixed to the head that wears it? The same process
of personalization which flattened the symbolic possibilities of the
Virgin cult now, within the limits set by a troubled Anglican
churchmanship, finally reduced the corporate universality of the
crown symbol to a function of little more than the direct adulation of the reigning sovereign. This adulation is given a religious
veneer by what amounts to the pseudo-canonization of the royal
person.

In his poem *An Extasie,* Nicholas Breton imagines himself
blessed by a vision of the lately departed Queen Elizabeth.

> . . . this heavenly apparition
> Bad me not feare, with sweete perswasion:
> For I am shee (quoth shee) that lately was
> Thy Sov'raigne: freed from this earthly Masse;
> I now can like an Angell with a trice,
> Shift place to serve the Prince of Paradice
> And I am come to thee by his permission,
> That (notwithstanding thy obscure condition)
> Thou shoulds't by me have light and clearly see
> (As in a Glasse) what shall hereafter be
> Touching this land. . . .[6]

Thus Elizabeth is canonized. Whereas the exultant Renaissance
patriot substituted the political offices of the Virgin Queen for the
heavenly offices of the Virgin Mother, Breton goes in for a higher
leap, awarding to Elizabeth the heavenly status of Mary. There is
this difference, of course: the new Queen of Heaven will, through
all eternity, keep an eye peeled for the temporal affairs of England. Henry VIII may have nationalized the church. Breton
nationalizes heaven. True, the French Louis long since, presumably, had taken his seat among the blessed saints—but *his* seat and
not another's. And this saintly eminence was not awarded to him
as a vantage point from which to signal political tips to his

---

[6] *An Extasie.* Published with *Microcosmos* (Oxford, 1603), p. 234.

countrymen here below. In any case, you will allow that this
prospect of Elizabeth dwelling above in the manner to which she
has been accustomed puts some considerable strain on the religious
layering of the crown symbol.

In fairness to Breton, and in order to demonstrate the ambivalence of the Elizabethan use of the crown as a symbol, let us look
at a stanza from an earlier poem of his.

> The Prince, anointed with the oyl of Grace
> Who sits with Mercie, in the seats of Peace
> Will long to see his Saviour in the face
> And all his right unto His hands release;
> (Whose onely sight would make all sorrow cease)
>   And lay both crown and kingdome at his feete,
>   But of His presence to enjoy the sweete.[7]

It is worth noting that the monarchy here, as in Shakespeare, is
treated symbolically. Not Elizabeth but "the Prince," the figure
of the English kingdom, lays his crown at the feet of Christ. Here
is the traditional mediaeval ideal of the anointed sovereign dis-
charging his proper function in the temporal order and present-
ing his good works to the greater King—who presumably then
joins them to the greater Kingdom. Here is something like the
mediaeval sense, not only of the dedicated function of monarchy
and of the corporate life of peoples, but also of the life of heaven
as a corporate participation in the Mystical Body analogous to the
lesser corporate participations of earth. Any self-sufficient nationalism is as far removed from such symbol-making as is the personalized idolatry of the other Breton poem. It may be significant
that the second poem is the earlier. Certainly it is more characteristic of a period in which the royalist formula of Hooker seemed
to apply to the actual facts of political reality. And certainly the
death of Elizabeth marks a decisive change in the poetic use of
the crown symbol.

We have already noted the thoroughgoing deterioration of the

[7] *An Excellent Poem upon the Longing of a Blessed Heart* (London, 1601),
p. 8.

royalist symbol in the plays of Beaumont and Fletcher. In much poetry of the more pious kind there is a simple withdrawal from any concern with the world of affairs. The analogical link between the world of affairs and the life of the spirit is sometimes wholly broken, a process far advanced in poets like George Herbert and a group of gentle otherworldly Anglicans who converse with Christ in remote parishes and quiet country gardens.

By the time of Charles, the crown symbol is accorded a religious or pseudo-religious layering only in the work of the less sensitive and the less gifted poets. But the same personalization of the symbol which we noted in Breton's unfortunate rhapsody to St. Elizabeth, Queen of Heaven, reappears in a considerable body of minor Jacobean and Caroline poetry. If anything, the Jacobeans outdo their Elizabethan predecessors. This striking passage from a poem of Christopher Lever's even suggests that Christ himself owes a proper reverence to earthly kings, especially English kings. Rome in refusing to accord such reverence is clearly Anti-Christ:

> Christ unto Caesar (not a Christian king)
> Exemplifies a dutiful respect;
> But bloodie Rome would to confusion bring
> All empire and command, her self except;
> Her greatness is with bloody practice kept.[8]

The thin veneer of Scriptural allusion fails, of course, to conceal a glorification of earthly power and an extreme and autonomous nationalism.

Side by side with cruder rationalizations of secular patriotic emotion in terms of traditional religious image and allusion, one also finds efforts by minor Jacobean poets to celebrate the king in his spiritual capacity as head of the church. Thus William Warner cries "our religion is authentical" because God "to our natural Prince grants sole supremacie."[9] Oddly enough, this emphasis on the king as Island Pope coincides with disturbances

---

[8] *Queen Elizabeth's Teares* (London, 1607). Reprinted in *Fuller Worthies Library*, III, p. 120.

[9] "How Our Religion is Authenticated." In *Select Poetry, Chiefly Sacred of the Reign of James I*, ed. Edward Farr (Cambridge, 1847), p. 296.

which threaten the king's power. The glorification of the Stuarts as "Defenders of the Faith" comes at a time when the Puritan cause is advancing and when doctrinal order is everywhere in jeopardy. What is most dangerous for the life of symbol is that these fervent royal image-makers, no longer able to identify crown and people in a symbolization of the ascent of the temporal to the divine, reverse the process, and invoke the authority of Christ to keep the crown on the king's head. The king is no longer the Defender of the Faith. The faith defends the king. Thus the nervous Caroline doctrine of the "divine right of kings," which is expressed well enough in these lines from John Stradling:

> The prototype of Sway and Soveraignty
> Directs his wholly to the rule of one;
> One God, one king, it holds analogy;
> This, under Him: He of Himself alone.[10]

This verse occurs in a section of the poem directed against the democratic political theories of the Anabaptists, a dangerous foreign tribe guilty of un-English activities. The gist of the whole passage is that the king is an incarnation of heavenly law. The crown is to be clamped down hard on the anarchistic impulses of the people. The crown is therefore becoming a token of partisan power. Christ the King is also (and inevitably) partisan, sallying forth to defend his defender, the distraught king of England.

As I have already observed, it was perhaps fortunate that patriotic Elizabethans were able to attach their confused religious emotions to the fact of their queen's virginity. Alas, the persons of the Stuart monarchy offered no such felicitous possibilities for the image-maker. Instead of a debased Mariolatry, there is in the Stuart period something rather like a debased Christolatry. The king in these frantic days of the gathering storm incarnates the will of Christ. More exalted than the Roman Catholic Vicar of Christ on earth, the king, like Christ, is attended by marvellous portents in the skies and is subjected finally to the sacrificial and redemptive Christ-death.

---

[10] *Divine Poems in Severall Classes* (London, 1625), I, st. 77.

In the Jacobean period it is the young Prince Henry who receives the lion's share of poetic flattery. The court poet dresses up all his old tricks in the adulations of Henry. Once more, religious allusion rubs shoulders with classical allusion. Once more, the person of the Prince is made to shatter the universality of symbol and to destroy any genuine religious suggestiveness in the image of the crown. However, it is the King and not the Queen of Heaven who is now identified with the English throne. The following excerpt from a poem of Joseph Hall's, though not to be taken too seriously, does point the direction now followed by those Jacobean royalist poets who still play with Christian allusion. The poem tells "of the Rainbow that was reported to be seen in the night over Saint James', and of the unseasonable weather ever since."

> Was ever nightly rainbowe seene?
> Did ever winter mourne in greene?
> Had that long bowe been bent by day
> That chased all our clouds away?
> It tells the deluge of our tears:
> No marvell rainbowe shine by night
> When suns yshorne do lose their light!
> Iris was wont to be of old
> Heaven's messenger to earthly mould:
> And now she came to bring us down
> Sad news of Henry's bitter crowne
> And as the eastern star did tell
> The Persian sages of that cell
> Where Sion's king was born and lay
> And over that same house did stay;
> So did this western breeze descry
> Where Henry, Prince of men, should die.
> Lo! there this arch of heavenly state
> Rais'd to the triumph of his fate;
> Yet rais'd in dark of night, to showe
> His glory should be with our woe.
>
> .   .   .
>
> The winter weeps and mourns indeed
> Though clothed in a summer's weed.[11]

11 "Lachrymae Lachrymarum." Reprinted in Farr, *James I,* p. 226.

There is nothing novel in the popular belief that signs in the sky may accompany the deaths of princes. Mediaeval and Elizabethan literature is full of the equivalence of macrocosm and microcosm. But here the macrocosm is Christ, the microcosm Henry. Just as the heavens told of the birth of Christ, they tell now, and quite properly, of the death of an English prince. That the dead Henry is flattered by way of the Christ simile is significant not so much because of the audacity as because of the frivolity of the poet. The Christ reference provides a kind of courtly interior decoration. In personalizing the religious layer of the crown symbol, the poet is driven to the Christ allusion. Mary, of course, is unavailable. But here the courtly play of wit, and the artificial trick of compliment, put a limit, happily enough, to the pretensions of the poem. The poem stops discreetly short of any serious identification of Christ and Henry. Hall has written an elaborate courtly conceit in which simile is never made to soar into symbol. However, it will not be long until the desperate Cavalier who witnesses the execution of his king will burn away pure simile in an intense emotive furnace. With an idolatry which must remind us of Japanese Emperor-worship, he will destroy the traditional symbolic possibilities of the English crown.

The following verse by John Cleveland reveals something more of this drift to Emperor-worship. The verse is from an elegy on the martyred Charles I. Note that the process of personalization inches a bit nearer to imaginative identification of Christ and king.

> Were not my faith buoyed up by sacred blood
> It might be drowned in this prodigious flood
> Which reason's highest ground doth so exceed
> It leaves my soul no anchorage but my creed;
> Where my faith, resting on the original,
> Supports itself in this the copy's fall
> So while my faith floats in the bloody wood
> My reason's cast away in this red flood.[12]

12 "An Elegy upon King Charles the First, Murdered Publicly by His Subjects." *The Poems of John Cleveland*, ed. J. M. Berdan (New York, 1911), p. 195.

The notion of Charles as a copy of Christ is in itself a notion not wholly impossible to the faith. The "imitation of Christ" does not, I suppose, necessarily exclude kings. And the martyrdoms of holy men have always been regarded as participations in the sacrificial suffering of Christ. I am more concerned with a less obvious statement in the poem. Reason is "cast away in this red flood." Only an inward faith offers any support in a churchless kingdom without a king. And, it must be remembered, it is precisely this impulse towards an utterly interior faith which marks the poetry of Herbert and Vaughan and other Anglicans whose spiritual integrity will permit no flirtation with trappings turned to tinsel.

But Cleveland is no Herbert. He is an incorrigible royalist not content to respect for long the proprieties of the faith. In these next verses, Charles is made into much more than a mere copy of Christ.

> How like a king of Death he dies!
> We easily may the world and death despise.
> Death had no sting for him and its sharp arm
> Only of all the troop meant him no harm.
>
> .   .   .
>
> In his grate name then may his subjects cry
> Death thou art swallowed up in victory.
>
> .   .   .
>
> And thus his soul of this her victory proud
> Broke like a flash of lightning through the cloud
> Of flesh and blood: and from the highest line
> Of human virtue passed to be divine.[13]

If anything, Charles has more divinity in him than Christ. Death has no sting for him at all. Spared the real agony of Christ, he demonstrates on the scaffold a light-hearted indifference to the world, the flesh, and the devil. And *his* subjects now may justly cry "Death thou art swallowed up in victory." What a pity that the Second Coming of Charles was to be rather less than Christlike in its epiphany!

13 Cleveland, *Poems*, p. 197.

But the Cavalier cult flourished before the "second coming." And with admirable discretion, the Cavalier refrained from putting out broad hints of the imminent resurrection of Charles I. However, Richard Lovelace, the prince of Cavaliers, does not stop very far short of the theme of Resurrection. The following is a curious compound of mere conceit and an unashamed religious personalization of the royalist symbol. Lovelace laments the failure of Reformation and the subsequent loss of public faith.

> Since none of these can be
> Fit objects for my love and me
> What then remains, but th' only spring
> Of all our loves and joys? The King.

Even a Stalinist would hesitate to go as far in his adoration of the state symbol as Lovelace goes in this next passage.

> He who being the whole Ball
> Of Day on Earth, lends it to all;
> When seeking to eclipse his right
> Blinded, we stand in our own light
>
> . . .
>
> Oh from thy glorious starry waine
> Dispense on me one sacred Beame
> To light me where I soone may see
> How to serve you, and you trust me.[14]

Charles is in his heaven—although all's not quite well with the world. And Charles is, mark you, prayed to that his sacred

[14] These passages are from "To Lucasta from Prison: An Epode." *The Poems of Richard Lovelace,* ed. C. H. Wilkinson (2 vols., Oxford, 1925), I, pp. 44–46, sts. XI, XII, XIV. It is worth recalling that in the mediaeval period the language of religious adoration was sometimes used in addressing royalty. (See J. Huizinga, *The Waning of the Middle Ages* [London, 1927], pp. 141 ff.) Nor may one overlook the ancient, even primitive, precedents for attributing religious and even godlike powers to the crown. Nevertheless, the great achievement of the Christian Middle Ages in this respect was the rejection of Caesaro-papism and the proper separation of spiritual and secular authority. The royalist rhetoric of the age, particularly at the end of the great liturgical cycle, referred to in Chapter II, sometimes exceeded and even contradicted the dictates of the faith and the demands of dogma. The point is, of course, that for the seventeenth century Cavalier there was no sure dogma to be exceeded or contradicted. Royalist rhetoric occupies the vacuum.

influence may shine upon the worshipper who solemnly dedicates his life and service to the heavenly English king. The cult of Elizabeth the Virgin gives way to the cult of Charles the Christ. Thus the crown symbol is reduced to a scandalous personal icon. The pathetic princely face peers out from a stylized Byzantine background of pseudo-religious allusion.

It is surely significant that this extreme species of Emperor-worship, the product at once of irresponsible verbal wit and desperate loyalty, is matched and, indeed, offset in Cavalier verse by a note frankly secular in tone, astonishingly materialistic and even cynical in attitude. At one pole, the crown symbol is destroyed by this preposterous identification of king and Christ. At the opposite pole, the purely political and polemical ancient Christian symbols are degraded to the status of party tag and slogan. The religious sense of the issue engaging Cavalier and Puritan sinks into a cynical *Realpolitik*. The Cavaliers, fighting openly and quite consciously in defence of ancient privilege, consistently represent their Puritan opponents as illiterate, lower-class buffoons who, behind a pretence of piety, seek to grasp the purse-strings of power.

The following stanzas from the Cavalier ballad "The Power of Money," betray the very secular and materialistic view of history characteristic now of the defeated and disenchanted Cavalier. For purposes of irony the ballad is put in the mouth of a Parliamentarian.

> 'Tis not the Silver and Gold for it self
> That makes men adore it, but 'tis for its power.
> For no man does dote upon pelf because pelf
> But all court the Lady in hopes for her dower.
> The wonders that now in our Days we behold
> Done by the irresistible power of Gold
> Our zeal and our love and allegiance hold.
> This purchaseth kingdoms, king, scepters and crowns
> Wins Battels, and conquers the conquerors bold;
> Takes bulwarks and castles and cities and towns
>
> .   .   .
>
> Stamp either the Arms of the State or the king

St. George or the Breeches, C.R. or O.P.,
The Cross or the fiddle, 'tis all the same thing
This [money] still is the Queen, whosoe'er the King be.[15]

This shaft of irony may be intended solely for the Puritan moneyman. But obviously the Cavalier is not unaware of the facts of life as they now are. A study of the Cavalier ballads makes it quite clear that men like Lovelace and John Suckling, no matter how scornful they may be of pious Puritan hypocrisy, are not blind to the political and economic implications of the struggle in which they are engaged—the struggle in which the new wealth of trade challenges the antique wealth of the land. Stars may fall at the death of a prince. Charles may still from the remote heavens flourish his ruined sceptre. Fancies such as these, howsoever fervent, do not blot out for the Cavalier the drawn lines of an actual struggle for power in a world which seems not to respond to the benign influences of late departed royal saints. Crown and mitre and all the insignia of the old state-church soon become little more than partisan devices useful in distinguishing the social traditions of the gentleman from the boorish pretensions of the monied upstart with his cropped head, steeple-hat, and chilly naked chapel. And I think it may be said that the extravagant worship of Charles the Christ and this cynical snobbish partisan realism of the war ballads are related as the heads and tails of the same broken coin.

We have in other words witnessed the fragmentation of a culture symbol. The multiple but simultaneous associations evoked by Shakespeare's symbolization of the crown have been wrenched apart, isolated, exaggerated, distorted, or stunted.

The process which we have been observing is neither accidental nor superficial. It affects poetry and the symbols of poetry because it presses upwards and outwards from the matrix of a decisive cultural convolution. In a succinct summary of W. H. Auden's theory of the dynamics of civilization, Monroe K. Spears puts

[15] Anon., *A Collection of Loyal Songs Written Against the Rump Parliament between the years 1639 and 1661* (2 vols., London, 1731), I, pp. 60 65.

ral ideas which will help to reveal the broader sig-
vhat is happening to culture in the seventeenth cen-
is convinced that modern civilization (and there-
~~~~, ~~~, ~~~ imaginative, symbol-making capacity of modern
man) has been perverted by a kind of false division which drives
us and our thinking and our symbol-making into opposite and
equally false extremes. To quote from Spears' restatement of
Auden:

> . . . he argues that civilization is based upon two presuppositions:
> (1) that throughout the universe there is one set of laws according
> to which all events and movements happen; (2) that there are
> many different realms of society, and that the peculiar laws of
> these several realms are modifications of the universal laws. He
> proceeds to identify the two corresponding heresies: (1) Dualism,
> "dividing the substance"—the denial of any relation between the
> universal and the particular. This produces an otherworldliness
> which regards all attempts to establish a social order as vain, or
> a secularism which regards progress as inevitable. (2) Monism,
> "confounding the Persons"—the assumption that the peculiar
> laws of one of the realms are universal laws from which all others
> derive. This produces either tyranny or violent revolution.[16]

If monism, in this sense, is the active assumption of the Calvinist revolutionary in the seventeenth century, a nominalistic
dualism, denying a relation between the particular church and
the universal church, produces simultaneously on the Anglican
side the otherworldliness of a Herbert and the extraworldliness
of the disgruntled Cavalier. The analogical act of the participation of the particular in the universal has been lost to view. A
new and very different compulsion is felt now by poets as un-
alike as George Herbert and John Milton.

[16] "Late Auden: The Satirist as Lunatic Clergyman," *Sewanee Review* (Winter,
1951), pp. 59–60.

George Herbert and the Humanist Tradition

CHAPTER SIX

UNLESS one is content with abstract definition, one can no longer discuss the meaning of humanism without concern and even trepidation. Perhaps if one is ready to admit that this meaning is subject to change, and that the persistence of the word from the Renaissance to the recent embalming of "The Hundred Best Books" is another indication of the poverty of language, one may avoid the trip and stumble that use of the term so often occasions.

In our day the word "humanism" has frequently been employed defensively by those who resist the implications of science for modern life and by those who seek to conserve amid the disturbing flux of social and cultural values some ideal construction of values gleaned from a reading of the past. For Irving Babbitt and Paul Elmer More (whose thought is characteristic of this defensive kind of humanism) the word clearly implies restrictive habits of thought and feeling, and this, I think, despite a healthy insistence on objectivity and aesthetic discipline. Unlike the humanists of a younger time, these men praise the fugitive and cloistered virtue, and draft an ethic out of inhibition.

Yet there are still among us those for whom the word is wide enough and deep enough to contain all of man's capacity and all of man's destiny. My own approach to the problem is historical and relativist. This chapter is, in a sense, a study in the contraction of a word-value, and will contend that the value of humanism, like the value stored up in any word of long life, is by no means constant and can even contradict itself in a changed historical context.

From this point of view it is instructive to re-examine the work of George Herbert, not only to gain a surer understanding of his poetry, not only to demonstrate the danger of static critical touchstones and catch phrases, but also to observe a cultural phenomenon in motion. Herbert's poetry has usually been regarded as the typical expression of Anglican humanism. However, by analyzing the imagery within the frame of its social reference one can detect the tradition in the process of transforming itself into something quite unlike the Anglican humanism of a generation before.

Most students have found in Herbert a quality of religious feeling intimate yet moderate in expression which places his work in the direct line of descent from the *via media* of Hooker and the spirit of the Elizabethan compromise. Hutchinson's critical examination of the text has saved Herbert's reputation from any taint of the romantic agony. Certainly there would seem to be no evidence, psychological or factual, to justify Palmer's "placing all the happier poems at the beginning of the Bemerton section, and then passing through poems of reflection and restlessness to poems of suffering and death." [1] The sense of crisis is never absent from Herbert, but it is crisis tentatively if not finally resolved in a quiet, reasonable, though intense faith.

While recognizing these qualities in Herbert which seem, by hindsight at least, to typify the spirit of the humanist tradition as it unfolds from the theology of Hooker, we must bear in mind that Herbert was not an Elizabethan and did not write under the pressure of those forces which went into the making of Hooker's *Ecclesiastical Polity*. The court of Charles may have been no more than a stone's throw in time from the court of Elizabeth, but it no longer represented the collective energies of

---

[1] F. C. Hutchinson, "George Herbert," in *Seventeenth Century Studies Presented to Sir Herbert Grierson* (Oxford, 1938), p. 151.

the English nation; and the church of Laud, no matter what it may have owed in theory to Hooker's conception of the Christian Commonwealth, was no longer, in the fullest practical sense, the Church of England. Division within the state and church (and finally *between* state and church) destroyed the Elizabethan synthesis, both secular and ecclesiastical. It is to this period of disintegration that Herbert's work belongs, and unless one is to regard humanism as wholly timeless and abstract, one is not apt to seek the Elizabethan synthesis of values in a Caroline country parish on the eve of civil war.

This is not to deny the resemblance of Herbert's "British Church" to the church of Hooker, or to deny in Herbert the presence of the humanist idea. On the surface at least the tradition seems unbroken, and it is from the Elizabethan compromise that Herbert derives his theoretical values. But to the historian of cultural change the exciting paradox is this: by his very reception of the Elizabethan humanist idea in a period of rapid disintegration and change, Herbert alters the tradition and imparts to it a new direction. The direction, for Anglican poetry at least, was to be away from humanism and towards mysticism. Elizabethan humanist values, persisting abstractly into a period which rejected their social origins, take on an independent life of their own. But it was to be a short life. It could not be sustained. The materialism of Hobbes and the nonconformist spirituality of Bunyan were the carriers into the next century of the motive forces of the English Revolution. There would be within the dominant hard-headed culture of the coming age no Anglican poetry and little Anglican prose to match in quality or intensity the work of a George Herbert or a Lancelot Andrewes. Such religious fervour as there was would be evangelical and quite outside the Anglican tradition.

To understand Herbert's unique place in a moment of cultural metamorphosis (for such this moment unquestionably was), it is necessary to look backwards as well as forwards. The origins of Elizabethan (and Anglican) humanism are clearly social and political. Paul Elmer More admits that "if challenged to state the motive that started the Church of England on her peculiar course, the historian is likely to reply that it was political rather than religious." [2] Sir Herbert Grierson, in assessing the spiritual quality of Elizabethan Anglicanism, states:

> . . . I do not ascribe it specifically to Anglican doctrine or to Anglican bishops generally—who were often as narrow and at heart as puritan as their opponents—but to the political situation, and not least to Queen Elizabeth. That strong-minded, worldly-minded, unscrupulous little lady it was who saved Shakespeare for us and gave him the chance . . . to present his picture of life which, whatever be its imperfections, is instinct with the finest spirit of a humanism, penetrating, just, and sympathetic. And it was she who saved England from passing from an infallible Pope to an infallible John Calvin; who in her endeavour to keep the door open for Catholic as well as Protestant made it possible for the English Church to retain and recover some of the most attractive and humane features of the old faith and . . . to cultivate reasonableness, to dispense with infallibility, and to appeal to history and reason, and produce men like Hooker, George Herbert, Henry Vaughan, Andrewes. . . . [3]

One notes here, despite the emphasis on the political genesis of humanism, the assumption of a continuous tradition from Hooker through the Caroline period, a position which, insofar as poetry is concerned, this essay questions. What Grierson overlooks, of course, is that the compromise between the old faith and the new spirit, between the old aristocracy and the new middle class, was no longer effective by the reign of Charles. But the recognition of the social origins of Elizabethan humanism is important, and particularly so because of the clear association within the humanist tradition of Shakespeare and Hooker, of the secular and the ecclesiastical.

One must remember that in Hooker's view "the English church and the English nation are identical in membership, for every

[2] "The Spirit of Anglicanism," in *Anglicanism,* ed. P. E. More and F. L. Cross (Milwaukee, 1935), p. xxi.
[3] *Cross Currents of English Literature in the Seventeenth Century* (London, Chatto and Windus, 1929), p. 205.

Englishman is a Christian and every Christian in England is an Englishman." [4] Hooker resists both Puritanism and Roman Catholicism as forces making for division between church and state, and his concept of the national church headed by the monarch fully reflects and complements the secular compromise effected between court and city by the unifying role of the crown. Indeed, Hooker's conception of the monarchy as the all-embracing symbol of national life corresponds to Shakespeare's. "Our Kings . . . when they take possession of the room they are called unto, have it painted out before their eyes, even by the very solemnities and rites of their inauguration, to what affairs by the said law their supreme authority and power reacheth. Crowned we see they are, and enthronized, and anointed: the crown a sign of military, the throne, of sedentary or judicial, the oil, of religious or sacred power." [5] The king becomes a symbolization of both secular and spiritual values. He is subject to law, but the law now natural to Englishmen is that very dynamic of national life which the monarchy embodies and expresses.

By adapting mediaeval political theory to the needs of the new nationalism, and by finding the just and workable balance between the claims of the feudal and bourgeois segments of society, Hooker presented the first clear rationalization of the Elizabethan compromise. Nor was his *Ecclesiastical Polity* idealist or abstract. It articulated the realities of Elizabethan political and church life. The love of moderation—the very accent of reasonable compromise implicit in the work—is evoked by the practical needs of the time.

Consequently, one cannot insist too strongly on the fact that at first Anglican humanism was a *rationale* possible for theology only because church and state coexisted as an organic whole. The *Ecclesiastical Polity* gave impressive sanction to a settlement arrived at in secular practice. Hooker's expression of the Eliza-

[4] G. H. Sabine, *A History of Political Theory* (New York, 1937), p. 441.
[5] *Ecclesiastical Polity*, VIII, II. Reprinted in More and Cross, *Anglicanism*, p. 689.

bethan spirit is paler than Shakespeare's because it is necessarily legalistic and formal. And it is in secular literature that the values of Elizabethan humanism are realized most characteristically. In reconciling the explosive force of Renaissance individualism with the demands of social order, Shakespearean tragedy gives profound (if unconscious) expression to the age. Shakespeare's prince is not only the fulfillment of the Renaissance wish for unrestrained power, but also, as in Hooker, he is subject to the very forces he symbolizes. Lear's kinghood is a mockery once the realm is divided, and individual aspirations, formerly collectivized in the symbol of the crown, are permitted to operate separately and therefore destructively.

Shakespeare's understanding of man alive, realizing himself not in spite of society but through it, is the essence of Elizabethan humanism, whether secular or churchly. Within a conception of freedom as an aspect of necessity the humanist idea grew. Acknowledging both the glory and the corruption of the flesh while savouring the life of the spirit, seeking the full realization of man's capacities, denying none of his appetites, yet countering boundless egotism with an awareness of the social limit, Elizabeth humanism achieved a fusion of the spiritual and courtly values of the past with the restless, aggressive, even pecuniary urge of the Renaissance. In Spenser an aristocratic Platonism mingles with a distinctly bourgeois ethic. In Bacon the love of good Latin is not yet incompatible with a devotion to science and the dedication of man's powers to the conquest of nature. In theology new confirmation is given to the doctrine, mediaeval in origin (and to be denied by Puritanism), that worldly and otherworldly values are continuous and cohere in a Christian humanism that need not divorce the orders of nature and grace.

This unified sensibility of Elizabethan humanism is neither restrictive nor exclusive. Its interest in the classical past is not antiquarian. It is not aloof, nor is its gaze turned inward. It is the thought and feeling of an age alive—and it wears good flesh!

The quality of Herbert's humanism must be seen and felt

against the fullness of the Elizabethan experience. This has never, in my opinion, been seriously attempted. Critical studies of Herbert have been limited for the most part to an analysis of the metaphysical element in the style, or to an appreciation of his specific religious sensibility.[6] Too little attention has been given to any concern Herbert may have shown in his poetry for the world about him. Although most critics have speculated as to why Herbert left the court for the church, the question has been approached biographically. In general, it seems agreed that no matter what attraction the secular life may have had for Herbert, and no matter what his reason for rejecting (or losing) it may have been, his essential nature as a poet and as a man was realized in the church. No one can doubt the sincerity of his religious convictions. No one can quite imagine him as a Cavalier poet writing Platonic masques for Henrietta Maria.

However, in considering the biographical problem, it should be recognized that the struggle in Herbert's mind, while intensely personal, is more than personal. The conflict of worldly and otherworldly values reflected in the poetry represents, surely, a crack in the great tradition. This conflict is foreign to the synthesis embodied in the *Ecclesiastical Polity* and, in its fullest implications, indicates a departure from the idea of a continuous Christian Commonwealth which is at once worldly and otherworldly. I am not suggesting that Herbert quarrels with Hooker's doctrine. I am suggesting that by Herbert's day the social assertion of Hooker's doctrine no longer fits the facts. This consideration cannot be overlooked in any estimate of Herbert's place in the humanist tradition.

A very un-Elizabethan world comes through in the texture of Herbert's poetry. As one would expect, the poems abound in references to the court. Indeed, the tradition of royalist symbolism persists even in a die-hard republican and regicide like John

---

[6] This is not meant to disparage the important work of scholars like Helen C. White and Rosemond Tuve. In Chapter VII, I shall attempt an analysis of the dogmatic content of Herbert's poetry.

Milton. The crown remains in Milton as the inevitable symbol of power and grandeur—despite the antiroyalist context.[7] Milton's contradictory use of the courtly tradition illustrates one aspect of the breakdown of the Elizabethan synthesis. Herbert's treatment represents still another aspect of this disintegration.

It is surely a significant paradox that the Puritan revolutionary makes positive use of the royalist symbol while the Anglican aristocrat uses it negatively. This does not, of course, imply that Herbert is more properly Puritan in tone than Milton. It is simply that Milton concerns himself with the realities of social power and, for lack of any other, must use an inappropriate literary tradition. Herbert, on the other hand, is not concerned with *Realpolitik* and the exercise of power. The strength-suggestion of the royalist symbol is thus lost to him. And the moral and spiritual values which the Elizabethan could also evoke with the symbol of the crown have detached themselves and dwell apart.

This denuding of a symbol once rich in positive suggestion cannot be explained by simple linguistics or attributed to personal caprice. Nothing points more clearly to the fragmentation of Caroline culture than the realization that both Herbert and Lovelace were the king's men. In the Cavalier group some semblance of the old tradition is left. Something of Spenser appears in the poetry of Lovelace and Suckling—the trappings, the gay colours, the grace, the chivalric stance. But the heart and brain have been removed. Compare the artificial and ornamental Platonism of the Cavaliers with the valid and real balance of ideas in Spenser, a balance in which Platonic idealism is tempered with a sense of present reality.

The "sage and serious" note of Spenser is proper now to the revolutionary moralist who would behead a king, or, refined from all association with courtly life, accompanies Herbert on his lonely walk with God.

Herbert's reference to the court, while negative, is not hostile,

---

[7] Malcolm M. Ross, *Milton's Royalism* (Ithaca, Cornell University Press, 1943).

never antiroyalist. He does not write like a man with a grudge. There is something more than personal disappointment involved in his representation of royalism. It is true that failure to win quick preferment at court may have affected his decision to take orders. It should be remembered, however, that Spenser felt keenly his neglect by the court and could lash out against it from a deep sense of injury. Nevertheless, the values held. Spenser is sometimes like an indignant child stamping his foot at his mother and threatening to leave home. But he never really does.

There is no such personal hurt, no sense at all of sharp injury straining for reconciliation, in Herbert's feeling towards the court. There is, instead, a quiet revaluation, a separation of what now appears as intrinsic from the mere crust of the tradition. This is a deeply meditative and not a willful or petulant process of mind which reshapes Herbert's whole universe of symbolic reference. He seeks:

> . . . the pliant minde, whose gentle measure
> Complies and suits with all estates;
> Which can let loose to a crown, and yet with pleasure
> Take up within a cloister's gates.[8]

The crown which Charles V of Spain put aside to enter a monastery has become more suggestive than the crown which still adorns the head of another Charles. In its social reference the royalist symbol is almost always used negatively by Herbert, although God retains his kingship in a completely otherworldly

---

[8] "Content." Herbert's treatment of royalism should be contrasted with the bitter, highly personal imagery of Donne's earlier work. (Cf. M. A. Rugoff, *Donne's Imagery* [New York, 1939], pp. 151–156.) One feels that in Herbert the court is not rejected *politically*, but rather is identified, through a religious insight transcending both political and personal considerations, with human pride and pretension. "Man is all weaknesse; there is no such thing/As prince or King" ("Praise"). Kingliness as a *virtue* is now proper not to the earthly state but only to Heaven:

> Where ev'ry one is King, and hath
> his crown
> If not upon his head, yet in his
> hands
> —"To All Angels and Saints"

realm. And the King of Kings himself is sometimes made to discard his formal majesty.

> Hast thou not heard that my Lord Jesus di'd?
> Then let me tell thee a strange storie.
> The God of power, as he did ride
> In his majestick robes of glorie,
> Resolv'd to light; and so one day
> He did descend, undressing all the way.
>
> The starres his tire of light and rings obtain'd,
> The cloud his bow, the fire his spear,
> The sky his azure mantle gain'd.
> And when they ask'd what he would wear,
> He smil'd and said, as he did go,
> He had new clothes a making here below.[9]

Splendour and pomp are appropriate to created nature, but not to man, not to the Son of Man. And even in the nature imagery the royalist reference can be negative.

> Then went I to a garden and did spy
> A gallant flower,
> The crown Imperiall. Sure, said I,
> Peace at the root must dwell.
> But when I digg'd, I saw a worm devoure
> What show'd so well.[10]

It is not surprising, therefore, that the soul's redemption and the song made for the soul's rejoicing should deny courtliness. Herbert seeks Christ in ". . . great resorts,/In cities, theatres, gardens, parks, and courts" only to find him at last amid "a raggèd noise and mirth of theeves and murderers." [11] One feels again and again in the poems that Herbert has reached for the unified experience of Hooker, for the synthesis of worldly and otherworldly values. And he has failed. As a poet he must make a different song, unaided by those who had been his fellows.

9 "The Bag."
10 "Peace."
11 "Redemption."

My God, a verse is not a crown,
    No point of honour, or gay suit,
No hawk, or banquet, or renown,
    Nor a good sword, nor yet a lute.

It cannot vault, or dance, or play;
    It never was in France or Spain;
Nor can it entertain the day
    With a great stable or demain.

It is no office, art, or news,
    Nor the Exchange, or busie Hall.
But it is that which while I use
    I am with thee; and Most, take all.[12]

Here the whole range and sense of the chivalric tradition are questioned. And in the last stanza the symbols of commerce fare no better. Indeed, the significance of Herbert's curiously negative treatment of the court cannot be fully understood unless one notices his distinctly hostile use of the symbols of wealth and trade. The court, in Herbert's symbolization of it, seems impotent. But the "Exchange" is vicious. The acquisitive urge menaces the present and will destroy the future. Everywhere Herbert sees about him the evidences of successful greed, sees the new vulgarity of money challenge and threaten the old dignity of the land. The strains and stresses that were to put the landed gentry under one violent banner and the merchant and the yeoman under another had been increasingly evident since the death of Elizabeth. Herbert cannot accommodate himself to the sharp new ethic emerging in Puritan sermonizing, an ethic which would justify the new man to the old God. Even John Donne could bless the Virginia planters and could find it in his heart to comfort the London merchant with the assurance that "Riches is the metaphor in which the Holy Ghost had delighted to express God and Heaven to us." [13] In Herbert,

---

[12] "The Quidditie."
[13] *Donne's Sermons*, ed. Logan Pearsall Smith (Oxford, 1920), p. 46.

Man is God's image, but a poore man is
    Christ's stamp to boot.[14]

Only once is Christ expressed in the metaphor of gold. Herbert
is addressing the Virgin Mary:

Thou art the holy mine whence came the gold,
    The great restorative for all decay
      In young and old.[15]

But this is an ironic flirtation with gold. While the suggestion of
wealth hovers in the word and thickens it, the supposed restora-
tive and medicinal properties of gold really inform the meaning
of the metaphor. And the specifically social virtue of wealth is
always clearly denied. Man has dug gold out of the dark cave
and made it bright; now it un-mans man.

    Nay, thou hast got the face of man, for we
Have with our stamp and seal transferr'd our right;
    Thou art the man, and man but drosse to thee.
Man calleth thee his wealth, who made thee rich,
And while he digs out thee, falls in the ditch.[16]

The active social role of wealth comes out in "The Church
Militant," Herbert's one deliberate poetic venture into the theory
of church, state, and history. He traces the flight of religion before
the successive invasions of sin from Abraham's time to Laud's.
Through Judea, Greece, Rome, Egypt, Spain, and Germany the
spirit of religion travels, coming to rest in England and "giving
the Church a crown to keep her state." This last is good Hooker,
and is meant to be. But sin "travell'd westward also." And sin
will prevail as it has in other lands and other times.

Then shall Religion to America flee.
They have their times of Gospel ev'n as we.
My God, thou dost prepare for them a way
By carrying first their gold from them away;
For gold and grace did never yet agree.

14 "The Church-Porch," st. 64.
15 "To All Angels and Saints."
16 "Avarice."

> Religion alwaies sides with povertie.
> We think we rob them, but we think amisse;
> We are more poore, and they more rich by this.[17]

There is surely a hint of irony in the suggestion that the exploitation of the colony will further degrade the English while ennobling their American victims. At least Herbert does not share Donne's trust that the planters are holy men prayerfully extending God's kingdom beyond the seas. Nor does the vision of a new empire kindle positive hope for the future. Even the virtues of poverty inadvertently raised up in America will perish soon.

> Yet as the Church shall thither westward flie,
> So Sinne shall trace and dog her instantly.
>
>   .   .   .
>
> The Church shall come, and Sinne the Church shall smother.[18]

Against the unleashed force of avarice, neither king nor church can prevail. Here and throughout the poems the treatment of the wealth symbol is as hostile as the treatment of royalism is negative. In one poem there is what appears at first to be a trade image with positive religious suggestion. Herbert sells his soul to God

>   . . . with open eyes
> I flie to thee, and fully understand
>   Both the main sale and the commodities;
> And at what rate and price I have thy love.[19]

But the transaction is in a commodity not to be had on the stalls or in the warehouses. And the price God charges is the world itself and all of the world's profit.

This distrust of riches, this fear of the merchant's world has, of course, nothing in common with the cry which later is heard

[17] "The Church Militant."
[18] "The Church Militant."
[19] "The Pearl." Herbert never uses wealth as *in itself* expressive of value. There is never, as there so often is in Donne, an equation between goods and the good. The opposition of spiritual to social wealth is consistent in Herbert.

from St. George's Hill. Herbert is no revolutionary. His ideal poverty has small reference to real or social poverty. He is never impelled, as Winstanley is, to banish wealth by banishing poverty. The mood, on the social level, is negative, passive, fatalistic.

Is this not a long leap backwards from the positive, all-embracing synthesis of Hooker's *Ecclesiastical Polity*? The crown no longer saves the church, nor does it "keep her state." The ideal which emerges from Herbert would seem to be pre-Elizabethan, pre-nationalist, pre-mercantile. It involves the renunciation of courtly and bourgeois values (both halves of the Elizabethan synthesis) and reaches after a society, admittedly unobtainable, where trade is little and princes need not be great.

Yet it is in the light of Hooker's philosophy of the *via media* that Herbert sees and interprets his own age. And Anglican thought and the still solid fact of the Anglican Church itself appear as the only constants in a world of flux. Herbert's mind is no *tabula rasa* receiving raw impressions from the social environment. He regards his world in a particular way. He looks for values he has learned to expect. Tradition—the tradition of Anglican humanism—directs his gaze, guides his appraisal.

In "The Church-Porch," a poem written before he took orders, Herbert presents his humanist ethic. The poem is a plea for the controlled life, the middle way between continence and abstinence ("Drink not the third glasse."). Balance is the prescription for the social as well as the personal life. Wealth and the profit motive already appear as dangerous, but not yet fatally so.

> Gold thou mayst safely touch; but if it stick
> Unto thy hands, it woundeth to the quick.[20]

Poverty is idealized, but only for the attention of the alms-giver. The good life still seems to be possible for the courtier or merchant whose ways are sane.

But even in "The Church-Porch" it is apparent that Herbert

[20] "The Church-Porch," st. 28.

is engaged in special pleading, without hope that his notions will easily prevail. The feeling that Englishmen are not what they once were is evident throughout the poem and, indeed, is the motive for preaching the verse sermon at all.

> O England! full of sinne, but most of sloth,
>   Spit out thy flegme, and fill thy brest with glorie.
> Thy Gentrie bleats, as if thy native cloth
>   Transfus'd a sheepishnesse into thy storie.[21]

In "The Church Militant" sermonizing and exhortation on the text of Hooker are to be abandoned for prophecy, a prophecy of relative failure for church and state within the limits of history. Herbert seems to have realized, as Simcox suggests, "that after the defeat of the Spanish Armada, the submission of the chieftains of Ulster, and the tardy pacification of the Netherlands, the English gentry were for the first time since the Field of the Cloth of Gold without a rational object of public concern." [22] Sloth has stilled the impulse of the gentry to action, and the drive of the age is no longer expressed in terms of a precarious but real alliance of the interests of land and money. Avarice destroys the old balance, and with it man's hope.

But the Church of England still possesses the solidity and rationality (if not the permanence) of the ideal construction of values. "The British Church" contains the congealed thought of Hooker.

> A fine aspect in fit array,
> Neither too mean, nor yet too gay,
>   Shows who is best.
> Outlandish looks may not compare,
> For all they either painted are,
>   Or else undrest.[23]

The gaudy Roman church on the hills and the bare Puritan

---

[21] "The Church-Porch," st. 16.
[22] G. A. Simcox, "Sandys, Herbert, Crashaw, Vaughan," *The English Poets,* ed. T. H. Ward (London, 1902), II, p. 194.
[23] "The British Church."

church in the valley represent the extremes which a rational
Anglicanism shuns.

> But dearest Mother, (what those misse,)
> The mean, thy praise and glorie is
>   And long may be.
> Blessèd be God, whose love it was
> To double-moat thee with his grace,
>   And none but thee.[24]

In the institution of the church itself, there persist values which
no longer characterize society. Within the church—and only
within it—Herbert contemplates a happy union of sense and soul,
of nature and grace.

> Doctrine and life, colours and light, in one
>   When they combine and mingle, bring
> A strong regard and aw.[25]

Nature, if not society, can still at times be regarded with joy.

> Heark, how the birds do sing,
>   And woods do ring!
> All creatures have their joy, and man hath his.[26]

It is this admission of sensuous enjoyment which marks Herbert
as a humanist, by contrast with the sober-sides Puritanism gain-
ing everywhere about him. The order of nature is not despised,
yet it is transcended.

> True beautie dwells on high. Ours is a flame
> But borrow'd thence to light us thither.[27]

The liveliness which Herbert finds in nature is akin to the loveliness of the church service, "neither too mean, nor yet too gay."
This is nature seen and felt through the glazed window of the
"British Church." It is nature enjoyed contemplatively rather
than experientially.

24 "The British Church."
25 "The Windows."
26 "Man's Medley."
27 "The Forerunners."

The humanist creed of Hooker, abstracted from Hooker's world, provides Herbert at once with a critique and a solace. The tradition is alive. It would be false to regard its persistence as merely static. For Herbert's work reveals a significant interaction between the tradition as such and the disturbing pressures of Caroline society. Only a crude and utterly mechanical criticism could find in Herbert's poetry nothing more interesting than the effects of social disintegration. But surely it is quite as mechanical to read Herbert only in the light of the tradition. A humanism emptied of its original social content and reference, and holding to its moral and aesthetic values in relation to a rapidly shrinking range of experience, is necessarily something other than itself. A new and different synthesis has emerged.

One must remember that even the "double-moat" does not always guarantee the church. Sin—the sin of avarice—will prevail. No institution, no construction of social values, is secure. The mind must turn inward to find the permanence it seeks.

Before the battle was joined, before the practical implications of Herbert's social fears were finally realized in the Civil War, an inner synthesis of values is discovered and held. The apparent contradiction between his devotion to the "British Church" and his fatalistic view of the church as a social institution can be resolved in a deepening sense of intimacy with God, which almost transcends the church as institution, as place of collective worship, and approaches mystical communion. By the music of the church service, Herbert is almost transported beyond churchliness altogether.

> Now I in you without a bodie move,
>   Rising and falling with your wings.
> We both together sweetly live and love,
>   Yet say sometimes, God help poore Kings.[28]

I say "almost transported"—but never quite. The consciousness of tension invades the mystical moment and curbs it. He is never

[28] "Church-Musick."

able to shake off a quite unmystical kind of awareness. He can rise over fear into a pity which still has in it the distant echo of fear. "God help poore Kings"—impotent prey of the world and bound to the world, as Herbert himself is bound.

As strong as this unfulfilled impulse towards mysticism is the yearning, again unrealized, towards mediaevalism. I have already noted the monastic ideal of poverty which underlines Herbert's despair for the unbalanced social order. On the religious level this direction is indicated not only in Herbert's priestly practice (which brings to mind Chaucer's "poure persoun of a toun") but also in the fascination which at times Roman Catholicism held for him. The saints and the Virgin beckon.

> I would addresse
> My vows to thee most gladly, blessèd Maid,
> And Mother of my God, in my distresse.[29]

The middle way is not so easy to travel when it is no longer in the middle. But travel it Herbert does. The inner balance is kept. The manner, though not the matter, of humanist thought, determines the nature of a synthesis which is almost mystical, almost Romanist, almost free of social conscience or concern— but never entirely any one of these. A delicately sensitive mind steeped, in a great tradition, turns from an outer tangible world upon which it can make no impress, and in which it can no longer "its own resemblance find," to the construction of an inner world where conflicts can be at least tentatively resolved. Conflicts recur: tensions return as quickly as they depart. One does not find evidence of a chronological development in Herbert's poetry. After the sermonizing of "The Church-Porch" his quality develops in depth and not in time. In this inner synthesis of awareness and withdrawal, crisis is never fully resolved, nor is the synthesis ever quite destroyed.

Herbert's more characteristic poems are, as Grierson has observed, love lyrics to God. The form and tone of these poems

29 "To All Angels and Saints."

are thus both old and new to English poetry. The courtly poem has been transformed into a verse prayer which is quite unlike any prayer before it or, indeed, after it. The style is of the court and not of the court. The tone is humanist and yet not humanist. The effect is unique in literature.

The values which coexist as an entity in Herbert could not coexist for long. One feels sure that if Herbert had lived into the Civil War, either a desperate loyalty would have made him partisan, a somewhat bewildered clerical Cavalier, or defeat would have hastened the impulse towards either the mystical or the mediaeval destination implicit in his view of contemporary life.

In the men who follow and who owe most to Herbert's influence, the spell is broken and the inner synthesis dissolves. For Crashaw the mediaeval flight is consummated in a highly romantic Roman Catholicism. Vaughan, dismayed by the triumph of the barbarian, turns away from the Renaissance tradition and carries forward Herbert's incipient mysticism. For certainly when Vaughan moves but one inch beyond his master, he enters a world of strange white light which would have set the eye of any sturdy Elizabethan to blinking. In his poetry the humanist tradition is finally cancelled out, to reappear and disappear in new forms and under new urgencies, at once traditional and novel, but always in motion, never still, never quite the same.

Before turning to a study of the more elusive problem of Herbert's use of Eucharistic symbol, I should like to stress this point: the antihistorical note of withdrawal in Herbert comes of no mere quirk in the personal devotional life but is a phenomenon characteristic of one considerable segment of piety in the Jacobean and Caroline church. And, significantly enough, it is in the work of poets whose integral churchmanship defies an easy institutional Erastianism that we hear over and over again the tone of disenchantment both with the pretensions of the court and the aspirations of the city. Men like Nathaniel Richards,

Charles Fitz-Geoffrey, Thomas Washbourne, and Joseph Beaumont share Herbert's social views to the letter. One can have no doubt that these views proceed from a Catholic Anglicanism unable to identify king and Christ, unwilling to descend with the embittered politicos of the Cavalier party to a commerce in the symbols of *Realpolitik*.

Nathaniel Richards in his *The Celestiall Publican* foresees the death of England's spiritual life in the courtier's thirst for monarchial favour as much as in the merchant's greedy hunger for worldly wealth. True, Richards prays for the king's safety and the kingdom's peace. Like Herbert, he remains royalist without becoming Cavalier. For he is convinced that it is the "vicious Courtier" who now destroys the proper and ancient function of the court and who deprives it of all religious relevance. And as in Herbert there is in Richards the backward glance over the shoulder at the lost mediaeval ideal, the Anglo-Catholic nostalgia for a world in which Christian and practical values had seemed for a while to commingle.

> O blest performance, Noble race of men,
> Worthy the praise of an Immortal Pen
> Your famous deeds, past stars, recorded stand
> For ever and ever, written by the hand
> Of Sacred Truth, to the Eternal shame
> Of the sin-branded Vicious Courtier's Name.[30]

One feels an almost Puritan vehemence and prurience in Richards' warning against the snares and temptations of the life at court.

> Whate'er thou art that careless shall resort
> To the Court of Vice, only to see the Court;
> Take heed, beware of that Enchanted Glass
> Where Pride in Mortals, Friends in Hell surpass.
> There shalt thou Masques, such midnight Revels find
> Such Music, Banquets to allure the mind
> As will affright the blood of Chastity
> Turn Virgin Love to Hot Love's Pleurisy.[31]

---

[30] *The Celestiall Publican: A Sacred Poem* (London, 1620). From the section subtitled "The World." The entire poem is relevant.

[31] *The Celestiall Publican*, from the section subtitled "The Vicious Courtier."

This reads more like Savonarola than it does like Herbert. And note that Richards warns against the relatively chaste court of the *first* Charles. Nevertheless, our man is no Presbyterian. His ethical emphasis is Catholic, he holds to a Catholic doctrine of sanctification, he shares Herbert's dislike of the money-grubber on the left.

> The deceitful Tradesman, that seems precise
> And is an arrant knave; to think the honey
> And only blessed life, still to get money,
> Mocks at the poor man's virtue and in pride
> Styles him a vertuous fool; thus knaves deride
> The poverty of men, which does as far
> (In Heavenly wealth) transcend them, as a star.[32]

The social ethic here is Franciscan rather than Calvinist, and represents a drift in Anglicanism of "the Catholic side" towards a pristine primitivism, towards a literalistic Scriptural reading of the virtues and vices of man in society. Within the context of the time such an emphasis could lead only to a deepening of the interior religious life at the expense of institutionalism and ultimately of any active corporate fulfillment of Catholic social ethic. For the exterior life of the institutional church was as remote and alien to this new Franciscan sensibility as was the exterior life of society, and the twisting and capricious convolutions of history.

Unlike Herbert, Richards lived into and through the Civil War, and he was forced, as Herbert was not, to choose sides. His *Poems, Sacred and Satirical* prove him to be, in his own way, a king's man. For decent order is threatened by these "new men," and Richards, like Herbert, is nothing if not conservative.

> . . . truth and all true Christians know Religion
> Consists in true obedience not Rebellion;
> Men that give way to ill, t'increase their good
> Bring famine on a land, fierce fire and blood.
> All villages in a kingdom, Sin does delude
> Leaves it a prey to the lawless multitude.[33]

[32] *The Celestiall Publican*, from "The World."
[33] *Poems, Sacred and Satirical* (London, 1641), p. 12.

This is not the tone of Emperor-worship—or of cynical realism, either. The enemy here is chaos. And men like Richards are all too aware that chaos is spawned as much by the "Vicious Courtier" as by the "deceitful Tradesman." When the storm breaks, the crown is defended as the traditional sign and guarantor of order, but without hysteria or myth-making. In none of these Catholic-minded Anglicans, for all their criticism of court and city, does one catch anything resembling the cry of violence which resounds through the verse of the dispossessed and the lowly. The pull of tradition and a "rage for order" subdue the tone of critics who write from beyond the right wing of existing political realities. And men like Richards have no hope of translating their words into deeds. But while they might recoil from the class-conscious anger of the stanzas which follow, could Richards or Herbert disavow the indictment of society contained in these outbursts from the extreme sectarian left wing?

> I smyle to see some bragging gentle-men
> That claim their descent from King Arthur great;
> And they will drinke and sweare and roar: what then?
> Would make their betters foote-stooles to their feet.
>
> · · ·
>
> And rich men gape, and not content seeke more,
> By sea and land, for gaine, run manie miles;
> The noblest strive for stale ambition's glore
> To have preferment, landes, and greatest stiles
> Yet ne'er content of all, when they have store;
> But from the shepheard to the King, I see,
> There's no contentment for a worldlie eye.[34]

Here is the indignation that bursts out not only at kings and courts but also, finally, at the stained glass window, the cross, and the altar. This is the way of the Negation of Images, and it is to be the revolutionary way. The other way, the way of Herbert and the "spiritual Anglicans," is towards the recovery, the re-affirmation of images. For if the indictment of the social order

---

34 William Lithgow, *Pilgrim's Farewell* (London, 1618). Reprinted in *Select Poetry, Chiefly Sacred of The Reign of James I*, ed. Edward Farr, p. 338.

and the way of history seems the same in both revolutionary and pietist, the sameness is on the negative side only. The left moves towards change, towards the positive act, separating the image from the idea, destroying the image in an urge to purify the idea, but losing the idea in the very act. The Catholic side of Anglicanism, just as painfully aware of the corruption of the image in the event, strives to purify the image and thereby to redeem the idea. But in an effort to recover the image by a return to an idea that lies outside the event, by a nostalgia for values which have been displaced by event, the "spiritual Anglican" purifies the image by abstracting it, by depriving it of "the historical concrete," and thus destroying its authentically *symbolic* possibilities. We must look now at the images of these "spiritual Anglicans."

The "Spiritual Anglicans"

CHAPTER SEVEN

IN THE VERSE of a Catholic-minded Anglican like Charles Fitz-Geoffrey, a pure Franciscan devotion to Lady Poverty prompts a mighty indignation at the privilege and avarice of Jacobean England. Fitz-Geoffrey preaches telling anathemas on "the cunning huckster," "the covetous merchant," "the greedy farmer." As in Herbert, a Franciscan love of the poor is fused here with an utter distrust of wealth and rank—and event. As in these others, there is evident in Fitz-Geoffrey a spirituality rooted in the doctrines of Catholicism and owing nothing either to the Erastian situation of the English church or to the immediate compulsions of English society. Not only does Fitz-Geoffrey hold to Catholic thought and Catholic image in poems on the Trinity and the Incarnation, he writes with something like Tridentine fervour and conviction on the person of the Blessed Virgin.

> No son like him, no Mother like to her,
> For such a Mother never was before
> And such a Mother never shall be more
>
> .   .   .
>
> Behold a field which nere by man was tilled
> Wheat whence is made, the bread of life doth yield.[1]

It would even seem that in the symbolism of Catholic Anglicans, the Eucharistic Christ once more takes the central place.

[1] *The Blessed Birthday Celebrated. Some Pious Meditations on the Angel's Anthem* (Oxford, 1634), pp. 10–11.

[158]

THE "SPIRITUAL ANGLICANS"

Not only does Mary return to the niche which had been usurped for a while by Elizabeth: Christ again is King. And once again the food and drink of the altar sustain those who truly hunger and thirst.

> There goes and flows from this celestial Mountain
> Bread against hunger and against thirst a Fountain.[2]

One notes, too, that the merits of Christ's sacrifice are applied to the faithful in the action of the Mass.

> A double virtue this one Fountain hath
> It quenches thirst and also is a Bath
> To wash and cleanse us from our sins pollution
> That so our filth may not be our confusion.[3]

Indeed, in Fitz-Geoffrey there seems to be an acceptance of something close to the Catholic faith in the Mass as efficacious *ex opere operato*. And it is not surprising that a yearning after the lost devotions to Mary and the saints and a heightened feeling for the ancient sacraments should be accompanied by a sturdy insistence on the integral and autonomous nature of the church. Thomas Washbourne, for instance, will not allow that the life of the church can be touched by the death of the crown. In the type of the "burning bush" he contemplates the indestructibility of the Mystical Body.

> Loe! here a sight
> Presented to the eye;
> A Bush on fire flaming bright
> Yet not consum'd; a wondrous mysterie.
> The Bush: the Church;
> Affection is the fire
> Which serves not to destroy, but search
> And try her gold, raising the value higher.
>
> . . .
>
> This Bush that flamed
> Could never long withstand

[2] *The Blessed Birthday*, p. 31.
[3] *The Blessed Birthday*, p. 31.

Unlesse the Lord were in the same.
'Tis He that doth uphold it with His hand.[4]

The "Bush" is near to being a thoroughly Catholic *figura Christi*. In the last stanza of the piece, however, the typological effect is seriously qualified.

For this fire shall
Like that which snatch'd away
The Prophet once, transport them all
From this world's sorrows to a world of joy.[5]

Washbourne's church is in essence divine. The gates of hell will not prevail against her. But, as in Milton's *Paradise Lost,* the church's triumph is to be by a transcendence of history and an abandonment of the historical concrete. Washbourne will not exalt the martyred Charles the Christ. The church resumes her own life, seeks her own integral fulfillment. The church is no longer of the world. She is scarcely even *in* it. And this is the danger. The very repugnance which the "spiritual Anglican" feels for a crude Erastianism forces him to an opposite extreme —to a sense of the church as a simple univocal reflection in time of the seamless spirit of Christ. One might almost say that it is the intense Catholicity of these men which, in the peculiar context of the time, finally makes them un-Catholic.

For there is a decided Catholic colour to the churchliness and the devotional metaphor of the "spiritual Anglicans." We have already noted an uneasy fluctuation in the religious sensibility of George Herbert. The discreet "British Church," set snugly between painted Rome and nude Geneva, by no means represents the full spectrum of Herbert's imagery. As we shall see in a moment, he often writes with a violence of physical image more characteristic of Crashaw and the art of the Counter Reformation than of the elusive Anglican "middle way."

Washbourne's "Scylla and Carybdis" may be read as an illumi-

4 "The Bush Burning," from *Divine Poems* (London, 1654). Reprinted in *Fuller Worthies Library,* ed. A. B. Grosart (London, 1868), I, p. 73.
5 Washbourne, p. 74.

nating footnote to Herbert's "British Church" and as a revelation of the contradictory pulls exerted upon the churchmanship
of the "spiritual Anglicans."

> Two gulfs there are 'twixt which 'tis hard to sail
> And not be shipwreckt: here prophaneness stands
> With all its brood of vices at its tayle,
> There superstition with its numerous bands
> Of false traditions; 'twas the main intent
> Of our late pilots between both to steere:
> But froward fate to seamen incident
> Made them mistake their way; for whiles they fear
> To sink into the gulf of superstition,
> They into the gulf of profanation fal,
> And in the furious heat of opposition
> 'Gainst Papists, are like to turn atheists all.
>
>   .   .   .
>
> . . . the faulte is in our eyes
> That wil not see; or rather in our mind
> That wil not keep the road and safest way
> Which by the best and wisest men is gone
> But rather through the unbeaten deserts stray
> Which lead to nothing but confusion.
> O God, be thou our pilot once again
> Or put some Pharos, that by the light
> Our ship the Church may saile safe through the main.[6]

One is aware here of an agonized longing for infallible light
like that light which flashes from the Triple Crown but not from
the crown of England. Certainly there is in this poem and this
attitude not the slightest trace of Erastianism. Indeed, no authority of any kind would seem to be left to preside over the
doctrine and practice of the Establishment. And until the prayer
for light is answered, the tortured conscience must continue to
choose, from this side and that, the form and content of a bind-
ing and efficacious worship. Unhappily, too, it must make its
choices by the exercise of a private judgment which shrinks from
judging privately. And so a yearning for Catholicity and for an

[6] Washbourne, pp. 188–198.

authoritative, supranational churchmanship is crossed by an inherited distrust of Rome and her "superstitious excess."

On Anglicanism the mark of this tension is a painful ambivalence rather than any *via media* securely realized. To recognize this ambivalence for what it is, is to place the poetry of the "spiritual Anglicans" in quite a new perspective. We have already noted the presence in Fitz-Geoffrey (and in Herbert) of a rhetoric more appropriate, one might suppose, to a Counter Reformation than to a Reformation art. It will be necessary to study Herbert in this connection. But it may be helpful first to develop more fully the context in which his poetry and his characteristic symbol stand revealed.

For the Catholic-minded Anglican, the church is no longer the church of Henry and Elizabeth, but the Church Universal, the Mystical Body of Christ. Nevertheless, it is *in fact* the Church of England, a national church. And as it is now, apparently, being rooted from the earth by barbarous sectarian snouts, its indestructibility, like its universality, must be of a wholly nonhistorical, nontemporal kind. The antitype of the "burning bush" is not the Church Militant here below but the Church Triumphant untouched by the waste and chaos of the historical order. The sacramental grip on time is thus inevitably loosened. And so is the sacramental grip on things. The process here is more complex than in the poetry of the Protestant Anglicans. For the *surfaces* of Catholic rhetoric are renewed. And the restoration to Anglican poetry of Mary, the saints, typology, and a feeling for the church as the Mystical Body would seem to be part of a strenuous effort, by way of analogical symbol, to bring the natural order once more within range of the divine. There is indeed such an effort. And there is failure. In the work of Joseph Beaumont, an Anglican even more Catholic than Herbert, we find a clue to the cause of this failure.

Beaumont, who took his M.A. at Cambridge with Crashaw in 1638 and was expelled with him in 1644 for "Catholic leanings," carries the Catholic possibility in Anglicanism to the edge of probability. To quote Eloise Robinson:

> Beaumont was not a Papist but he was a High Churchman and one who lived in a spiritual world which was in all its details Romish. Ceremony, church tradition, and ritual meant so much to him that the travails of his own soul seem fused in or subordinate to the experience of the saints and martyrs.[7]

Miss Robinson goes on to say that Beaumont, despite this devotion to Catholic-looking ritual, had none of Crashaw's power to make the agonies and ecstasies of the saints seem alive. "His poems on the saints lack symbolism." [8]

But Beaumont's failure to fulfill the symbolic possibilities of traditional Christian image cannot be put down simply to a deficiency in the man's imaginative powers. His work shows forth the predicament of the Catholic-minded Anglican in poetry and reveals for us the new texture of the Christian firmament of symbol as rhetoric separates itself from dogma.

In Beaumont, as in Herbert, one finds the ancient language of the sacramental possession of things—the language of analogy. And yet such language is employed by Beaumont, as by Herbert, to its own destruction. The rhetorical surfaces of this poetry are often fully Catholic, and in individual poems the analogical capacity of traditional symbol sometimes seems to survive. But it would not do for us to rest altogether in the item, in the poetic unit. One must be aware of a kind of motion between poem and poem, even between image and image, a motion which frets to decay the texture of the tradition in which Beaumont and Herbert seek to work.

On the surface of most of Beaumont's pages, the Romish devotional colour leaps at once to the eye. For instance these stanzas from the "Annunciatio" seem to come from the very heart of the restored Mary cult:

[7] *The Minor Poems of Jos. Beaumont* (New York, 1914), Introduction, p. xli.
[8] Ibid.

[163]

HAILE FULL OF GRACE
May we have place
To heap our prayses on they crowne,
    About whose wreathe
    All sweets doe breathe
And Heav'ns illustrious Joyes are throwne.

May we have leave
To think old Eve
No more unhappy, who have found
    The Cure, and may
    With Triumph say
Eve's Gall in Marie's Sweets are drownd.[9]

In "Love" one cannot miss the authentic patristic paradox and tension of this taut image of the creative agony of Christ:

. . . Mark that crosse Tree
No other Bow but that brought Hee:
    And on ye same
    Stretch'd with full strength
    Himself at length
And shot at Death and Hell.
But since these Monsters fell
    He aims His Darts
    At none but Hearts.
He heals by wounds, by killing
                Life imparts.[10]

This would seem to be safely within the firmament of the Catholic baroque. Moreover, one encounters frequently in Beaumont those images of pain crucified so characteristic of Southwell and Crashaw—and of the ecstatic devotionals of the Spanish mystics.

Burn us, whilst Thou letst us freize
In our dull aridities;
Wound, yet never shoot a dart
At the wounded bleeding Hart
            .   .   .
Wounds and Death brought Life for me
Wounds and Death my life must be.[11]

[9] Beaumont, p. 170.
[10] Beaumont, p. 24.
[11] Beaumont, "The Complaint," p. 310.

Dear *Love,* thou needst not send a Dart
To finde the bottome of my Hart:
'Tis found already by that Spear
Whose barbarous point Thine own did tear.[12]

The bitter-sweet language of agonized exultation veering, as in Crashaw, from the simple patristic paradox to thick Italianate verbalism, hints at something more than a mild flirtation between Beaumont and the Scarlet Woman. And then, too, there are the saints. Beaumont has poems to Paul, James, Andrew, Mark, Philip, John the Baptist, and, notably, to Peter, who is accorded a veneration quite unique in the poetry of Anglicanism. Beau-mont rhetorically admonishes the Roman tyrant who crucified Peter:

For thy proud Rome shall see his Throne
Flourish, when thine is dead and gone.
What though He but a Fisher be?
Illustrious is his Trade, for He
Useth no bait, but what is more
Worth, then this Imperiall store:
His Hook's a noble Crosse, and this
With a Kingdome baited is;
Eternal Crowns are fastened on it;
Do Thou they Selfe but Bite, and He
Can catch, and thither draw up Thee.[13]

Beaumont seems almost ready to kiss the fisherman's ring. But not quite. These Catholic-looking surfaces are deceptive. And it is now that we must try to detect that motion which runs restlessly between poem and poem, between image and image to their mutual consternation and eventual destruction.

One is soon struck by the fact that these saints of Beaumont's are never invoked. What is more, they are confined, discreetly but firmly, to their narrow moment in the historical order. They were here; they are gone from us; we praise the memory; we take heart

[12] Beaumont, "The Wound," p. 312.
[13] Beaumont, "St. Peter," p. 229.

from their example. Only Peter is thought of as in any way "present," and his presence is merely a metaphor for the continuity of the church. If Mary is hailed as "full of grace," she is most decidedly not asked to "pray for us." There is therefore in this Catholic-Anglican poetry no sense of a living exchange between the Church Militant and the Church Triumphant, no sense of an actual and active communion between the temporal and eternal orders. These are plaster saints, these saints of Beaumont's. They decorate the static surfaces of piety. They are able to set moving a stream of emotional-religious associations to the enrichment, no doubt, of the interior act of worship. But the saint-image is shorn of its proper symbolic possibilities in being, first of all, isolated, deprived of its living, analogical function in the Communion of Saints, and then psychologized, deprived of its objectivity, reduced to a metaphor of the spiritual way.

This "high" church lowering of the saint from symbol to metaphor is quite explicit in Washbourne's "Upon All Saints Day."

> . . . wel may
> We solemnize at least one annual day
> Unto their honour yet not guiltie be
> Of superstition or idolatry.
> When we observe this day, we do no more
> Than reverence them as saints, not them adore.
> God's the sole object of our invocation
> They but the pattern for our invitation.[14]

The saint still decorates the stained glass of the church window. His example illuminates the dark path before the wayfaring Christian. But the "Communion of Saints," a phrase still retained in the Anglican liturgy, is drained of symbolic possibility because the saint is consciously excluded from any living *present* participation in the timeless corporate totality of the Mystical Body. This passage from John Donne illustrates the essential individualism of the Anglican compromise as it affects crucial symbol, an individualism of dogma and of concept which, despite deceptive

[14] Washbourne, pp. 204–205.

Catholic surfaces of rhetoric, is unmistakably Protestant at the core:

> Other men's crosses are not my crosses; no man hath suffered more than himself needed. That is a poor treasure which they boast of in the Roman Church, that they have their exchequer, all the works of supererogation, of the martyrs in the primitive church that suffered so much more than was necessary for their own salvation, and those superabundant crosses and merits they can apply to me. If the treasure of the blood of Jesus Christ be not sufficient, Lord, what addition can I find to match them, to piece out them! And if it be sufficient of itself, what addition need I seek? Other men's crosses are not mine, other men's merits cannot save me. Nor is any cross mine own which is not mine by a good title . . . from whose hands can I receive any good thing but from the hand of God? [15]

Thus Donne is, after all, an island entire to himself. This theology of utterly individual salvation destroys what had been, in the Catholic economy of redemption, a cohabitation of the visible and invisible worlds. One danger is that the Church Militant, with all lines of communication down between itself and the Church Purgatorial and the Church Triumphant, will no longer have a body proper to its own essence and function. It must conform to the contour and texture of the body politic—or vanish. Certainly, this Protestant theology of individual salvation fails to give dogmatic sanction to that corporate social sense which comes through in so many of Donne's *Sermons and Devotions*. For Donne has the Thomist feeling for society as an organism. This feeling would seem to persist out of sheer habit well after Donne's rejection of the theology that had mothered it. For with the loss of the living Communion of Saints in that Mystical Body which compounds time in eternity, a real participation of the social body in the Mystical Body is inconceivable. That "continent" of which all human lives still seem to be part is a flat continent roofed over by the merely historical. And if there are holes in this roof, they

---

[15] Sermon LXXII (1640 Folio). Reprinted in *Seventeenth Century Poetry and Prose*, ed. R. P. T. Coffin and A. M. Witherspoon (New York, 1946).

are large enough for only one leap at a time. Therefore, Donne's Catholic-sounding "sociology" is semantically treacherous. Great words feeding on the bread but not on the Body shrink suddenly like Alice in Wonderland and are in danger of disappearing.

This contradiction between traditional modes of thinking and feeling on the one hand and the foreshortened symbolic possibilities of Reformed dogma on the other, rapidly transforms the firmament of Christian poetry. Perhaps the kernel of the contradiction is to be found in the Eucharistic symbolism of the "spiritual Anglicans" because, if my thesis is well founded, the Eucharist burns like a sun at the centre of the Christian firmament of symbol. All the peripheral symbols and images of Christian poetry must be seen in the light of this sun.

Joseph Beaumont's view of the Eucharist is "higher" than George Herbert's. We shall see that Herbert controls by specific definition the Catholic-looking rhetoric of his liturgical poems. But Beaumont tries to hide the point of controversy with the trick of ambiguity. In "The Holy Sacrament" Christ is said to have borrowed man's frail flesh from Mary, the "chosen maid."

> What He once had borrowed Hee
> Ment to keep eternally
> Yet in debt He would not be
> Unto poor Humanitie.
> But e'er He went to Heav'n contrived how
> To bear it hence, yet leave it still below.
> Moulded up in *Mystick Bread*
> And into a *chalice* shed
> Flesh and Blood He rendered:
> Ordering we should be fed
> With this high Diet, and incorporate
> Againe with Him, who had assured our State
> Bounteous *Jesu,* thou hast more
> Then discharg'd thy loving score:
> And we, richer than before,
> Happily find ourselves most poor;
> We never can repay this love of thine;
> God ran in debt, to make man more Divine.
> If ourselves our offering be
> Thou wantst not Humanitie:
> Love forestalled halfe what wee

With most right might offer Thee.
We yeeld, Great Lord, Thou hast subdued us quite
And unto Thee belongs e'en our *selfe-right*.[16]

Beaumont seems, without equivocation, to grasp and hold the Catholic paradox of the simultaneous Presence of Christ in heaven and in the sacrament. The Heavenly Christ returns to man in the Flesh and Blood of the altar. But is this an altar? Is there sacrifice? Although it is to "incorporate" man "againe with Him," the sacrament seems to be effected only by reception. We are incorporated in Him by being fed "with this high Diet." The faithful receive Christ in the act of communion. To pay their love debt, the faithful offer themselves, their souls and bodies, their "humanitie," their "selfe-right." They do not, together in the proper orders of the Mystical Body, offer Christ. The sacrifice, if such it is, is manward and not Godward. It terminates in reception.

Beaumont is, of course, more Catholic than Cranmer and his "low" Anglican progeny. Here the Real Presence is indeed affirmed and in a liturgical context which had been framed specifically to deny that Presence. Beaumont keeps to a corporate language. The sacrament is for "poor Humanitie"; it is "We" who are fed and thus made "incorporate" again with Him. And yet the analogical character of Eucharistic symbol is threatened if not impaired by Beaumont's dismissal of the sacrificial act. The Eucharist is no longer properly an action analogous in time to the eternal action of redemption, and *participating* in that action. The Mystical Body does not act. There is in the poem no integral symbolization of the Mystical Body. For we are "incorporate againe with Him" only *after* communion. This suggests the inconvenient and Daliesque image of the Head joining Himself to His member trunk and limbs *after,* and yet by means of, the sacramental banquet. The Mystical Body is therefore not quite formed and jointed until the faithful rise, one by one, from the altar rail. And it will disintegrate again, presumably, before the first communicant can return to his pew. . . .

16 Beaumont, p. 109.

The actual dogma of the Real Presence can scarcely live secure in a context which denies the analogical function of the liturgical act. For it is not just that the sense of the historical concrete is ultimately destroyed by this kind of Eucharistic emphasis: a religious interiorism amounting, in the end, to full-blown psychologism is inevitably induced by the exclusive emphasis on communion as apart from sacrifice, by this closed concern with the reception of sacramental favours. In other poems the passivity of Beaumont's Eucharistic dogma is even more explicit. And it is a passivity which infects the Eucharistic symbol of the "spiritual Anglicans" as a group. For instance, in his "Thursday in Holy Week" Beaumont imagines Love feasting his "faithfull Guests" with "choice Dainties of all Heavn." Here, as everywhere in Beaumont, there is more than the hint that it is by "faith alone" that the Presence is made real in the reception of the sacrament. In the same poem the chalice is said to hold

> A Cordiall Wine, which onely can
> Truly cheere up ye Heart of man.[17]

One remembers again the ritual words of Cranmer: "Feed on Him in your heart and be thankful"—words intended to define explicitly the subjective mode of the Presence and to limit sacrifice to a giving of thanks. Certainly the poem stresses and is meant to stress the interior spiritual benefits of reception.

> All Heavn is melted and doth drop
>   Into ye Cup:
> Which smiling there, invites each Guest
>   To come and taste.
> Come taste, sayes Love, and drink in Mee
> At one short draught Eternitie.[18]

Each Guest tastes the "Cordiall Wine which onely can truly cheere." The dogma, only partially concealed by the ancient rhetoric of Flesh and Blood, is clearly individualist rather than corpo-

17 Beaumont, p. 151.
18 Beaumont, p. 152.

rate, receptionist rather than sacrificial, and therefore inescapably subjective, rather than objective.

It is not my intent to push Beaumont further into Protestantism than he belongs. His predicament is that of the Catholic-minded Anglican who hunts the Real Presence in the liturgical context of a Real Absence. There is uncertainty, vacillation in the use of the familiar words. One is convinced that the Eucharist offered for "poor Humanitie" means, really, a communion for each separate (and separated) guest, and that the bread of the sacrament is Christ to the heart's faith alone. Yet one is left uncertain about the weight of Catholic images as they rest in Protestant scales.

This uncertainty reflects, of course, the double-edged and indecisive dogmatizing of the Anglican prayer book. A Catholic Anglican like William Strode, who was popularly believed to be a Papist, can shift in the twinkling of an eye from a seemingly orthodox celebration of the objective Presence to a thoroughly antisacramental exposition of the Lutheran doctrine of justification.

> See how the Rainbow in the sky
> Seems gaudy through the Sun's bright eye;
> Hark how an Echo Answer makes,
> Feel how a board is smooth'd with wax,
> Smell how a glove puts on perfume,
> Taste how their sweetness pills assume:
> So by imputed Justice: Clay
> Seems fair, well spoke, smooth,
>   sweet each way
>   The eye doth gaze on robes appearing,
>   The prompted Echo takes our hearing,
>   The board our touch, the scent our smell,
>   The pill our taste: Man
>   God as well.[19]

A deceptive world of "seeming," without integrity or intelligibility proper to itself, issues from a univocal theology that denies to man any active part in the economy of redemption. One begins to

[19] "Justification." *The Poeticall Works of William Strode* (1600–1645), ed. Bertram Dobell (London, 1907), p. 55.

suspect that there is an inner logical consistency between the "receptionist" view of the Eucharist, the "fictional" Lutheran view of justification, and the subjective-idealist view of nature and the historical order. The Christian who feeds upon God invisibly in his heart, the Christian whose invisible justification leaves no mark upon his will, is concerned, *as a Christian,* neither with the structures of time nor with the substance of things. Just as the analogical validity of the historical order is reduced by such thinking to a set of signs either univocal or equivocal in bearing, so, by the dogma which now spins towards the centre of the Anglican firmament, the order of intelligible, significant object is depressed to the level of the merely illustrative or the purely illusory. "Clay" *seems* fair, but it is not.

The extreme Cartesian separation of word and thing is not yet fully evident. The "word," in Beaumont's Eucharistic poetry, is, as we have seen, pulled simultaneously in opposite directions—towards a Catholic sacramentalism and towards a Protestant abstractionism. But as dogma slowly sets below the horizon of uneasy rhetoric and concept, the images of poetry fall into shadow and the landscape is without substance. Things become fragmented ciphers, manipulated arbitrarily. These lines from Beaumont's "House and Home" will help to illustrate the process:

Seek no more abroad, say I,
House and Home, but turne thine eye
Inward and observe thy breast;
There alone dwells solid Rest
That's a close immured Tower
Which can mock all hostile Power.
To thy selfe a Tenant be
And inhabit safe and free.
Say not that this house is small,
Girt up in a narrow wall;
In a cleanly sober Mind
Heavn it selfe full Room doth find.
The Infinite Creator can
Dwell in it, and May not Man?
Contented heer make thy abode
With thy selfe, and with thy God.

Heer, in this sweet Privacie
Maist thou with thy selfe agree
And keep House in Peace; though all
The Universe's Fabrick fall
No disaster can distress Thee,
Nor no furie dispossess Thee:
Let all war and plunder come
Still mayest thou dwell safe at home.[20]

The poem constitutes a significant footnote on the corporate and objective language of Beaumont's specifically Eucharistic poetry. One suspects that the Eucharist is for him primarily a source of consolation, a means of spiritual entry into a godliness that transcends the body even as it transcends history. In this poem the fear of "war and plunder" connives with a Protestant theology of interiorism to extricate the soul of the poet from the menace of flesh and time. For if this is a flight from history, which it obviously is, it is also a flight from the relevance of things, from the claims of the material order. Let "the Universe's Fabrick fall" with the fall of throne and sceptre. "Still mayest thou dwell safe at home"—within the solitary self. Images from history and nature alike are *outside,* suggesting the reality within, only by the harshest contrast. And there is not in this poem anything like the mystical search for God through the Dark Night of the Soul— the search that must issue in a dazzling illumination of place and time, of the practical, the actual, the tangible. In Beaumont's flights from place and time there is no thought or hope of return, of renewal.

Thanks still unceasing Turmoils; I
Mistook you heertofore.
But now I learn no more
To chide with that uncertainty
Which hunts me out in every place, and tosses
My settling hopes through new disturbances and crosses.

.   .   .

Blow then the worst of Blasts and beat
My bark about the World;

20 Beaumont, pp. 60–61.

Still can I not be hurled
Beyond the ken of my Hav'n, nor meet
One place more distant than another from
The heavenly Port, to which alone I pant to come.[21]

Restless images of motion and turmoil, suggesting at once the staggering, unpredictable spaces of the Copernican universe and the chaotic skirls of history, are made into a flickering hieroglyphic for the spiritual *Angst*. The brutal "a-morality" of matter and the frightening convolution of event provide the signs, but not the symbols, of an insubstantial purgatory of the inner, hidden life. This is a storm of metaphor, relevant only as illustration. The uniqueness and incarnate dignity of things vanish from the poetry of the "spiritual Anglicans," just as the sense of history as true analogue of God's traffic with man dissolves into accident and chaos. Note, too, how Beaumont abstracts, interiorizes, and dehydrates the simple political image:

The lower House, the Commons of my Breast
My traiterous Passions, speciously drest
    In Liberties bewitching cloke;
    First trampling down my Will and Reason
    As useless Peers, in triumph broke
    Into the gulf of deepest Treason
And murdered their *royal Lord* again,
Whose guilt was nothing but his Gentle Reign.[22]

Here, it is true, is the distrust of both Lords and Commons to be found everywhere in the poetry of the "spiritual Anglicans." But the war in the state has become nothing more than a sign-shop for the war in the soul.

This declension of the natural and the historical from the status of divine analogue to that of metaphorical sign or exterior counter is unmistakably evident in Thomas Washbourne's poem on the circulation of the blood. Here, at first glance, all the elements of the analogical grip on reality seem present and active. But, in

21 Beaumont, "The Pilgrim," p. 318.
22 Beaumont, "ενεθλιακόν," p. 378.

effect, the poet makes sport of the analogical possibilities of his material.

> Our famous Harvey hath made good
> The circulation of the blood
> And what was paradox we know
> To be a demonstration now.
> The like in bodies doth befall
> Civill as well as naturall
> Such revolutions in them found
> That they are always turning round.
> We know a kingdome which of late
> Converted was into a State.
> And from the hands of many men
> That State devolved to one agen.
> We know the wealth, which now doth flow
> I' th' City veins, did lately grow
> I' th' Country furrows, and the same
> Soon runs to th' place from whence it came.
> We know our bodie's frame, of dust
> At first created was, and must
> Crumble to dust ere long; we see
> Not one from dissolution free.
> We know, or what's equivalent,
> Believe our souls, which God first sent
> To make our bodies move and live,
> Shall go to Him who them did give.
>
> . . .
>
> Thus we see almost everything
> Circling about as in a ring.
> The winter-season of the yeer
> Is now turned Summer everywhere.
> This summer will to Winter turn
> And that freize which before did burn.
>
> . . .
>
> Sure nothing under heaven hath rest
> But floatings up and down; 'tis
> To look above, and fix mine eyes
> Where not a shadow of change lyes:
> No variation there, but all
> Stand still in state pacifical.
> Go then my dust to dust, but thou my soul
> Return unto thy rest above the pole.[23]

[23] Washbourne, *Divine Poems*, "The Circulation," pp. 107–109.

Clearly, what might have been, in the light of Harvey's study, an effort to illuminate the lively participation of the microcosm of men and things in the vast macrocosmic motions of being, is here only a witty reduction of an analogical relationship to playful metaphor. For as Washbourne actually *places* his images, there is no sense left of the analogy of being in this circular motion of seasons, societies, and persons. These floatings up and down, these swirlings about in the world of appearance, are alike only in their inability to arrive anywhere. They are equally and simultaneously meaningless and in shadow. Only "above," beyond these circlings, in a realm of being which has no possible analogical relation to the shadow-world of appearance, may the soul find peace—and proper symbol. Harvey has merely provided the poet with a novel set of signs for the delineation of illusion.

Seventeenth century Anglicanism can no more absorb the findings of the new science into an account of the world appropriate to an incarnational theology than it can make relevant to itself the forces alive in the historical order. A Romish surface of saints, surplices, and stained glass may deceive for a while. But at the core of this "spiritual Anglicanism" one finds a withering away of dogma and therefore a subtle dislocation of rhetoric and a loosening of the sacramental grip on time and things.

George Herbert, of course, is the finest poet of this group. He shares the dogmatic and therefore the artistic predicament of the group. We have already noted his Franciscan repudiation of court and city, his lonely walk in the mystical garden, his half wistful withdrawal from the temporal and social order. We have yet to observe his Catholicism, or rather the uncertain tension which obtains in his work between a Catholic sensibility and an urgent, if uneasy Protestant dogmatism.

Herbert is joined to the Catholic tradition not so much by his use of traditional typology and iconography as by his intense and immediate feeling for the Person of Christ. The vivid Catholic intuition of the Crucifixion, of the suffering God-man, is as much Herbert's as it is Crashaw's. Herbert sees, as if before his very eyes,

A man so wrung with pains, that all his hair,
His skinne, his garments, bloudie be.[24]

Herbert's dark night of the senses is identified with the ever-present agony of the Cross.

My thoughts are all a case of knives
　　Wounding my heart
　　With scatter'd smart
As watring pots give flowers their lives.
　　Nothing their furie can controll,
　　While they do wound and prick my soul.[25]

And there is no Anglican reticence in the very Tridentine relief of those tears which flow so often to put out the fire of Herbert's pain.

I have not lost one single tear:
　　But when my eyes
Did weep to heav'n, they found a bottle there
　　(As we have boxes for the poor)
Readie to take them in; yet of a size
　　that would contain much more.[26]

. . . O Mother deare and kinde
Where shall I get me eyes enough to weep,
As many eyes as stars? [27]

As in the art of the Counter Reformation, images of Christo-centric pain and cosmic weeping are crossed with images of purification and ecstasy in an almost Teresan yearning after the "wound of love" which hurts much yet is desired.

Oh my dear angrie Lord
Since thou dost love, yet strike;
Cast down, yet help afford

[24] "The Agonie." I am indebted to Miss Mindele Black for a detailed treatment of Herbert's Catholic-seeming imagery in an unpublished Honours thesis "Herbert and the Counter-Reformation," which she prepared under my direction at the University of Manitoba, 1948–49.

[25] "Affliction."

[26] "Praise."

[27] "Church Rents and Schisms."

> Sure I will do the like.
> I will complain yet praise;
> I will bewail, approve:
> And all my sowre-sweet dayes
> I will lament and love.[28]

Similarly, the fire which "shall consume the world" may also "kindle the heart." [29] The flaming dart of grace pierces, but it caresses, too.

And there is in this poetry a ravishment of soul and sense at an intensity scarcely proper to the experience of the staid "British Church."

> O what sweetnesse from the bowl
>   Fills my soul,
> Such as is, and makes divine!
> Is some starre (fled from the sphere)
>   Melted there,
> As we sugar melt in wine? [30]

This is the gourmand's anticipation of the Eucharistic feast:

> Come ye hither all, whose taste
>   Is your waste;
> Save your cost, and mend your fare.
> God is here prepar'd and drest,
>   And the feast,
> God, in whom all dainties are.[31]

The actual symbols of the Eucharist are sometimes far closer to Rome than anything that could have been imagined by any blinkered traveller of the *via media*. In "The Invitation," Herbert speaks of the wine "which before ye drink is bloud." And in "The Banquet," after celebrating the "sweetnesse in the bread," he affirms that this "perfume" is truly of God's flesh.

But even in poems like these which come close to implying that "carnal" view of the sacrament which has always been repellent to

28 "Bitter-Sweet."
29 "Love."
30 "The Banquet."
31 "The Invitation."

Anglicanism, there are hints which tend to qualify the Tridentine effect of the poems and which raise pointed questions about Herbert's whole frame of reference. In "The Banquet," after a taste of the cup,

> Wine becomes a wing at last
> For with it alone I flie
>   To the skie:
> Where I weep mine eyes, and see
> What I seek, for what I sue;
>   Him I view
> Who hath done so much for me.

The image of wine as "a wing" which lifts the soul out of itself is at least appropriate to Cranmer's spiritual communion, to a religious experience of an individualist and utterly psychological kind. And if God "flesh assumes," He does so in order to perfume the "heart" (that magic organ of spiritual digestion in Cranmer's liturgy). Therefore, one is by no means sure that the God Who is here "presented" is indeed *made present*.

But it is necessary to go to Herbert's carefully articulated doctrinal poem "The Holy Communion" for a reliable gloss on the Eucharistic symbols of the poems we have been discussing. "The Banquet" is meant to do no more than evoke the spiritual awareness of the celebrant. The traditional Catholic symbols are therefore readily, perhaps even recklessly, released into the stream of religious emotion. But in "The Holy Communion," Herbert is engaged in exact definition, in a conceptualization of Eucharistic dogma. And we are forced to look below the Catholic surfaces of these other poems, to note the disengagement of Catholic rhetoric from Catholic dogma, to recognize the emergence of a perplexing new firmament in which the surface of rhetoric at first conceals and then belies the inner sun and centre of the theology. For in Herbert's "Holy Communion," bread and wine, spreading through the physical body of the communicant, carry only the "name of Christ" and in themselves may not leap "the wall that parts our souls and fleshly hearts."

But by the way of nourishment and strength
        Thou creep'st into my breast;
        Making Thy way my rest.
    And they small quantities my length,
Which spread their forces into every part,
        Meeting sinnes force and art.

Yet can these not get over to my soul,
        Leaping the wall that parts
        Our souls and fleshly hearts;
    But as th' outworks, they may controll
My rebel-flesh, and carrying thy name,
        Affright both sinne and shame.

Onely thy grace, which with
        These elements, comes
        Knoweth the ready way
    And hath the privie key,
Op'ning the souls most subtile rooms;
While those to spirits refin'd, at doore attend
        Despatches from their friend.[32]

Not only is the world of sense here cut off cleanly from the world of spirit (there is only a pretty Cartesian porch between them for the exchange of "despatches"), but also the physical elements of the Eucharist are given as wholly separate from the reality of Christ's Presence. They carry His "name," they are signs. Christ is present in this Eucharist only by the grace "which with these elements, comes." The physical act of eating and drinking is accompanied by a spiritual act on the other side of the high wall. The physical act is given as a sign that there is indeed a spiritual act.

In the light of this, one realizes that the objective surfaces of poems like "The Banquet" are deceptive, that even the Eucharistic typology of a poem like the "Bunch of Grapes" must not be read at the level of rhetoric alone.

This is not meant in depreciation of Herbert. There is a quality to his poetry wholly unique, and no one could wish it away. There is nothing here of the blunt and imageless Puritanism of

---

[32] "The Banquet."

the "low" Anglican. For this is sunset and not raw dawn. But in this light the loveliest things may not be quite what they seem.

Professor Kenneth B. Murdoch makes a penetrating comment on the apparent sensuousness of Anglican poetry. He finds that sense images abound but that, generally, "beauty of words and images only typify or represent the idea of what is holy." No matter what the image from the physical or natural order "the emphasis was put on a doctrine, or a truth, a moral dogma or holy emotion, not on the natural object itself." [33] In brief, the analogical participation of the natural order in the divine now disappears. One clearly observes in Herbert and the Catholic Anglicans the spectacle of analogical symbol dissolving into simple metaphor.

From Shakespeare to Herbert through Donne, as poetry moves step by step away from the dogmatic core of the mediaeval firmament, the language of analogy declines without halt. S. L. Bethell argues that in Shakespeare, for whom the hierarchical structures of the mediaeval world-view still held, multiple planes of reality rise and cohere along each link of the chain of being. In Shakespeare, therefore, images from the natural order may function simultaneously at the moral, the social, and the spiritual levels of experience. But for John Donne "the great chain of being was rather badly damaged." The analogical sense has shrunk to a feeling "for the spiritual element being implicit in" or "somewhere just behind" the concrete situation. While Donne can never, therefore, achieve "the shifting functional metaphor of Shakespeare," (the fully analogical symbol), "his imagery is nevertheless capable of striking a genuine metaphysical relationship between two terms: a relationship in the realm of being." [34]

But as Bethell justly observes, this analogical activity is often

[33] *Literature and Theology in Colonial New England* (Cambridge, Massachusetts, 1949), p. 27.

[34] S. L. Bethell, *The Cultural Revolution of the Seventeenth Century* (New York, 1951), pp. 86–96.

compromised in Donne by the mere play of wit. There is imbalance, instability in the style. In a phrase like this—"One might almost say her body thought"—Bethell contends that the "interpenetration of mind and matter is a reality." The analogical grip holds. But, he adds, quite as characteristic of Donne is the witty but clearly univocal metaphor of the compass in "A Valediction Forbidding Mourning." It is as if Donne strained simultaneously towards Shakespeare and Cleveland. And as we have already noted, this tension between true analogy and mere metaphor is equally apparent in Donne's religious expression. He can state in one breath his fully Eucharistic belief in the corporateness of man—and in another breath reject flatly the corporate doctrine of redemption in and through the living Communion of Saints.

If in Donne true analogy and mere metaphor coexist in an uneasy, although fruitful, state of tension, in Herbert the relation is simpler and less fruitful. Metaphor succeeds analogy with the immediacy of a first echo—and with the poignant loveliness of something very near, yet very far because irretrievable.

In addition to all the forces proceeding from the new thought to the destruction of traditional cultural patterns, the reform of Christian dogma itself has obviously been to the detriment of analogical activity in poetry. No wonder that the firmament fell into fragments and that the several orders of being now seemed alien one to another. The centre did not hold. And even the revival, in Vaughan, of a neo-Platonic, Cabbalistic doctrine of correspondences is no more, can be no more, than a shadowy and precarious substitute for an analogical awareness grounded anciently in dogma. The shadow soon passes. Perhaps the metaphysical mode is a clutching after straws as the ancient bricks crumble. But if the seventeenth century is an age of disintegration, it is also an age of revolution. And in poetry, as in all things, there are no losses without gains. With the poetry of John Milton we enter a new firmament of symbol over the lovely ruins of the old.

Milton and the Protestant Aesthetic: The Early Poems

CHAPTER EIGHT

MILTON IS the last great Christian poet until Gerard Manley Hopkins. Between these two there are poets of stature who are Christian, but there are no Christian poets of stature. It would therefore seem that Milton failed to transmit his most deeply felt values. This has been generally assumed. Such a view, however, is only superficially true. It fails to take proper account of the untraditional nature of Milton's theology and of the aesthetic consequences of his highly individual religiosity. For while Milton comes at the end of the universal Christian culture and preserves much from the mediaeval heritage (as from the more recent "orthodoxy" of the Reformation), it is also true that he projects into the secular culture which succeeds him values and techniques which already in his most characteristic work contradict and repudiate significant aspects of the traditional Christian aesthetic.

It is not merely that Milton comes at the end of the great Christian tradition. In a real sense he ends that tradition. His role in the process of cultural change must be recognized as active. He carries Christian poetry, and in particular the poetic use of the Christian symbol, to a limit beyond which it cannot go and remain Christian. In its ultimate reaches, Milton's art is distinctively Protestant, but Protestant edging on the purely secular. For this reason the abandonment by the poets of the next century of Milton's awesome theological framework was by no means an abandonment of the direction Milton had set for English poetry. Indeed, the heterodox nature of Milton's theology is already sign enough of the rapid disintegration of theology. This process of disintegration merely continues after Milton—and it will not stop with mortalism and Arianism.

My aim here is to isolate the specifically Protestant character of Milton's aesthetic in its shift from tradition to innovation. I am aware that it is no easy matter to discuss an aesthetic problem touching on belief without betraying a bias. With Milton the task is doubly difficult. For Milton scholarship is increasingly thin-skinned. The defenders of Milton have lately been very much on the defensive. Those who are not entirely with them must be entirely against them, and no quarter is given. The revival of Christian humanism in contemporary critical thought seems to have coincided with the scholarly defence of Milton against his detractors. There has been, consequently, a tendency to refuse any distinction between faith in Milton and faith in Christ. The heretical ideas of *Paradise Lost* are minimized until, in the view of Mr. C. S. Lewis, Milton emerges as more traditional and orthodox than Archbishop Laud.

Formerly, the detractors could be scattered by a parade of learning. Milton's thought was disinterred and laid in line like the splendid bones of the dinosaur. But it was, perhaps, not altogether economic to save the man's skin by producing his skeleton. Certainly, there is a great gain in the fact that it now seems possible to locate in the consciousness of our time a core of sensibility hospitable to the assumptions of a Christian aesthetic. The Christian scholar is encouraged to abandon the antiseptic illusion of "disinterested objectivity" and to say out loud that the doctrine of original sin is much more than a rationalization of "class guilt," and that the Christian notion of the free will is not just

[184]

a display of aristocratic impudence. The Christian scholar may even admit agreement with Milton on a point of faith without dread of having committed an intellectual indecency.

One would hope that as a result of this particular liberation from the respectable academic conscience, the dichotomy in our criticism between a "sound," if abstract, knowledge of Milton's ideas on the one hand and an impressionistic "appreciation" of his poetry on the other might be succeeded at last by a fused response and judgment, by a criticism which can assess Milton because it can first possess him.

But one suspects that the gain, great as it is, may bring not peace but the sword. To restore Milton now to a critical Christian awareness is to revive and sharpen the Christian memory. As Christianity becomes conscious of itself again, it must become conscious of its ancient quarrels and ruptures. Anglo-Catholic, Methodist, and Quaker may not be able to inhabit forever the common shelter of Milton's Christian humanism without inspecting the roof—and the exit.

It is my own conviction that the recent tendency to regard Milton as a latter-day St. Augustine, equally agreeable to Catholic and Protestant habits of thought and feeling, has done much to obscure the unique quality of Milton's art and has led to blurred aesthetic appraisals. A fascinating example of this "blurring" comes out in the argument advanced by Wylie Sypher[1] to the effect that Milton "represents an Anglican art of the Counter Reformation." Milton, with his vast, external poetic "ritual," is the type of Catholic artist, and T. S. Eliot, who disapproves of Milton's rhetoric, is the naked Protestant purist. Milton's style properly parallels the Catholic tradition of worship. Eliot's poetic style and critical method are both inconsistent with his professed Anglo-Catholicism. Mr. Sypher's conclusion is that "a more sympathetic evaluation of Milton may be the first

1 "The Metaphysicals and the Baroque," *Partisan Reader* (New York, 1946), pp. 567–581.

token of a reaction in poetry that has already occurred on one level in Anglo-Catholicism and on another level in Mr. Eliot's royalism."

Briefly, then, Milton the poet is a Catholic, and Milton the Protestant theologian is quite irrelevant to the poetry. The obvious danger of such an approach is, of course, that it takes us back in a new way to the besetting sin of the impressionist critics. Style and thought are put out of proper relation, unless Mr. Sypher is willing to contend (as I am sure he would not be) that Milton's "ritualist" manner encases a Roman matter.

Mr. Sypher's error lies in his easy identification of the baroque with the Counter Reformation. No one will now dispute the relative usefulness of the term baroque as applied to Milton, nor need one dispute that in the obvious external sense Milton's art has therefore certain formal similarities with the art of the Counter Reformation. But (paradoxical as it may seem) Milton is most baroque when he is most Protestant, and it is doubtful indeed if his aesthetic "whatness" should be sought beneath the shadow of a Jesuit cathedral. For poetry is not architecture, or sculpture, or painting. It deals in words which one may rightfully expect to have meaning of some precision. The typical Miltonic symbol and the typical Miltonic rhetoric are not Catholic unless one is willing to exclude from his symbol and rhetoric all ideational reference.

Part of Mr. Sypher's difficulty is in his attempt to make the term "ritual" synonymous with rhetoric or embellishment. There is, of course, a Buddhist ritual, a court ritual, a Masonic ritual, and a ritual of the Stock Exchange. But if we fix our use of the term in the context of the Counter Reformation (as we must), ritual can be understood to mean only a code of symbolic practices and values with fully established Christian associations and therefore having definitely calculable powers of evocation. A simple comparison of the ritualistic rhetoric of George Herbert with the highly selective and arbitrary rhetoric of Milton will reveal profound differences between the Anglo-Catholic and Protestant habits of mind and consequently between Anglo-

Catholic and Protestant poetry. Nor can we assume, as Mr. Sypher seems to, that the ritualistic symbolism characteristic of Catholic poetry is external or artificial because it supplies a spinal column of value to an entire tradition of art and not merely to a single work of art. It is the loss of this "spinal" symbolism which one observes in Milton's work, and it is precisely this loss which characterizes the Protestant aesthetic of the period of the Counter Reformation.

It will become clear, I think, that the rhetoric which Milton invents destroys ritual. The Christian symbols in Milton's poetry are indeed externalized, but in the Protestant context of Milton's thought and by an intriguing kind of dialectic, they cease to be ritualistic at the very point of externalization.

It is not within the scope of this essay to define Milton's theological position. But we know his Puritanism to have been impure. Always Protestant, he is sometimes Catholic in his differences with Calvin and Luther. Characteristically humanist, he is sometimes Manichean in abrupt fits of reversion to a pre-Augustinian sensibility. It is this eclectic quality in Milton's thought, this will to the uniquely personal synthesis through a radical process of rejecting wholes for parts, this habit of picking and choosing to a shifting pattern of values, which marks the specifically Protestant temper, a temper which holds steadfast no matter what quirk of Protestant doctrine may be summoned or dismissed. Milton is more and not less Protestant when his ideas on creation, the death of the body, and the Person of Christ seem as heretical to the Calvinist as they do to the Catholic. In fairness to the Reformation orthodoxy with which Milton's thought is often so unfairly lumped, it must be remembered that just beyond the strained boundaries which are finally put to Milton's Protestantism, there looms the empirical rationalism of Locke and its opposite, the "imaginative" Christianity of William Blake —that spider's theology spun from the gut of the wish. But it must be remembered, too, that this was the way which the Protestant aesthetic by its very nature must take.

The direction in which Milton was carrying Christian sym-

bolism was already evident in the early poetry, before the hetero-
dox quality of Milton's thought was clearly shaped and while
Milton's ecclesiastical allegiance was still outwardly Anglican.
The symbolization of Christ is, as one would expect, the test.
Modern critics have frequently remarked on the abstract effect
of Milton's Christ. In the *Nativity Ode,* says J. H. Hanford,[2]
Christ is not a Person but "a symbol of purity and truth." And
Hanford sees no little significance in the fact that Milton soon
abandoned his scheme for "a series of lofty religious poems cele-
brating the successive events in the life of Christ and the festivals
of the Christian year."

It seems beyond doubt that Milton was unable to imagine
poetically the humanity of God. His symbolization of Christ is
never incarnational. This is not to say that Milton denied the
doctrine of the Incarnation. One might argue that the Arian
heresy seriously qualifies the meaning of the dogma in Milton,
as indeed it does. What is more important is that a point of
dogma, however orthodox, is not yet a poem. To take on flesh,
to incarnate itself, the article of belief must invade the will; it
must be perfected by love.

In the Catholic and Anglican tradition (from which Milton
departs with such profound consequences for poetry) this process is effected by the sensible and visible sacrament. In the Eucharistic sacrifice "the material universe also, to which man's body
unites him, is taken up into Christ; the consecrated bread and
wine are the pledge of the first fruits of the new heaven and
the new earth. Thus the Eucharist is literally a foretaste of the
Kingdom. In it the whole creation is joined to Christ, super-
naturally perfected, and brought into its proper relation with
the Father."[3]

Despite the verbal acceptance of the doctrine of the Incarnation
(modified, and seriously so, by Arian heterodoxy), Milton's

[2] "The Youth of Milton," *Studies in Shakespeare, Donne and Milton* (New
York, 1925), pp. 123–124.
[3] G. R. Bentley, *Catholic Design for Living* (London, 1940), p. 75.

poetry nowhere expresses the incarnational and operative sense of Christ which had infused Christian theology from St. Paul to St. Thomas Aquinas and which is still present in part to Anglicanism. The outright condemnation of the sacramental system in the *De Doctrina,* and the bitter repudiation of the whole visible church from the Apostolic Age to the Second Coming of Christ in *Paradise Lost,* Book XII, demonstrate how completely Milton finally detached his Christ symbol from traditional associations and from understood techniques of communion and participation.

In the *De Doctrina* he gives an orthodox enough statement of the doctrine of the Communion of Saints and the Mystical Body. He acknowledges "the mutual fellowship of the members of Christ's body among themselves" in the invisible church. But the church is *utterly* invisible, as is the fellowship it is said to contain. And the faithful enter this invisible fellowship, if at all, by equally invisible means. The old lines of communication between the visible and the invisible are discarded. The Mystical Body is retained as a thoroughly bodiless concept. Indeed, Milton's assertive individualism threatens the concept itself: "But since it is only to the individual faith of each that the Deity has opened the way of eternal salvation, and as He requires that he who would be saved should have a personal belief of his own, I resolved not to repose on the faith or judgment of others in matters relating to God." [4]

This is scarcely compatible with any view of the church visible or invisible as the Mystical Body of Christ. In Milton, the living sense of the Christian person growing through actual, sacramentally realizable fellowship within the total community of a church stretching beyond time is put aside for ingenious and original biblical exegesis.

Ultimately, it is the loss of the corporate Christ in whom "the whole creation is joined," the loss of an imaginative and imagin-

---

[4] Chapter XXIV, *Student's Milton,* ed. F. A. Patterson (New York, 1933), p. 1020.

able vision of the Mystical Body, which determines the nature of Milton's religious symbol. Instead of St. Augustine's simple but bottomless confession that "all mankind is in Christ one man," one meets in Milton either the Perfect Idea, or the Perfect Hero who marches ahead and apart to lead His redeemed into Heaven. And the army of saved saints dwindles to a platoon as deserters break line and vanish into Satan's "perverted world." Christ, in *Paradise Lost,* is the warrior-victor whose prize is in the end much less than had been anticipated. The Pauline-Augustinian image of Head and Body, developed by the Christian tradition into a mystical symbol of union and communion, is transformed gradually in *Paradise Lost* into the exterior and quite unmystical image of the leader and the led, the captain and the broken ranks.

New and impressive symbolic content is created by Milton. His power and originality as an artist must be understood in terms of his genius for innovation and measured by the extent of his departure from the traditional symbol and its characteristic kind of evocation. In the early work the process of detachment from conventional symbolic value seems uppermost, but even here the new (and Protestant) direction is evident.

The Christ of the *Nativity Ode* is a novel poetic conception. One must observe with Hanford [5] that Christ becomes a symbol of abstract values rather than a Person. The poem proclaims but never realizes the Incarnation. The "light unsufferable" enters "a darksome house of mortal clay" without illuminating it, certainly without transforming it. While the heavenly Christ of the prelude is the consubstantial Trinitarian Son, He becomes in the hymn, Son of God but never Son of Man, wearing Divine Nature but never sharing human nature. The redemption of nature ("pollute with sinful blame") and of man (who is either blood-stained king or unthinking peasant) is effected entirely from outside nature and man through those distant and divine prin-

[5] Hanford, pp. 123–124.

ciples of order and light which Christ is intended to actualize. Atonement is vicarious indeed. Man is the passive spectator (and astonished beneficiary) of an abstract and remote performance. Mankind is not "One Man in Christ" but a less than innocent bystander. There is, therefore, no poetic continuity—no "character"—in the representation of Christ, but rather a series of separate symbolizations of the might and goodness of God. The muscular Babe who can rise in His crib to "control the damned crew" of pagan gods symbolizes the power of God exerted, just as the Prince of Light in the opening stanzas of the hymn symbolizes that same power in benign but pregnant repose. The Babe who finally sleeps in the stage-prop arms of the Virgin, sleeps only that the poem may end, sleeps like a picture on a falling theatre curtain. Nothing in the poem has proceeded from a union of the Child with the children of earth. The form and the strength of the poem, as Professor Arthur Barker [6] has shown, derive from the active images of harmony and light. To these the Person of Christ is subordinated, and from these man is excluded.

One must be conscious here of a significant reversal of value. Christ is no longer, as in typical Catholic art, the all-inclusive and constant symbol towards which the fractional and derivative symbols of Truth, Justice, Order, are directed as to a source. Christ, rather, has become a variable symbol dependent for meaning upon superior and controlling ideas. The later poem on the Passion fails, obviously, because Milton has not, as in the *Nativity Ode,* hit upon a controlling idea which Christ can be made to serve. The "Perfect Hero" of *The Passion* becomes static and nominal because Milton has not found for Him a fitting task to perform.

The Christ symbol will be imaginatively idle until called upon to run a sufficiently urgent allegorical errand. The important point here is that already in Milton's first deliberately Christian

---

[6] "The Pattern of Milton's *Nativity Ode,*" *University of Toronto Quarterly* (January, 1941), pp. 167–181.

poem, the Christ symbol has been externalized and can be manipulated on the periphery of a central concept. Such an externalization constitutes in the Christian tradition a change of place between means and end.

Powerful new impulses are soon to enter Milton's creative thought. An ethical principle of dedication takes hold of the artist's craft, shaping and pointing the poetry to deliberate moral and social ends. As Professor A. S. P. Woodhouse [7] has rightly noted, there is no turning back from the sonnet "How soon hath Time," in which Milton submits his powers to the great taskmaster. The reality of Milton's "conversion" one cannot question. Its fruits are seen in the giant resolve which proceeds from it. But the conversion is essentially ethical in character. It is in no sense mystical. The isolation of the Christ symbol from traditional associations is therefore not overcome. Nor is there need to overcome it. The peripheral use of the symbol, freed finally from clustered Catholic suggestion, is to be a positive gain as far as Milton's artistic freedom of movement is concerned. An ethical Christianity, increasingly individualist, attaching itself to successive partisan causes, could only be hampered by a strained compromise of Catholic and Protestant values.

English poetry before Milton had felt no pressure of this kind. The mingling in Spenser, for instance, of universal-Catholic with national-Protestant images is never fatal or forced, although the transition from the sly beads of Archimago to the blameless rosary of the House of Holiness is at least troublesome.

However, with the Second Reformation the sacramental principle is abandoned by the Puritan side; nationalism is turned inside out; individualism finally displaces the lingering corporate sense even on the secular level; and Puritan art is forced to absorb and to rationalize these new and disparate realities. The ethical mind must seek ethical sanction for the side it chooses, must find in conflict the opportunity for a higher unity, must

[7] "Notes on Milton's Early Development," *University of Toronto Quarterly* (October, 1943), pp. 66–101.

somehow seek in the triumph of its side the triumph of the whole over the part. The theology which accompanies such a miraculous process cultivates strenuously the sense of difference, while pretending to a more catholic synthesis. For a poetry which would be at once ethical, political, and theological in such a situation, the difficulties of symbolization are consequently enormous. As the old ritual is abandoned (as it must be, because it goes with the other side although it cannot take sides), a sharpened Puritan ethic is let loose on the whole body of culture. When the Christ symbol is no longer central and all-inclusive, it can no longer spread its benediction, tolerant and unafraid, over the lovely profane. Pagan beauty will be suspect. A self-conscious ethical selectiveness will prevail, sterile to art if no positive impulse appears powerful enough to absorb restrictive moral energies into activity on a different level.

There is the difficulty, too, of consistency. The artist must avoid that infection which is carried by the old flying fragments of broken images. And it is no easy task to create a new and distinct framework of poetic allusion, Christian but clearly Protestant, out of the scattered bits and pieces of a Catholic culture. A cross may suddenly suggest an altar; a Presbyterian saint may look suspiciously like a monk. Yet, on the other hand, a "purification" of imagery, if rigorously attempted, can easily lead to bleak negation.

Such were the difficulties in the way of an imaginative Protestant aesthetic in Milton's period. They were real difficulties for Milton. The measure of his success can be taken in the distance of *L'Allegro* and *Il Penseroso* from *Lycidas*. For it must be recognized that Milton did share for a time in the old tradition. Professor Douglas Bush [8] points out that in *L'Allegro* and *Il Penseroso*, Milton for the last time "celebrates the Anglican ritual." The full implications of this comment need to be explored. In the companion poems we have not only the sensuous

---

[8] *English Literature in the Earlier Seventeenth Century* (Oxford, 1945), p. 363.

beauty of the cathedral with its "storied windows" and "antick pillars," and its soaring liturgical song; we have not only the prophetic hermit, the nun rapt in adoration, together with the rich pageantry and rustic jollity of a most un-Puritan England; we have as well a conspicuous lack of strain, an absence of pressure. Conflict relaxes into contrast. The ploughman and the knight blend into a congenial feudal landscape. Courtly love and religious ecstasy dwell not far apart. The British goblin and the Grecian sprite consort with Chaucerian compatibility.

How different this is from the skillful, yet forced, effort needed to control the pagan allusions of the *Nativity Ode*. There, by an ingenious process of reversal, the sensuous value of heathen legend is brought in through the back door to add poetic "body" to the positive but chaste images of light and order—yet never to merge with them. The lovely nymphs are there only to flee. But they are none the less lovely. And the poet must not seem to invite us *quite* to follow. The skill with which the right effect is achieved is a self-conscious skill. The same self-consciousness is to reappear in *Comus,* where the Cavalier lustre of pagan beauty is not altogether depreciated and controlled by the dark rites of Cotytto, the cool logic of the Lady, and "the sage and serious doctrine of virginity." Yet one is always aware that the appropriate moral effort is being exerted. In both the *Nativity Ode* and *Comus* there is a strenuous ethical core and the evidences of a busy Puritan conscience that has turned the artist into his own censor.

But *L'Allegro* and *Il Penseroso* record a brief excursion into the freer realms of Chaucer and Spenser. Milton's characteristic ethical note is not absent, but neither is it central. For once the self on holiday from stern and mighty labours is lost in what it enjoys. For once even an ethical dogma can be fondled rather than brandished. It has been claimed that in these poems the traditional Christian imagery is used ornamentally rather than piously, and that the inspiration is always more literary than personal. Yet one cannot mistake here the relish of the poet for images he must presently destroy. Because of this relish it will be no easy task for Milton to make "the beauty of inner Sanctity" outgleam the "dim religious light" of the Anglican cathedral.

It is the fully Protestant Milton who will soon give us the Lady of *Comus* in place of the Nun of *Il Penseroso*. The difference between the two is highly significant. The Nun makes Contemplation visible. Her virginity is not presented as a supreme value in itself. In her, purity is for the sake of devotion and achieves the rapt soul sitting in the eyes, the ecstatic veneration which forgets the self to marble.

It is this loss of the self through communion which characterizes the Christian temper of the poem as a whole and lifts it above antiquarian ornamentalism. For once in Milton, a dominant Christian symbol fully within the context of the old tradition, and drawing its energies from that context, spreads through the whole poetic conception, absorbing alike into the centre, by a kind of contemplative love and self-forgetfulness, the high things of the mind and the kindly things of the senses. The ecstasy of the Nun is never isolated. It overflows permissively into the "Platonic" speculation, the gorgeous tragedy, the sage and solemn tunes, sanctifying sylvan loves, dissolving drear enchantments. Never again, one feels, will Milton be less alone than he is in the rare charity of that "high lonely tower" of *Il Penseroso*.

The Lady is the ethical symbol of *Comus*. She does not forget herself to marble. She has no capacity for ecstasy, except in the contemplation of her own virtue and the means for its defence. The creed she speaks in a forest echoing with "the sound of riot and ill-managed merriment," is of the greatest value not only for what it tells us of the Lady, but also of the nature of Milton's Christian symbolism at this stage of his development.

> O welcome pure-eyed Faith, white-handed Hope,
> Thou hovering angel girt with golden wings
> And thou unblemished form of Chastity,
> I see thee visibly, and now believe

That He, the Supreme Good, to whom all things ill
Are but as slavish officers of vengeance,
Would send a glistering guardian if need were
To keep my life and honor unassailed.

Faith, Hope, and *Chastity*. And the greatest of these is chastity!
The substitution of chastity for charity is the reduction of the
highest supernatural grace to a secondary practical virtue. And
the substitution is too startling, too exposed, to have been accidental. The fact is that the poem is entirely lacking in the Christian sense of charity, in that love of God which contains the love
of one's neighbour. The Lady is wholly self-regarding. Faith and
Hope minister solely to her chastity. Chastity rises to the "sage
and serious doctrine of virginity," which is meant to convey the
absolute quality of the supreme good. One should not be sur-
prised, however, if it fails to do so without the sound of brass
and the tinkle of cymbal.

The grace of charity is the lifeblood of the Mystical Body, the
living energy of the Christ symbol. It is Love who bids the tortured George Herbert to sit and taste His meat. It is this same
Christian charity that in Chaucer's *Franklyn's Tale* transcends
the logic of courtly love, dissolving in a single mercy the plight
of the wife and the sensuality of the lover. It is this same Love
which fills the rapt eyes of the Nun in *Il Penseroso* and radiates
from the central symbol to the outer circumference of the poem.

The Lady of *Comus* does not love. Her life is, as far as one
can judge, a rear-guard action. Yet Milton's effect is not inten-
tionally negative. The full scheme of *Comus* properly understood
in its "intellectual frame of reference" has been convincingly
presented by Professor Woodhouse. After showing that the
ethical movement of the poem begins on the natural level of
temperance and continence, advances to the level of chastity
which is common to both nature and grace, and reaches finally
through the doctrine of virginity the exclusive level of grace, he
concludes: "In *Comus* Milton does not repudiate the order of
nature; he does not deny an area common to nature and grace,

or the ascent through it from natural wisdom to divine; he does not seek to divorce the two orders. But he believes that experience on the level of grace will cast a light back upon nature and enable one to realize its true significance." [9]

Certainly Milton has overcome for the time any Manichean tendency to disparage "most innocent nature," and has clearly striven for the paradoxical humanist conception of grace in which man acts freely yet under the divine condescension. But it is not so certain that Milton realizes his intention poetically.

The trouble is not, I think, that Milton by his striking substitution of chastity for charity signals a departure from traditional values and thereby creates new expectations. This in itself is legitimate in the light of the ethical Protestant direction which Milton is now taking. The trouble, rather, is that the new expectations are not fulfilled within the main framework of action and symbolization. The epilogue is added to rescue the main symbolic pattern from negation.

The Sabrina episode is the climax of the masque. Until the invocation of Sabrina, the Lady for all her chastity is held "in stony fetters fixed and motionless." Although Comus seems shaken by her proclamation of "the sage and serious doctrine of virginity," the Lady remains under his spell. The power of chastity has been relative and not decisive. The Elder Brother, like the Lady, had placed an almost smug confidence in it. But the Attendant Spirit had no such confidence and speaks of "the aidless, innocent Lady." Evil shall not "back on itself recoil" because of the "complete steel" of chastity with which the Lady believes herself armed. That it is, in fact, much less than complete, the presence and action of the Attendant Spirit—divine aid—amply demonstrate. Nor will heroic force avail against the grip of evil. The rescue of chastity may be effected, it seems, only through the protective virtue of "haemony," with its suggestion of poetry and philosophy working bright miracles with the help of heaven.

[9] "The Argument of Milton's *Comus*," *University of Toronto Quarterly* (October, 1941), pp. 46–71.

Then we have the almost scholastic seduction scene in which the Lady argumentatively pins her faith and her hope on the "sun clad power of chastity," but, as though to a second line of defence, points to the godlike power of virginity, that high and irresistible mystery of heaven and grace.

Characteristically, the Lady seems to overestimate her own role in the workings of grace. She thinks that if she should but try, "the uncontrolled worth of this pure cause" could be made to shatter the devil and all his works. But when the Brothers rush in to the rescue, the Lady is found senseless (though otherwise intact) under the dread spell of Comus. Self-sufficiency has failed. The saving doctrine of virginity is presumably transcendent beyond the Lady's faithful but egotistical comprehension of it.

And now it is, in the Lady's release from the spell, that Milton attempts to symbolize concretely this high doctrine of virginity. He does so with a kind of bastard ritual which combines pagan and Christian elements. Sabrina, the goddess of the river, can "unlock the clasping charm." She will be "swift to aid a virgin such as was herself."

The Attendant Spirit invokes the virgin Sabrina in a ritual which suggests, however distantly, the invocation of the Virgin Mary. And that the episode is intended to represent the saving operation of grace on the highest level after human heroism, art, and self-reliance have failed, is certain from the order of events and from the participation in the ritual of the messenger from heaven. After an elaborate prayer-song chanted by the Attendant Spirit, Sabrina performs a baptismal rite over the Lady, who then rises, cleansed, one supposes, by water and the spirit.

The total effect of the scene, however, is not to lift the doctrine of virginity to the shining regions of heavenly grace but to destroy the doctrinal abstraction by *actualizing* it. The virginity of Sabrina is as specific and unmystical as the virginity of the Lady. The Communion of Saints, distantly but inevitably suggested by the invocation of the virgin and by the baptismal imagery, becomes nothing more than a special league for the protection of unchaperoned girls. Virginity turns out to be nothing, after all, but virginity—in the utterly physical sense. One's hope for a metaphysical realization of the doctrine is flattened. There is no doctrine.

The Christian and pagan ingredients of the symbolism have cancelled each other out. The Christian images, dissociated from charity, remain static and merely picturesque. They cannot transform the pagan detail into the soaring significance one had been led to expect. And the pagan material reduces the Christian associations to the merest magic. Sabrina is localized to a particular shore with a particular occult office to perform. In the process, evil as well as grace loses universal significance. Comus becomes a merely local devil:

> Come Lady, while heaven lends us grace
> Let us fly this cursed place
> Lest the Sorcerer us entice
> With some other new device.

In short, the transcendent conception of victorious grace towards which the poem has been striving in a series of ethical affirmations is thus spoiled by confused and inadequate symbolization.

Milton's dismissal of traditional expectations by the substitution of chastity for charity had prepared us for new effects in which the ethical Protestant motif might claim its own proper texture. Despite the negative personality of the Lady herself, one was hopeful for a poetic realization of her doctrine. In the debate with Comus, her social philosophy of natural justice for the just man seemed to point in the direction of a genuine content for the ethical doctrine. Again, through the symbol of "haemony," and later in the Chaucer-Spenser associations of the Sabrina legend, one was made to anticipate the idealization of the poet-priest and the active role of art in the ethical task. Nevertheless, the wider ethical implications which seemed to develop on the way are sloughed off at the climax. The great doctrine towards which time and the will of heaven have been leading us is nothing more than practical sexual prudence.

Christian symbolism to be effective in a poem which clearly disallows any organic conception of the Mystical Body alive with the grace of charity would have to be fully externalized, and to the same degree that the Christian symbolism of the *Nativity Ode* is externalized. Such externalization is possible only if a heterodox idea of sufficient power captures the centre of the poem. In the decisive *Comus* episode, the Christian images cannot give their traditional evocative value because of the ethical context of the poem as a whole, and because of the adroit dismissal of traditional Christian expectations in the Lady's first speech. And yet these images seem to have meaning beyond their capacity for meaning because no countermeaning of any positiveness has emerged. There can be no externalization when there is no core. The result is anticlimax and negation.

The epilogue is an attempt to compensate for the central symbolic pattern. Here the Lady symbolism is wholly reversed. Images of fertility replace the images of sterility hitherto associated with the doctrine of virginity. On the level of grace,

> Two blissful twins are to be born
> Youth and Joy, so Jove hath sworn.

In an entirely humanist ascent of pictures and symbols, no Christian virgin without charity appears to interrupt and confuse the sense. Milton is now on surer ground. But he has not unified his poem. The epilogue is spoken by the Attendant Spirit and has no relation symbolically to the character or behaviour of the Lady. It completes the sense of the poem by changing and correcting it. For Youth and Joy are both alien to the spinster-like debater of the main fable, and the fine expansive lift of the epilogue has nothing in common poetically with the fumbling descent of the Sabrina scene.

Consequently, the poem lacks focus. The dedicated Milton of the sonnet "How soon hath Time" expresses his individualistic sense of dedication lyrically in the epilogue as he contemplates the elevation of the moral man. But the ethical life still lacks positive content. The ethical sense must attach itself to an intelligible and actual purpose or wither away. In *Comus,* on one level, Milton expresses the exhilaration of the dedictated moral self. On the other level, he is entangled in the treatment of a restrictive moral technique. On one level, the riches of classical and natural allusion are employed with unambiguous daring. On the other level, obsolescent Christian images collide with classical allusion. Milton fails to unify the two levels in any comprehensive and comprehensible purpose. Thus the note of exhilaration and the note of restraint remain distinct.

Comus stands half-way between the consistent Anglicanism of *Il Penseroso* and the fully developed Protestant aesthetic of *Lycidas.*

In *Lycidas,* the Christian and classical symbols confirm rather than confound one another. The exteriorization of the Christian image is completed with a consequent consistency of style. The difficulty of lingering Catholic associations is cleared with a single sweep, and Milton moves now with magnificent ease.

The whole poem is a masterpiece of enlivened conventionalization. One need not stress here the skill with which Milton handles the classical framework which is not only conventional but allegorical. It invites "translation" at every point, and its train of pagan gods and nymphs can no more be taken literally than can the shepherds on the hill be taken for real shepherds. In the same way, the sensuous beauty in which the poem abounds is never permitted to propose or even suggest sensual values. Milton is in complete control of his effects.

What has not been so fully appreciated, I think, is the equal clarity with which Milton controls his Christian symbols. St. Peter appears in a procession of mourners which includes a pagan river-god. But the effect is not one of inconsistency. By a technique of exteriorization, which the allegorical pastoral convention makes possible, Milton converts St. Peter from a fixed to a variable symbol. With quite a brilliant Protestant audacity, Milton has St. Peter (keys and all) repudiate his apostolic successors, both Anglican and Roman. St. Peter is thereby freed of ecclesiastical associations and becomes the rock of a reformed structure of Christian symbols which henceforth draw their value from a new and wholly untraditional motivation. St. Peter ushers into the poem precisely what was lacking in *Comus*—a specific problem involving actual definable conflict. The poem is unified by division. The personal ethical theme of *Comus* is absorbed into a wider morality of struggle, and the dedicated chastity of the poet is at last directed to an object. As a result, conventional classical and unconventional Christian images cohere, their evocative powers equally exploited for novel and positive ends. River-god and saint are allies in a conflict which overrides the proprieties of tradition by assaulting tradition itself.

The first movement of *Lycidas* recapitulates the problem of *Comus* and concludes with the assurance that a chaste dedication to art and learning will have its fame in heaven. But from this point the poem advances to a fusion of personal and political values. The Protestant St. Peter with his abrupt violence culminating in the image of "the two-handed engine at the door," discharges into the nerve fibre of the poem energies which transform all the succeeding fragments of Christian symbol into a new, consistent, and meaningful pattern. This energy soon reappears in "the great vision of the guarded Mount" and turns homeward the gaze of the warlike Archangel Michael. No longer must the patriot and his guardian angel stare defiance across the waters at Spain. Holy strength is now dedicated to a closer struggle and the reformation of the Reformation itself.

Lycidas is mounted high not to the court-room heaven of "all-judging Jove" but to the swirling active heaven of Revelations. And one knows at once that the saints who move above "in solemn troops and sweet societies" are sturdily Protestant, not only because St. Peter has already, in effect, presented their credentials, but also because the ascent of Lycidas constitutes the

[202]

final symbolic realization of the whole Protestant-revolutionary theme of the poem.

The joy of the *Lycidas* heaven is very different from the kind of exhilaration achieved solely on the moral-personal level in the epilogue of *Comus.* In *Lycidas,* the personal conclusion—the promised "fame in heaven" of the first movement of the poem —is indeed achieved finally in images of tenderness and love, images of ultimate personal security. But this personal fulfillment is not attained in the terms set by the first movement of the poem. The almost perfunctory assurance of "Jove" that individual dedication will have its reward has now been deepened as a result of the extra-personal problem hurled into the poem by St. Peter. The serenity of the *Lycidas* heaven comes from the fusion of hitherto separate levels of experience, the personal and the political. It comes from the discovery of a cause which can translate dedication into action. The self is secure in a new context of expectant and progressivly realizable meaning.

In the rush of active strength-suggestions released by the explosive speech of St. Peter, even the specific Christ symbol has been touched and moved into place.

> So Lycidas, sunk low, but mounted high
> Through the dear might of him that walk'd the waves.

The *mighty* Christ, the warrior angel, and the angry Saint have been pressed into active service which leads on to "fresh woods and pastures new." We look through the open ending of the poem to a horizon of struggle. The peace of the *Lycidas* heaven is like the stillness at the centre of a moving wheel. The might and the tenderness of Christ hold together in a masterfully baroque tension.

There is left behind a "Genius of the shore" who shall "be good to all that wander in that perilous flood." We are reminded of Sabrina. But Lycidas is not reduced and localized as Sabrina was. Lycidas has become something more than the man Edward King drowned in the Irish Sea. Lycidas has become the cause. His ascent is the ascent of Milton's hope. His guardianship of the shore is a guardianship of the aggressive new faith. He is not put down to succour harassed damsels but to stand as the sign of victory, and to point the way.

Significantly, both the Christian image of heaven and the pagan image of the "Genius of the shore" move on a single surface. Finally separated from any possibility of traditional Catholic intention, and put to a combative ethical-social purpose, the Christian symbols easily assume new relationships, new dialectical possibilities. Saints and druids, Christ and the river-god, can be conscripted into one regiment now that the regiment has been made to march.

The artistic consistency of *Lycidas* is a thoroughly Protestant achievement. New means serve a new end. A shaping idea born of the Protestant temper recasts with daring and originality traditional Christian symbols and prepares a new and different tradition. The gain is apparent. An almost infinite artistic freedom is made possible. But, as far as the Christian tradition itself is concerned, the dangers are correspondingly great. For the movement of the specifically Christian symbol from the centre to the periphery of the work of art implies a decisive shift of value and anticipates the emergence of a dominantly secular culture. The exteriorization of Christian symbolism opens a vacuum at the centre which must be filled. And even the massive theological barricade of *Paradise Lost* will not shut out the invader for long.

Poetry, Belief, and Paradise Lost

CHAPTER NINE

THE QUARREL in modern criticism over the meaning (and worth) of *Paradise Lost* can, I think, be made to yield striking proof of the semantic and theological originality of Milton's firmament of symbol. Not that the modern critic is always aware of this originality. Indeed, the unresolved clash between the Milton zealots and the Milton detractors is to no small degree the consequence of a disinclination on both sides to credit Milton with that audacious independence of mind which, with "no middle flight," pursued "things unattempted yet in Prose or Rhyme." The very children (and they are legion) of Milton's mighty heterodoxy do not, will not acknowledge their own father. Milton must be treated as though he were respectably pre-Miltonic, the dutiful if brilliant heir of Reformation and Renaissance. Or else the religious symbols of *Paradise Lost* are pushed aside as no more than the accidental vessels of a moral message or a "pure" poetic vision. Thus we read into Milton's symbolism much more than it will hold, or we shrink it and even remake it in our own image.

By a critical examination of some of our characteristically modern difficulties in the reading of *Paradise Lost* with anything like agreement among ourselves, we may be able to clean and adjust our spectacles. We then may be able to catch a glimpse of a distant revolution occurring at the very centre of the Christian firmament of symbol.

Two provocative studies of *Paradise Lost* (those by John Diekhoff[1] and the late A. J. A. Waldock[2]) will serve to illustrate
the modern difficulty with the symbolism of *Paradise Lost*. These
books are not, of course, put forward as either the best or the
worst of their kind but as convenient indicators of a dilemma
in the modern approach to Milton which is typical and, I think,
instructive.

It is hard to believe that Diekhoff and Waldock are writing
within the same cultural framework, at the same point in time,
about the same literary subject. Here is no simple difference in
taste, but rather a difference in assumptions so vast that the reader
is driven to scrutinize his own assumptions and to put desperate
questions to himself. One's possession of the past is lost, the de-
pendable pendulum stops its predictable beat, and in this topsy-
turveydom of value, while the textbook falls apart, one begins
to guess in panic at the concealed romanticism of the heroic
couplet, the implicit piety of Restoration comedy, the secret sa-
lacious Bohemianism of *The Idylls of the King*!

And it is not reassuring to remember that the differences between Diekhoff and Waldock, while fundamental and typical
of the chaos of critical method in our time, are by no means ex-
haustive. We are confronted in these latter days with every conceivable interpretation of *Paradise Lost*. Further novelties in the
reading of the poem are not possible.

Paradise Lost is mainly about the conflict in man's soul between
the principles of reason and unreason, says Professor Edwin
Greenlaw.[3] According to Paul Elmer More,[4] the true theme of
Paradise Lost was not the Fall, not the justification of the ways
of God to man, not Paradise *lost* at all but Paradise itself and

---

[1] *Milton's Paradise Lost* (New York, 1946).

[2] *Paradise Lost and its Critics* (Cambridge, 1947).

[3] Waldock, pp. 4–8. A comment on Greenlaw's "A Better Teacher than
Aquinas," in S.P., XIV, pp. 196–217.

[4] Waldock, pp. 119–121. A comment on More's view of Milton in "The Theme
of Paradise Lost," *Shelburne Essays*, Fourth Series (New York, 1907), pp. 239–
253.

man's eternal longing for the Garden, the Golden Age. Professor E. M. W. Tillyard [5] finds clear evidence in the poem of a deepening pessimism. Professor Arthur Sewell, on the other hand, finds equally clear evidence of a rising optimism, a final childlike trust in God Almighty.

These are only a few of the divergent judgments of Milton's meaning that now illuminate the subject. They are playfully rehearsed by Waldock in the course of his own provocative commentary on the poem. He also has a word to say of Miss Maud Bodkin's approach [6] to the Miltonic symbol by way of Jung's racial myth. He might have noted the revival of variations on the "Satanic" view, not only in the essay by G. Rostrevor Hamilton but also in the work of Marxists like Christopher Caudwell and the Soviet critics. Moreover, the problem of *Paradise Lost* in our time is made more slippery by Professor E. E. Stoll and his disciples, who both simplify and complicate it by their artful separation of life and art. Notable, also, is the current "aesthetic" drift, which reconciles—or bypasses—conflicts between Milton's conscious and unconscious intention by gracefully regarding such conflicts as part of "the baroque sensibility" of the age. For this school, the troublesome problem of meaning is, in effect, raised to a problem of design and referred to architectural analogies. (Here, at least, is a window that lets in fresh air, if not light.)

To thicken the "darkness visible," it is only necessary to recall that Milton himself is now bestuck with darts wondrous if not slanderous. He is still, for some, the hard and sour Puritan. He is for many American scholars the last voice of the High Renaissance. Mr. C. S. Lewis places him at the centre of the Augustinian-Catholic tradition. Professor Bush regards him as a Christian humanist next door to the Cambridge Platonists. He is, besides, all other things to all other men—an Aristotelian, a masked ma-

[5] Waldock, pp. 9–15. A critical evaluation of Tillyard's *Milton* (London, 1930).

[6] Waldock, pp. 129–135. His reference is to Maud Bodkin's *Archetypal Patterns in Poetry* (London, 1934).

terialist, a sinister apostle of the Zohar, a prim Victorian liberal, a "protofascist," a ruddy forerunner of Marx, Lenin, and Stalin! Of his kingdom, seemingly, there is no end.

These views are not mutually exclusive. They have relevance in varying degree to aspects of Milton's thought and influence. But can we go on mistaking parts for wholes? It may be that knowledge is now so enormous that we must wear blinkers as we charge down our "special field." It may be that we have been forced to narrow our critical judgments to the narrowness of precise research. But, in any case, it is no longer gratifying to claim that our critical morass is teeming with furious life, or to claim that so many sects and schisms prove a splendid vitality both in Milton and in ourselves. Unless we are to acquiesce in a shameless relativism—"Blake's Milton was true for *him*, and you, too, can have a Milton all your own!"—we must concern ourselves strenuously with critical method in the light of absolute value.

Unless we are to esteem poetry chiefly for its impact on the nervous system, and as a patterned emotional therapy that can operate apart from the conceptual and contemplative intent of the poet, we must be impatient with this capricious diversity of our judgments. A poem is first of all and last of all a *creation;* it is not an invitation to infinite irresponsible acts of re-creation —or improvisation. There may be obstacles (technical, factual, ideological) between us and the poem. The critic's task is to force these aside, to discover the conditions in which objective evaluation is possible.

Why has this been so difficult with *Paradise Lost?* What has made for so much misunderstanding? Is the peculiarity in Milton or in us? Waldock thinks the fault is largely in Milton; Diekhoff not only insists that the fault is ours but proclaims his belief that an acceptance of Milton's central values would cure our world of all its ills! He seems to offer *Paradise Lost* as a moral handbook for the Security Council of the United Nations. Without identifying himself with Milton's theology, Diekhoff accepts the whole of Milton's ethical intention as he understands it. He claims, moreover, that his understanding of the ethical intention guarantees a proper aesthetic response to the poem.

Waldock finds serious aesthetic flaws in the poem where Diek-hoff sees only the purest beauty. It should not be surprising that Waldock dislikes Milton's ethical intention and does so because he dislikes the theology. The point to be observed here is that the aesthetic response is governed finally in both cases by a kind of belief, by agreement or disagreement with what is thought to be Milton's belief. And surely this element of belief (whether theological, ethical, or social) determines to a very large degree the shades of interpretation in the other critics to whom I have already alluded. I shall not argue that it is impossible to "enjoy" *Paradise Lost* without sharing or without understanding Milton's theology. (Tillyard enjoys *Paradise Lost* without sharing Milton's theology. Saurat enjoys *Paradise Lost* without understanding Milton's theology.) I contend, however, that any full critical estimate of Milton is determined first by the degree of our understanding of his thought, and second by the extent of our sympathy with it. Here we cannot forget that Milton's thought is involved at every point in belief, and what is more troublesome, in belief that is heterodox. Consequently, understanding will not necessarily imply sympathy.

Waldock, for instance, understands Milton at least as well as Diekhoff does. He does not approve, however, of what he understands. He knows, but he does not like, Milton's God. Therefore, he cannot believe in the justice of Milton's God, and he cannot respond intellectually or aesthetically to a poem that would justify what seems to him to be the injustice of this God. For Waldock, inevitably, the whole design of the poem falls apart. In his view the God of Genesis, to begin with, "does not show to advantage." He is harsh. He is not the Christian God of mercy. Milton, in expanding the little "myth" of Genesis into epic, only enlarges the spectacle of God's harshness and can find no justification for it that is humanly acceptable. Eve's act is surely not so damnable as Milton's God makes it out to be, and Adam's crucial loyalty to Eve is the noblest realization of love in the entire poem. Milton would have us condemn Adam for possessing that godlike quality of mercy and love so lacking in His God. "There is no way out. *Paradise Lost* cannot take the strain at the centre, it breaks there, the theme is too much for it." [7]

It might be argued in rebuttal that Waldock is suffering from a sentimental humanism, that he cannot think theologically, and so on. This would miss the mark. Waldock knows the theological tradition. I think he understands it. But he cannot believe in what seems to him to be the pompous Egoist of Milton's heaven, afraid for His dignity, constantly on the defensive, not a little vindictive, soliciting the flattery of the Son, seeking to demonstrate His mercy by that incredible call for the volunteer.

Milton suffers here, thinks Waldock, by comparison with Dante, whose method with God was "to keep him hidden: to lead us toward him, it may be, by degrees of mounting suspense, but to refuse the final revelation." [8] Milton's method is an invitation "to stare God full in the face." [9]

Waldock's fault—and fault it is—should now be obvious. This critic seeks to explain his dislike of Milton's God on purely artistic grounds. Very simply, Milton's technique is, he believes, inferior to Dante's. While sometimes admitting that Milton's God is as he is because Milton "liked God in just that way," Waldock prefers to find crudity, carelessness, clumsiness in Milton's portraiture. One cannot deny that telling points are scored. No blemish escapes Waldock's scrutiny. In the main, however, the approach on the purely technical level fails because of the assumption that Milton's God might have been like Dante's God if only Milton had been a good craftsman. In short, Waldock confuses his own issue. In recoiling from the forbidding surfaces

[7] Waldock. The analysis of "The Fall" in Chapters II and III deserves careful study.
[8] Waldock, pp. 98–99.
[9] Waldock, p. 100.

of Milton's theology—and in preferring Dante's vision—Waldock
has not had sufficient respect for the imaginative laws that determine the poetic symbol. A God who is conceived as the end
of contemplation will not come off poetically like the God who
must be made to symbolize justice in a gigantic post-mortem of
the nature of evil, like a God who must be made to perform the
post-mortem himself. One must not overlook the very great difference in belief (and purpose) between Dante and Milton.

Obviously no amount of learned explication will change the
minds of those who honestly dislike the theism of *Paradise Lost*.
The day will not be saved for Milton by further evidence of
Milton's knowledge of Wollebius, and the Talmud, and Tertullian. Such knowledge clarifies but does not finally clear the
central difficulty of response to *Paradise Lost*. After the rabbinical
readings, after the Fathers and Plato, after the most meticulous
examination of seventeenth century habits of thought and feeling, we must still decide if it is possible to dislike the theism of
Paradise Lost, to dislike theism outright and altogether, and yet
respond aesthetically to ideas that may be repellent to us as ideas.

Two factors must be considered: Milton's belief and our own.
We must be precise about both. Scholarship is beginning to
achieve the necessary precision with regard to the first, but we
have not been sufficiently precise about the second. In seeking to
be objective we have attributed no beliefs to ourselves. The result
has too often been that we have, instead, attributed our own beliefs to Milton. This phenomenon has done much to distort the
interpretation of Milton and to obscure the actual relation of
poetry to belief.

T. S. Eliot, in his essay on Dante, sought to put the whole
question of this relation quietly to rest. "What is necessary," he
said, "to appreciate the poetry of the *Purgatorio* is not belief but
suspension of belief." If you know how "to read poetry as poetry
you will 'believe' in Dante's theology exactly as you 'believe' in
the physical reality of his journey; that is, you suspend both belief and disbelief." He admits that a Catholic has an easier time

with the meaning of Dante than has an agnostic, but this is "not because the Catholic believes, but because he has been instructed." [10]

As a critical canon this is misleading, despite the partial truth it contains. Apply it to the reading of *Paradise Lost*. Waldock is "instructed." He "believes" in Milton's theology as he "believes" in the description of the war in heaven. The theology and the war alike serve the poetry as "myth." His dislike of the theology, however, has consequence for his criticism that no cavil about the art of Milton's war could possibly have. Suspension (or rejection) of belief in Milton's war, or of Dante's journey, is of a very different order from suspension of belief in the central vision of the poetry. In both Dante and Milton this central vision is theological and is inseparable from "the poetry as poetry" because it *is* the poetry. In the final analysis, then, Waldock dislikes Milton's poetry because he dislikes the vision that is the poetry.

Eliot, of course, would not rule out sympathy for "the high dream" of the poet. In the case of *Paradise Lost* this sympathy cannot be achieved at all by the reader who permanently suspends belief in the theological and ethical matter that the poet's vision informs and from which that vision gains its substance. The contention of Yvor Winters [11] that the non-Christian may share a wide community of ethical belief with a poet like Dante and yet fail to ascend with him to the mystical levels of the *Paradiso* is surely correct and is appropriate to my argument here. Full enjoyment depends upon an imaginative agreement that is not really possible without theological agreement (or similar mystical experience), just as a lesser enjoyment depends upon a lesser or partial belief and at least some capacity to accept the ethical understructure of the vision. We can enter the imaginative world of Dante (or anyone else) only to the extent that we can enter the assumptions of that world. The non-Christian who

10 *Dante* (London, 1929), pp. 32–33.
11 *In Defense of Reason* (New York, 1947), p. 476.

inherits through his culture the moral assumptions of Christianity will penetrate Dante's world or Milton's more deeply than will the anti-Christian who repudiates these assumptions.

It is equally true that the serious Christian can enjoy the poetry of the pagan-classical tradition only to the extent that he has assimilated classicism to his own belief. There have been, and are, Christians who have never succeeded in doing this, or who have refused the attempt. No Christian, however, can regard the myth of Homer and the "myth" of Genesis as of the same kind. Likewise, while the Christian may very well recognize in the "slain god" of the Golden Bough a groping primitive forecast of the Resurrection and may even use these primitive myths as poetic symbols of the Resurrection, he will all the time be making a distinction between a primary and a secondary kind of Christian symbol. The whole of traditional Christian theology is symbolic in the primary sense; that is, it is imaginative without, to the Christian, being imaginary. It derives ultimately not from a primitive or poetic guess at the nature of things but from a divine revelation of the nature of God.

Criticism of Milton is bound to fail when it takes no account of this distinction of the primary from the secondary symbol, *of the creatively received from the creatively conceived, of the adorned truth from the true adornment.* At the level of primary symbol the Christian poet seeks imaginatively to realize a vision already revealed; at the level of secondary symbol he may seek to convey his vision by analogy, indirection, or invention. The war in heaven, the palaces of hell, the blush of the angel, properly belong to the second level; the revelations of the angel as to the nature of God, sin, and redemption belong, or should belong, to the first.

One must be aware, of course, in one's treatment of poetry in the Christian tradition, of historical moments when the "imaginary" nature of the secondary symbol invades and threatens to displace the imaginative revelation of the primary symbol, when the "myth" of Genesis reverts to the status of the myth of Homer, when the idea of God nods and is made malleable to the privately inspired idea of the poet, when the Christian dogma becomes a secondary and exterior illustration of a primarily secular or non-Christian thesis. This process is far advanced in the poetry of the nineteenth century. It had begun in Milton's time and makes our problem more complex than is sometimes realized either by the orthodox Christian or by the wholly agnostic student of Milton.

The critic who cannot share any part of Milton's belief is, of course, in danger of blurring together these levels, of assuming too simply that the imaginative vision is nothing more than imaginary myth weighted with its own unique poetic revelation. For such a critic, the primary Christian symbols become altogether secondary, serving the higher vision of "what Milton really meant": the higher vision of the Golden Age, the triumph of pure reason, the rout of the libido, and all those other "unconscious meanings" we have been hearing about. Symbol is at first reduced to image in this process and then re-imagined. The wishful fruits are all about us.

A critic like John Diekhoff, who honours Milton's theology as one honours the aged parent of a strong son, is limited in his view of *Paradise Lost* by the limits of the moralistic approach. Such an approach to *Paradise Lost* has some of the weakness of the liberal Protestant approach to Christ as "the great moral teacher." It must by its very nature and at its very best be incomplete. For Milton's poetic vision, while ethical, is always more than ethical. Nevertheless, by understanding the poem as an essay in moral persuasion, Diekhoff does share a wide community of belief with Milton and enters the world of Milton much further than the man who tries to improvise his way.

In a nontheological age such as ours, it might be asked, is this ethical approach not the only one that offers a way into Milton? Assuming that we are unable to believe theologically what Milton believed, are we not constrained with Diekhoff to adopt the only approximation to Milton's full belief that now seems possible for us? Must we not do this or retreat to pedantry, impressionism, or formal aesthetics?

I do not think so. The problem is difficult, but it is not insoluble. One must conclude that Diekhoff's method in terms of objective judgment fails almost as badly as the method of the impressionist. In Diekhoff, sympathy for the part—the ethical part—of *Paradise Lost* colours the understanding of the whole, thereby falsifying the whole. For example, Diekhoff, working from his ethical agreement with Milton, easily accepts the justice of Milton's God. He does so because he accepts the assertions that Milton has his God make. Waldock, on the other hand, is as much concerned, and properly so, with the tone of voice as with the word, with the performance of God as with His assertions. The difficulties, at once theological and aesthetic, that Waldock exposes cannot be covered by any simple contention that Milton's God must be as good as His word and that therefore all's well in heaven.

The merely ethical approach seems to involve not a "suspension of belief and disbelief" but rather, after a certain point, the suspension of understanding and the extension of sympathy. While I agree that the non-Christian can enter the world of a Dante by sympathy with the understructure of ethical belief, I could not agree that he therefore can interpret or possess the superstructure of religious vision by any extension of this minimum kind of sympathy. He may get enjoyment from the play of his limited belief at its proper level. If he is a critic, he should seek an understanding (if not the full enjoyment) of the rest by a suspension of his disbelief, and by a scrupulous awareness of the distinction that obtains between sympathy and understanding. He must never assume that his affection for the foothills gives him a knowledge of the mountain-top or, what is worse, gives him the right to insist that there can be no mountain-top.

In dealing with a Christian poet like Dante or Milton, we must be prepared to separate, tentatively at least, the factor of understanding, which need not involve sympathy, from the factor of appreciation, which must. If we assume with Eliot that the one guarantees the other, we are lost. Diekhoff's appreciation kills his understanding. Waldock's understanding kills his appreciation.

I do not think that Diekhoff's is the right appreciation or that Waldock's is the right understanding. Both men fall short of an objectivity of method which is quite possible to the scholar, whether he be Catholic, Protestant, agnostic, or Marxist. Moreover, this objectivity is prerequisite both to full understanding and to legitimate appreciation. The effort to attain it must begin with a precise knowledge of Milton's theology. The critic must indeed be "instructed" (as both Diekhoff and Waldock are to no small degree). But the critic must also sharpen his sense of history and his sense of what poetry is. Particularly, he must sharpen his sense of what the absolutes of Christian poetry can become when pressed by the compulsions of history. Waldock errs in merely comparing Milton's God with Dante's instead of trying to find just why He is often so *different* from Dante's. Where Waldock complains that Milton's God is without mercy, he might better have wondered why this God sometimes talks as if He had mercy and sometimes acts as if He had not.

The contemporay critic, Christian or non-Christian, can at least detect in the theological poem the presence of both primary and secondary Christian symbols. He can at least define the symbolic use to which doctrine has been put by the poet. In reading *Paradise Lost,* even without faith but with some good sense, he can observe, I am sure, the phenomenon that clears the main difficulty of interpretation for us. This is the passage of the primary into the secondary symbol, of the creatively received into the creatively conceived, of the revealed God into that fictional, stage God who does not employ but who is employed.

The moralistic critic avoids such distinctions—the poem is all of a piece to him. The critic like Waldock, who is hostile to Milton's theological representation, makes the mistake of attacking the secondary symbolization as though it were primary, of equating Milton's half-fabricated God of vengeance, who sometimes appears in *Paradise Lost,* with the scriptural God, who also puts in an appearance.

To avoid this error we must keep in mind the pressure of the historical moment on Milton. I shall not develop again a point that I have sought to develop elsewhere.[12] I am bound at least, however, to suggest that further attention needs to be paid to Milton's symbolic treatment of God in relation to his treatment of history in Books XI and XII. In these dark pages, illuminated only briefly by the abstract Christ, who soon vanishes, Milton's justification of God is surely never an attempt to make His ways *agreeable* to men. The ways are dark, and for the mass of men are meant to be so. Milton is expressing here his own angry despair for society and for history and at the same time is seeking to salvage his personal religious hope. Like his Adam of the last few lines of the epic, he both despairs and hopes at once. A harsh and violent God, the vindictive stage God whom Waldock cannot abide, treads upon the lost history of men. Yet quite another God assures "the paradise within."

Milton's poetic vision, then, is more tortured than Dante's, compelling the "conceived" symbolization of a God who is never quite Dante's "revealed" God, and yet always reaching towards the symbolization of the God who is. This much at least can be discerned without the operation of belief. The fallacy of the critic who tries to tidy up Milton's orthodoxy can be avoided. The fallacy of the critic who ignores the orthodoxy and re-imagines Milton's myth can also be avoided. The true structure of the epic emerges, as what seemed to be a theological and artistic blunder becomes more nearly like an imaginative necessity. The difficult structural unity of the work as a whole will be found, I think, in the fluid juncture of the "received" and the "conceived" symbolization—not only of God, but of Christ and Satan, of sin and redemption, of the whole Christian story and doctrine. The study of Milton will advance, I am convinced, only in the direction of a discriminating symbolic interpretation.

[12] *Milton's Royalism* (Ithaca, Cornell University Press, 1943).

A correct even if limited understanding of the poem is possible, it would seem, not by means of a "suspension of belief," but *in spite* of disbelief. Beyond this, the range of appreciation must depend upon the kind and degree of our belief. Assuming that we can finally see the poem as it is, that we can read the poem and not our own shadows on the page, we shall still debate its merit. We may find the secondary symbolization of Christ disturbing in itself and amounting in its effect to a mischievous vision of man's fate. Or we may feel that the "conceived" symbolism overwhelms the "revealed" symbolism, giving a result more secular than Christian. As this estimate is more than half true, I suspect that the non-Christian may be able to appreciate Milton more deeply, or at least more honestly than he can appreciate Dante.

Whatever our feelings about the poem, let us not mistake these feelings for the poem itself. Our likes and our dislikes are relative. The essence of the poem is fixed. It is only by temporarily disentangling our sympathies from our understanding, by recognizing that relativism infects the subject and not the object, that we can see a poem as a creation, as a thing-in-itself. It is only then that we can begin to appraise it.

As we have seen, the simple Puritanism of the "low" Anglicans results in a flat and imageless style. In the verse of Lok and Turke and Lever and Gascoigne, the act of purification is negative. Theirs is the poetry of the negation of images. The "spiritual Anglicans" reaffirm the images, even as they revise or qualify or deny the dogmas of Catholicism. The rhetoric of their poetry, now insubstantial but still lovely, is the afterglow of a sinking sun. The tone of this poetry is wistful, nostalgic, elusive. The sensibility of a Herbert or a Beaumont reaches after a past that cannot be recovered and feeds, vicariously, on a dogma that may not be allowed. Time and the flesh *dissolve* in an imagery which glances with the *shadows* of time and the flesh. History ceases, and nature is now the distant hieroglyph of the soul. Herbert's rhetoric is a displaced rhetoric, a Catholic rhetoric Protestantized but always looking backward. It is the end-point of a moving cycle, of a steady process of deterioration in the analogical symbol from Shakespeare onwards, a cycle in poetry reflecting a decline in dogma and in habits of mind and heart that were rooted in dogma. With Herbert the cycle is closed.

Milton is not enclosed in this cycle. His poetry opens into wholly new areas and possibilities. His Protestantism is never merely negative. Although Milton makes short work of the dogmas and the liturgical images of Catholic worship, he refuses to rest in Puritan abstraction. Nor does he cling wistfully to the Catholic surfaces of dogma, at once fascinated and repelled by what is known to lie beneath. With a boldness (and a strength) impossible to a Herbert *or* a Donne, Milton will risk a reform even of the Reformation itself. As "pope of his own church" he will make his own *ex cathedra* pronouncements. He will pilfer from the Fathers and the scholastics, as from Luther, Calvin, and Boehme, but always to his own peculiar purpose. He will twist the economy of redemption to fit his own private intuition of the nature of things. Thus his doctrine of free-will is more Catholic than Protestant, yet for Milton the consequence of man's freedom is as dark as if man in the mass had been predestined to damnation. Milton's free conceptualization (and improvisation) of dogma permits a parallel freedom in the use of rhetoric which startles us, not by the incongruity which we might expect to result from these montages of Catholic, pagan, and Protestant surface, but by the incredible propriety of the mongrel effect. For Milton neither negates nor affirms the images of particular and exclusive dogmatic traditions. He uproots them; he rearranges them. And they come somehow to cohere in living novel patterns.

This is not to say that on the negative side Milton's poetry escapes the pressures which have shaped the symbols of the Cavaliers and the "low" and "high" Anglicans. No one writing in the Christian tradition and in a time of urgent crisis could be untouched by the process we have observed. The firmament of Christian symbol is in motion. And this is now the motion of chaos. The historical concrete is lost to Milton as surely as it is to Herbert. Milton wastes no time in driving Eucharistic symbol from his poetic firmament. The analogical sense of time and event goes with it. Christ the Warrior-God may hurl Satan over the battlements of the Miltonic heaven, but He has no way of joining Himself to the flesh of men in history. For, as we have seen, the invisible unity of the invisible church, achieved by way of the invisible act of an invisible grace upon the invisible and individual soul, stands as the very antithesis of the corporate, Eucharistic, incarnational assertion of the analogical symbol. Poetically, the sanctification of time under the sacramental benediction of the liturgical year is abandoned by Milton with his incomplete (and inept) poem on *The Passion*. In *Paradise Lost,* time runs on and down, benign only to the evil. History, like the will, is opened to a helter-skelter freedom—and to damnation.

Significantly, it is only in the Garden and before the Fall that nature is seen to rise on an analogical ladder to the divine. There man is truly the "image" of God, and it is by a connatural knowledge of the real that he gives "names" to those lower creatures which in their proper order are analogues of the whole order of being. The Garden is a little world of harmonies and hierarchies opening upward from the order of the inanimate to man, and from man and the order of the family (the hierarchical social unit) through angels innumerable in choir to final uncreated Being. The complex hierarchy of being is broken by the revolt of Adam, and at every level, spiritual, psychological, social, and natural, the harmony of creation is lost. No more do the analogical mirrors glisten and receive the clear impressions of successively higher levels of being. The link between high and low has snapped; the chain of being lies in ruins. Nature and history are cut adrift and in themselves are unredeemably lost. It is only in "new heaven, new earth" that a restoration will be effected of the corporate, hierarchical analogical character of original creation. And this lies outside time and space.

It is a typically Miltonic stroke, this, to apply the Thomist ontology to a world which no longer exists and which cannot exist again within the horizons of time. The enemy schoolman is turned upon himself, and in such a way as to illuminate, in a lightning flash of contrast, the world of Milton's private Protestant vision. For Milton's world is clearly one in which the analogical symbol is meaningless. Only in the Garden, the lost prelapsarian Garden, could man know with surety by analogy. And while Milton can call Christ the "second Adam," he will not permit to Christ his timeless Eucharistic strategy for redeeming the time. And if Milton's God will indeed clear man's senses dark, it is not so that man may *know* again as Adam knew, but that he may by faith impute to himself in a cheerful fiction the real righteousness of Christ.

Milton thus rejects the very possibility of the analogical symbol. But this is a positive rejection and not just a wistful and wavering farewell. It is a beginning, and a strong beginning, of a new and uncharted voyage of style. And if Milton's Christ is never the Eucharistic Christ, neither is He the pallid abstraction of the "low" puritanizing Anglicans. As early as *The Nativity Ode,* Christ has become a secondary and peripheral rather than a primary and central symbol. But on the periphery this displaced Christ symbol is manipulated with amazing artistic skill and power. It is pointless to identify the Christ of the poems with the simple Arian Christ of the *De Doctrina.* Milton's Arianism permits a freedom of treatment wholly impossible to a poet of Trinitarian views. And while *conceptually* the Son is inferior always to the Father, Milton has no compunction in giving free rein to rhetoric and developing to the full the dramatic and exclusively aesthetic possibilities of his own adaptation of the Christ symbol.

In *Paradise Regained,* Christ is at times almost a self-portrait of Milton. It is significant that the centre of this poem is ethical (the temptation in the desert), and not mystical, not the Eucharistic Sacrifice of the Cross. Here is the adopted Son of the Father, symbol of the strenuous, wayfaring moral life and the ultimate "paradise within," who saves only those whom Milton will have saved, and who scorns, as Milton scorns, the wholly unmystical body of man in history. Here, surely, is the voice not of the Saviour but of the defeated and disillusioned revolutionary:

> And what the people but a herd confus'd,
> A miscellaneous rabble, who extol
> Things vulgar, and well weigh'd, scarce worth the praise.
> They praise and they admire they know not what;
> And know not whom, but as one leads the other;
> And what delight to be by such extoll'd,
> To live upon thir tongues and be thir talk,
> Of whom to be disprais'd were no small praise?
> His lot who dares be singularly good.[13]

It is only within the typological frame of the *Samson* that Milton manages to convey a sense of the redemptive Christian act as sacrificial and corporate. Read in the full context of Milton's Christology, Samson is clearly not the type of the whole Christ. He is the type of Man, not the God-man, not the Son of Man. Yet, held within the vise of an evocative typology, Samson is much more suggestive of the Christ of Catholicism than is the scornful, snobbish Miltonic demigod of *Paradise Regained*. Thus the poem simulates, however precariously, the liturgical act, catching up the private destinies of the many members in the fruitful consequence of the one organic sacrificial offering of the Head. History is again made valid. Once again the fact in time seems to participate in values which have no dependence on time. This is a recovery of the analogical symbol. This is Milton's most perfect poem.

Significantly, the analogical effect of the poem is achieved by the exclusion of any overt Christ reference. Samson cannot, by any trick of exegesis, be *equated* with Christ. He is carefully and

---

[13] *P. R.*, Book III, ll. 52–57.

completely humanized. But he is given the *function* of Christ in the symbolization of self-sacrificing—and victorious—love. And the typological patterning of the poem controls the symbol, holding it within a firmament of dogmatic reference which Milton consciously, at least, had long ago disavowed. Christ the Person is never in Milton the Christ of tradition. Embarrassed intellectually and emotionally by the humiliating agony of the crucified God-man, Milton discreetly deploys the Scriptural Christ as a dramatic, ethical, and psychological image. It is only through the un-named half-Christ of *Samson Agonistes,* and by the use of a typological technique which encloses the hero in the swaddling and inescapable dimensions of the Catholic firmament, that Milton discharges for once into his poetry something like the Eucharistic knowledge of things and event. The poem stands as the miraculous and solitary victor over Milton's antisacramental theology.

But it is the Milton of *Paradise Lost* who changes the direction of poetry, who creates a new and usable firmament of symbol. For if in *Samson Agonistes* Milton approximates the liturgical effect of the Catholic tradition, in *Paradise Lost* he discovers a brilliant substitute for liturgy, he invents a liturgical surrogate. He does so, negatively, by a thoroughgoing abandonment of any pretence to analogy. As we have noted, it is only in the Garden that analogical knowledge holds. The fallen world is a world of dislocation, dislocation within the human faculties and between these disordered faculties and exterior nature. Nor can the "justification" of the separate soul by faith mould again the shattered fragments of time or heal the wound of nature.

But if for Milton, "reality" inhabits only the "paradise within," if nature and event can provide no proper analogue of this higher province, nevertheless the world of sense and act is not abstracted into an arbitrary set of lifeless signs for the contemplation of the spiritual life. The umbilical cord between sense and spirit is cut. But the world of sense is given a vivid and positive role to play. The gorgeous palaces of Milton's Heaven and Hell do not dissolve, are not reduced to mere sign, until all their sensuous possibilities have been exploited. Indeed, free of the proprieties dictated to the poet by the properly analogical imagination, Milton can build imagistic structures and relationships quite beyond the reach of a traditional Christian art. The Protestant Peter, arm in arm with the pagan river-god, marched early through Milton's imagination. And he marches late. Pictorially, the pomp of a despised feudal chivalry and a godless courtliness decorates Heaven and Hell alike, and if, pictorially, Milton's Heaven is distinguishable from his Hell, it is by the addition of that very ritual which, presumably, is the mark of anti-Christ.

> See Father, what first fruits on Earth are sprung
> From thy implanted Grace in Man, these Sighs
> And Prayers, which in this Golden Censer, mixt
> With Incense, I thy Priest before thee bring.[14]

Milton is the last man to intend a sacramental Catholic heaven, or, for that matter, the Greek heaven of Mulciber. The key to Milton's free and ingenious handling of sensuous rhetoric is given by Raphael just before he relates to Adam the revolt of Satan.

> High matter thou injoinst me, O prime of men,
> Sad task and hard, for how shall I relate
> To human sense th' invisible exploits
> Of warring spirits;
>
> · · ·
>
> Yet for thy good
> This is dispenc't, and what surmounts the reach
> Of human sense, I shall dilineate so,
> By lik'ning spiritual to corporal forms
> As express them best, though what if Earth may
> Be but the shadow of Heav'n, and things therein
> Each to other like, more then on earth is thought?[15]

At the beginning of the speech, Heaven and earth are said to be in an equivocal relationship one to the other. But metaphor

[14] *P. L.*, Book XI, ll. 22–25.
[15] *P. L.*, Book V, ll. 563–576.

will do its best. However, at the end of the passage, in the form of a question which surely no angel need ask, the possibility of a simple univocity between heaven and earth is suggested. It is not that the angel does not know, or that Milton does not know. The war of the angels is no more like the battle with the Spanish Armada than Heaven itself is like the sensuous Roman cathedral. The multiplicity and inconsistency of Milton's images of heaven clearly rule out this possibility of univocal correspondence between high and low. But the suggestion of such a possibility titillates the imagination, gives to metaphor a nervous life by making it *reach* even when it cannot, must not, touch. Thus a mighty façade of sensuous metaphor, pilfered from every known tradition, is made to cohere aesthetically. By a suspension of disbelief, by the intriguing "who knows?" of Raphael, Milton imparts an excited vitality to a picture-rhetoric compounded from pagan legend, biblical history, Catholic worship, military adventure, courtly pomp. No detail in the façade functions analogically. Consistency of idea, while necessary still to the inner and ultimate vision of the poem, is not demanded, with any exactitude, of the outer façade. What is demanded at the outworks is a consistency of colour, of pattern, of evocative power. The surfaces of pagan, ecclesiastical, and feudal rhetoric merge in an overpowering evocation of the *feeling* of power and grandeur from on high, and in a sense of man's mighty doom. As I noted in an earlier study,[16] Milton the antiroyalist does not scruple to deck out God, Satan, and even, at times, Adam in the brave trappings of the tyrannical king. Difficulties in interpretation and in the total aesthetic effect are thereby created, as they are unquestionably created, too, by Milton's freewheeling use of the Christ-image. But perhaps we read the poem too often with the wrong expectations. Perhaps, almost instinctively, we look for analogy, for a real participation of Milton's image in that which we think *should* be symbolized. And thus, according to our in-

16 *Milton's Royalism.*

dividual bias, we can somehow get for ourselves a Calvinist or a Quaker or a Catholic *Paradise Lost* with all the unmanageable images tidied into a nice dogmatic row.

It would seem to me now that whatever the inconsistencies between Milton's royalist imagery and his avowed and doctrinal republicanism, the massive effects conjured up by the crown and its almost endless cultural associations merge with an equally inappropriate Catholic and pagan set of images to create in the reader the feeling appropriate to and necessary for the reception of Milton's personal vision. We are prepared to feel the weight of *Milton's* power-God; we are prepared to feel the plight and the hope of *Milton's* Adam. The style puts us in Milton's hands. If we read aright, aesthetically, we make no attempt to translate secondary into primary symbols; we do not read Milton's God as if he were Dante's. Rather we allow ourselves to be moved by this tremendous if wholly artificial liturgy which accompanies a very personal and private vision of the nature of man and things. There is no analogy of sense and spirit; there is now no need of it. The epic action, the sensuous façade, even the novel conceptualizations of dogma, are made to play upon us, and we are moved. But we *know* that this God is not God, that this Christ is not Christ, that this Adam is not Adam. We also know, even if we explain our knowledge badly, that we have experienced greatness.

We still need dogma to measure Milton's effects, to appraise the startling originality of his vision. But the dogmatic symbol moves to the periphery of Milton's firmament. *Paradise Lost* is anthropocentric, not Christocentric. The artist himself is at the centre of the new firmament of poetry, Milton's firmament. He is free to *use* dogma, to *use* typology, as he is free to use whatever concept or image that can be made to serve *his* vision. It is but a step, albeit a step down, to the clever machinery of "The Rape of the Lock." It is another step, although this time on the same level, to the gnostic mythology of Blake and Yeats and to the visionary revival of our own day that would have the source and end and *test* of "truth" to be in the "imagination," in the myth-making faculty.

Milton's art is a mighty leap forward from the pallid abstractions and nostalgias of the Reform. A new firmament is born out of the decay and death of the old. But was this death? And is this life?

We must look now at that poetry contemporary to *Paradise Lost* which was still conceived within the orthodox Catholic firmament of symbol. And we must, in conclusion, come to some judgment about the durability of that ancient firmament and the relevance of the analogical act to the poetic process itself.

Conclusion: The Firmament Arrested

CHAPTER TEN

WE HAVE NOTED the unmistakable deterioration in seventeenth century poetry of the traditional firmament of Christian symbol. Dissociated in one degree or another from its generative core of dogma, the rhetoric of Anglican poetry either dissolves into bloodless abstraction (as in the poetry of men like Lok and Gressop) or, with a kind of half-life, haunts nostalgically the edges of ancient symbol (as in the poetry of Beaumont and Herbert). Most significant is the loss to such poetry of the analogical grip on the "historical concrete." For it would seem that a living relationship between the dogmatic, conceptual, and rhetorical levels of Christian symbol can be ensured only by an abiding faith in the spiritual relevance of the human *act*. A faith without works is the ultimate solvent of the old firmament of symbol, separating the soul of man from the carnality of time, because separating the word from the deed. But the deed will nevertheless be done, the flesh will glow with a lustre quite its own, time will not stand still. By denying its own initiative, by refusing its own imperative to redeem the natural order through a consecrated effort to redeem the times, in short, by undedicating itself to "good works," to significant act, the Christianity of the Reform shattered the creative potential of the old firmament of symbol, and by dividing the natural from the historical from the divine released each for its own separate and hazardous adventure.

CONCLUSION: THE FIRMAMENT ARRESTED

The old corporate sense of all men as potentially One Man reaches its final corruption in the idolatrous royalism of the Cavaliers and is only caricatured, at different and drastically opposed levels of society, in the narrow Calvinist doctrine of the Elect and the specious Digger version of the classless Utopia. Human experience, generally, is fragmented by the repudiation of the act. And at root this repudiation is antisacramental, welling up into the thought and feeling of the seventeenth century from the extreme Protestant annihilation of sacrament. If ever for Luther, Christ is actually present in the bread and wine of the altar, it is because Christ is everywhere and inescapably present, ubiquitous, and not because Christ as Head of the Mystical Body has *acted* out of eternity into time, not because man in the Body of Christ participates in the sacrificial offering. Christ is present because he cannot but be present. And man receives Him; he cannot conceivably give, offer, *act*.

Yet he must act. He must create. And if his act and his work have now been denied analogical dignity, if they no longer partake in their inmost being of the nature and order of worship, they are by this very fact set free. Indeed, the different but related provinces of the historical act and the poetic act will now grow into mighty and utterly separate kingdoms, mutually exclusive autarchies. They will even in time declare that a state of war exists properly and permanently between them. And in our final Babel of freedom and self-sufficiency, the "naturalist," the "realist," the "surrealist," and the "suprarealist" will each deride the works (and the faith) of the other.

If the germ of such a progress towards ourselves is to be found in the passive Eucharist of Luther, it is Calvin who gives the actual signal of release. An extreme iconoclast, Calvin forbids all use of the representative arts in the act of worship. But he does recognize that the genius of the artist is a gift from God and therefore not to be despised: ". . . I am not so scrupulous to think that no images ought ever to be permitted. But since sculpture and painting are gifts of God, I wish for a pure and legitimate use of both; lest these things which the Lord hath conferred on us for his glory and our benefit be not only corrupted by preposterous abuse, but even perverted to our ruin. We think it unlawful to make any visible figure as a representation of God because he hath himself forbidden it. . . . We conclude, therefore, that nothing should be painted or engraved but objects visible to our eyes." [1]

As Leslie Spelman [2] has shown, Calvin forced the artist to turn away from religious theme and symbol. Paradoxically enough, Calvin thus aids and abets the antireligious impulse of the hated Renaissance. He abandons to the world what the world is willing and able to have and to hold. In this way the Reformation connives with the Renaissance in the secularization of the arts. To the severe Calvinist cast of mind, art at best is a distraction, not only from formal worship but also from the serious duties of every day. At worst, art is the occasion of sin. In any case, the artist is invited to go his own way. It should not be surprising that this invitation is extended by a theology which confines the Incarnation to a pinpoint in time and separates the spiritual and ethical values of the Eucharist from the species of the temporal and the physical.

As we have seen, it is Milton, alone among seventeenth century English poets, who creates anew out of the new freedom implicit in Reformation dogma. In his representation of the Deity and in his use of sacred image he takes liberties that Calvin would certainly have condemned and a decent Puritanism must surely still abhor. The Anglican poet of the time worked within the fading outlines of the ancient firmament of symbol even as the sun at its core darkened and gave place. But Milton built freely, to his own design, and out of every particle and fragment that lay at hand. It is the Miltonic firmament which displaces the old Catholic firmament. And until Gerard Manley Hopkins,

---

[1] *Institutes,* Book I, Chap. XI, p. 12. Quoted by Leslie P. Spelman, "Calvin and the Arts," *Journal of Aesthetics and Art Criticism* (March, 1948), pp. 246–252.
[2] "Calvin and the Arts."

it was within this free, elastic, chameleon firmament of Milton's that the poetry most characteristic of post-Renaissance English culture was conceived. It is against this firmament that T. S. Eliot protests. And it is the ancient analogical firmament of Dante which Eliot has now, in part, restored.

In the seventeenth century the analogical firmament of traditional Catholic poetry was displaced but not yet destroyed. Under the pressures of the time, central dogmatic symbols though conserved by Catholic theology were unable to function poetically at their full height and depth. For the purification of ritual and the clarification of crucial dogma by the Council of Trent, no matter what the consequences for continental baroque, did not really penetrate the poetic situation in England, did not restore to function and life the full Catholic firmament of symbol. An appropriate rhetoric was restored. Dogma was even reinforced. But the miracle did not happen, could not happen. For if the English Catholic poet of the seventeenth century was an Englishman, he was an Englishman without England, an exile in space and time.

A new cycle in liturgical development begins with Trent. The corporate character and sacramental relevance of the Mass is once more made fully articulate. But one must note, too, that in the face of the Protestant revolt, Catholicism, by a precision of canonical definition that is almost frightening, asserted, more forcibly than ever before, the authoritarian power of the hierarchy. After Trent, until the fury of the Reform had spent itself, there would be permitted to Catholics far less freedom than the mediaeval churchman had enjoyed in metaphysical speculation and in the development of theological concept. With the principle of order and discipline uppermost in its mind, the Church drew up in rigid battle-line. True, the Jesuit is an avowed humanist and is able to adapt to the needs of a Church at war even the voluptuous flesh of the Renaissance itself. But this strenuous forcing together of mediaeval piety and Renaissance humanism is done in the heat of battle and by a kind of tour de force. The real glory of the Counter Reformation is to be found not in the façades of the baroque cathedral (as splendidly defiant as a battle-shout) but in the mystical vision of a St. John of the Cross and in the social thought, at once corporate and personalist, of Bellarmine and Suárez.

However, in technical Catholic metaphysics one detects a reluctance to meet, on fresh untried ground, the challenge of the new science and all the speculative problems that now emerge. The ancient dogma of the Eucharist is reaffirmed, but there is not, as there was in the time of Aquinas, any reconceptualization of dogma in the light of contemporary movements in thought. Indeed, it may fairly be said that whereas Protestantism fell into the error of confusing dogma with concept and then, under pressures both ideational and historical, of rejecting dogma *as though it were concept,* Catholicism went to the opposite extreme of protecting dogma behind a prickly barrier of concept no longer persuasive or even properly intelligible. The chief Catholic metaphysician of the time, Suárez, never gets much beyond a commentary on the philosophy of Aquinas with innovations that have little pertinence to the formidable new question marks now writ large in men's minds. And, as Professor Louis Bredvold [3] has demonstrated, Catholic apologists of the seventeenth century even used the weapons of Pyrrhic scepticism, disclaiming the relevance of reason to truth and, amidst the winds of doctrine, pointing mutely to the Rock. Thus the sceptical, fideistic, nonconceptual, nonhistorical Catholicism of John Dryden, and the abandonment by Catholic poetry itself of the living firmament of Catholic symbol.

Trent had salvaged the liturgy by erecting an unscalable canonical wall between Eucharistic dogma and the shock troops both of Renaissance rationalism and Protestant irrationalism. The strategy is inevitably defensive. Further Catholic advances in the conceptualization of dogma must await a calmer season when it will seem prudent to sally forth again. The shape and texture of

[3] *The Intellectual Milieu of John Dryden* (Ann Arbor, 1934).

the ancient firmament remain intact. But the living motion of the firmament has been arrested.

In England the free, expanding, visionary firmament of Milton contains creative possibilities wholly absent from the orthodox but motionless firmament of a Crashaw. Deprived of that analogical principle so necessary, I believe, to the highest art, Milton is nevertheless in better stead than the poet who holds to a set of dogmas in which analogy is implicit but may not become explicit, may not function *outward,* vivifying and enlarging the rims of concept and rhetoric.

The Catholic philosopher Jacques Maritain persuades us that a higher truth does not necessarily guarantee a higher art.

> I do not believe that the greater or less perfection in intrinsic truth of the universe of thought of a poet matters to his poetry save in quite a remote manner. The mediaeval universe true as its highest metaphysical principles may be, was, on the other hand, lacking in a great many truths that the modern man has discovered at the price of internal unity. Moreover, great poetry was to live in universes of thought quite different from Dante. . . . What matters to poetry in a close and direct manner are, I think, certain extremely simple but basic *presences* or existential certainties, assured by the universe of thought which constitutes the vital environment of poetic intuition: for instance, a certitude both of the mysterious irrefragable existence and the exigency of intelligibility involved in things; a certitude of the interiority of the human being and of its importance; a certitude that between man and the world there is an invisible relationship deeper than any material interconnection, a certitude that the impact of his freedom on his destiny gives his life a movement which is *oriented,* and not lost in the void, and which has to do in one way or another with the whole fabric of being . . . natural as they may be, these certitudes exist with greater force or stability if they are integrated in an articulate universe of thought. They cannot exist in us when the universe of thought that we have received . . . from our age of culture is a disintegrated universe which rejects or denies them.[4]

It was, on the whole, within the heretical firmament of the seventeenth century that these "many truths" lacking to the

[4] "Dante's Innocence and Luck," *Kenyon Review* (Spring, 1952), pp. 313–314.

mediaeval universe of thought were reached for and partly gained. The price was to be not only the "internal unity" of man but also man's sense of purposeful participation in creation itself and therefore, finally, all those certitudes which Maritain has catalogued. But not yet—not until the vast, visionary, explorative excitement of the Miltonic firmament had exhausted itself.

For a poet like Crashaw, the certitudes of faith, while real and intense, are limited not only by a Tridentine conservatism of the intellect, but also by something more crucial to the poetic activity, by a loss of the certitude "that the impact of his freedom on his destiny gives his life a movement which is *oriented* . . . and which has to do, in one way or another, with the whole fabric of being." The poetry of Crashaw is "a-historical." In it, as surely as in the poetry of Herbert and Beaumont, interiority of religious experience leaves no room at all for the *corporate human act*. Not only does Crashaw hold to Catholic values in "a disintegrated universe which rejects or denies them"—he cannot *act* within that universe. The movement of his life is inevitably oriented inward, away from the unruly order of event, and even, in the properly analogical sense, away from the fragmented order of things. Crashaw's witty and capricious reordering of the physical image is quite at variance with an analogical solicitude and respect for the thing-in-itself, for nature as nature.

Crashaw's poetry stands at the last extreme of the aesthetic predicament of Catholicism in seventeenth century Protestant England. We must consider for a moment the nature of this predicament.

As a Christian, writing within the tradition, both poetic and pious, of his own tongue, the seventeenth century Catholic poet can scarcely be exempt from those pressures and contradictions which worked to the disintegration of the ancient firmament of symbol. If George Herbert, dismayed by the secularizing tendencies of his day, is driven to an interior and otherworldly piety, how much greater must have been the pull of a pure and detached spirituality on the will of the hated and persecuted Catholic! Certainly, Catholic poets from Southwell to Crashaw proclaim a contempt for the world which seems to be just as anti-historical as the typical note of the disenchanted spiritual Anglican. Southwell longs fervently for martyrdom and a quick release from life and time. Is this very different from that profound distrust of the evil moment which prompts Anglicans like Herbert to drop time like a hot coal?

Catholic otherworldliness is not of a piece. For instance, Southwell and Crashaw, despite similarities of rhetoric and common dogmatic assumptions, are far apart in their sense of the *use* of history. Southwell's yearning for martyrdom, for an exodus from the historical, is preeminently a yearning, by way of the addition of the merit of his own sacrifice to the corporate treasury of merit, to strengthen the practical life of the visible church, the church which Southwell believes to be a leaven in the world and therefore fully involved in history. His own death, while a personal release from history, is an oblation intended to further the action of the church *in* history. Here, then, is contempt of the world in the interests of the redemption of the world. This is the central paradox of a fully Catholic spirituality. Southwell's sacrificial zeal is no more like Washbourne's ideal of the church triumphant over history by an act of transcendence than the contemplative withdrawal of a St. Teresa is analogous in any real way to Vaughan's flight into the golden childhood garden. In St. Teresa, withdrawal is an act of renewal; it is a moment in the rhythm of fulfillment, a coiling up of hidden powers which soon will spring into actualization, into history—just as in St. John of the Cross detachment from the images of the created order is a high strategy to repossess them, as they really are.

The poetry of Southwell and the verse of the Catholic balladeers from the Pilgrimage of Grace to the accession of James I is the poetry of Crucifixion. The blood of martyrs waters the ground of history. Beyond question, the Catholic poetry of the persecution is informed with a sense of the Eucharistic immediacy and relevance of the human act. The wounds of the scaffolded Jesuit are joined to the Five Wounds of the Cross. For a while, no matter how rigid and precise the conceptual life of the Counter Reformation, English Catholicism, through its suffering subjugation to time, is vivified in the flesh by that intense sun at the core, the Eucharist firmament.

Rhetoric gives again living answer to a dogma that penetrates the marrow of the human act. Southwell's "Burning Babe" is the realization, direct and by analogy, of the naked simplicity and inescapable agony of Christ and of the Christ-life as here and now it must be lived.

However, the story of recusancy in England is finally to be one of retreat, compromise, and exile. The hope of a Catholic restoration flickers and fades, and Catholicism finds itself driven into scattered country pockets. Meanwhile, the tremendous vitalities of Elizabethanism prove irresistible to men of itching genius like John Donne. As we have seen, the new corporate mystique of royalism diverts honest men from the ancient fact of unity in the Mystical Body, seducing the mind with glittering and plausible concepts, and capturing, for secular ends, the need and capacity of the will to act. The recusant made his peace with Leviathan—or fled to Douay. For him, as surely as for Herbert, the analogical link between the political and the Mystical Body was broken. And by the selfsame agencies. The recusant was either assimilated or cast aside. He was no longer what he was, nor could he now distinguish his own face in the mirror of event.

As confusion of identity increased with the waning of Elizabethan exhilaration, and clear spirits like Southwell were extinguished one by one, the force of recusancy began to surrender its independence and merge into a compromise with its adversaries. . . . Recusancy proper may be said to have ended where men could no longer think of a return to mediaeval values as a feasible course of action; where the gulf became too wide for the eyes of their memory to span, and they were obliged to recognize that the spiritual reserve which had been lost or spent during the Renaissance could never be recovered in the old forms; that they must look to the future for a rebirth of faith and valid ethics.[5]

In short, the English Catholic, like the extreme sectarian, was forced to project his values and his hopes into a remote future. But unlike the sectarian, he had no illusion that the future could be brought close by any act of his. If he kept to his communion, he belonged still to a faith corporate and active (as well as personal and contemplative) in its assertion and in its practical demands upon him. But he was denied the corporate, active Catholic way of life. He heard the urgent dogmatic dictates of the Mass privately, below floors, behind drawn blinds. Liturgically, he adored the Wounds of the Cross; practically, he saved his own skin. Between the motion and the act there fell a shadow. And while his imagination could still swirl with Jesuit emblems of the suffering, ecstatic Flesh, and with the brave new legends of churchmen militant abroad and beyond, the Blood of Christ must now seem to run through other veins than his. He might indeed contemplate the Blood, but at a distance and secondhand. The great firmament stands motionless if it is abandoned by the living act of intellect and will. If the symbols of the corporate Eucharistic act are reduced to the icons of a private devotion, they lapse into metaphor, stained glass, the mere frostings and façade of worship.

In the Eucharistic verse of these years of withdrawal and inwardness, one detects an almost Protestant individualization of the sacramental symbol. Henry Constable's "To the Blessed Sacrament" is characteristic.

> When thee (O holy sacrificed Lambe)
> In several sygnes I whyte and liquid see
> As in thy body slayne I thynke on thee
> Which pale by shedding of thy blood became.
>
> And when agayne I doe behold the same

[5] John Chandos, "Recusant Poets of the English Renaissance," *The Month* (January, 1950 [New Series, vol. III, no. 1]), pp. 5–18.

Vayled in whyte to be receav'd of mee
Thou seemest in thy syndon wrapt to bee
Like to a corse whose monument I am

Buryed in mee unto my soul appeare
Prysen'd in earth, and bannisht from thy sight
Like our forefathers who in lymbo were,
Cleere thou my thoughts as thou did'st gyve them light,
And as thou others freed from purging fire
Quench in my heart the flames of badd desyre.[6]

Constable accepts, in the Catholic sense, the reality and immediacy of the Eucharistic sacrifice. The dogmatic assumptions are far enough from Herbert's in his "Holy Communion." But the feeling of the poem is receptionist and individualist. Despite the dogmatic intention, the poetic attention is directed exclusively to the action of the sacrament upon the passive moral rim of the soul. In his narrow lonely room, the recusant compresses the public, corporate act of the liturgy into a species of private devotion, into a ritualized prayer for personal spiritual benefit. Thus the dogmatic core of Eucharistic symbol is conserved but, in effect, sealed tight and immobilized. The firmament is arrested.

However, in a poem like Richard Verstegen's "Our Blessed Ladies Lullaby," a deep devotion to Mary still lends a Catholic immediacy and warmth to the poetic realization of the humanity of Christ.

Upon my lap my severaigne sits
And sucks upon my breast,
Meanwhyle his love sustaines my lyf,
And gives my body rest
    Sing lullaby my little boy
    Sing lullaby my lives joy.[7]

There is a homely Catholic intimacy here and in the following

---

[6] *Poems and Sonnets by Henry Constable,* ed. John Gray (London, 1847), p. xxxviii.

[7] *Odes, In Imitation of the Seaven Penitential Psalms, with Other Sundry Poems and Ditties* (London, 1601), p. 50.

stanzas in which Mary seems to open her arms to her infinite
family in the Church-to-be.

> Let heaven and earth, and saints and men
> Assistance give to mee,
> That all their moste occurring ayd
> Augment my thankes to thee
>> Sing lullaby my little boy
>> Sing lullaby my lives joy.
>
> And let th'ensuing blessed face
> Thow wilt succeeding raise
> Joyne all their praises unto myne
> To multiply thy praise
>> Sing lullaby my little boy
>> Sing lullaby my lives joy.[8]

This is surely the spirituality of the Catholic Communion of
Saints, corporate, time-annihilating, and yet personal, close, ten-
der. But somehow even this corporateness becomes a private
thing, kept warm for the hours of the rosary and the vigil. It is
lovingly compounded of nostalgia and far-off hope. For in Verstegen, the present, the realm of event and act, stands wholly external and alien to the devotional life.

> The golden world long since is worne away,
> As now the golden yeare hath taken end,
> The Iron world doth stil remain and stay
> And in his rust doth to his ruyne tend,
>> And in the shew of vertue and of truthe
>> Seeme-good seeme-gospel turneth all to ruthe.
>
> At Babel tower where tounges confusion came
> It stayed the woork that fond advice begun
> But fond advice now seeketh to disframe
> A tabernacle seated in the sun.
>> And tounges confusion church-war hath procured
>> Lately begun and yet to long endured.[9]

True, the "tabernacle in the Sun" will never be "disframed."

[8] Verstegen, p. 54.
[9] Verstegen, p. 48.

The anguish of time can and will be endured. The Catholic waits. Although he feels, as painfully as Vaughan or Traherne, the loss of the Golden World, the Catholic does not, as they do, venture to counterfeit the gold in the secret fastnesses of his own fancy. He does not play with the philosopher's stone. He waits. And with him the ancient firmament waits, intact but still.

Less patient men of Verstegen's faith will come even closer to the idolatry of Cavalier royalism than Verstegen comes to the garden retreat of the "spiritual Anglicans." John Abbott, a Catholic convert who took refuge from the fury of event in an Antwerp monastery, sees a prospect of a Catholic restoration in the proposed "Spanish Match" of Prince Charles of England. Abbott blesses King James, gulps down the whole doctrine of the Divine Right of Kings, and even calls upon England to smite down in Catholic righteousness the plebeian Protestant democracy of the Netherlands. From Antwerp he addressed his about-to-be Catholic English countrymen.

> My worthy countrymen, why are you slaves
> To Brewers, Cobblers, Basket-making Knaves?
>
> · · ·
>
> You answer that you part of Holland take
> For the Lord's word and for his Gospel's sake.
>
> · · ·
>
> But if you nearer to their Gospel look
> You'll find it is a Machiaevellian book
> Wherein each leaf containeth damned things
> Conspiracies and treasons against Kings.
>
> · · ·
>
> Must they forthwith up in rebellion band
> Against their King, and take from him his own?
> If so: what Prince can sit safe on his throne?
> Let's pray that Princes may do what is right
> And not with trait'rous arms against them fight.[10]

The poem is charged with the soundest Catholic dogma. Ab-

[10] *Jesus Praefigured: Or a Poem of the Holy Name of Jesus* (Antwerp, 1623), pp. 38–39.

bott even plays with surprising skill on the ancient instruments of typology and iconography. Saints and martyrs are called upon to redeem the pledge of Eucharistic sacrifice and love. But at the heart of the poem, nullifying everything else, one meets not only a Cavalier contempt for the common man, not only a failure or refusal to see and admit the real motion of the historical order, but also an opportunistic and crawling itch to make peace with the devil, and to do so on the very terms proposed by the devil's party. The natural alliance of Catholicism with the people's cause in the Pilgrimage of Grace has given way to a confused and desperate expediency by which the deepest symbols of the faith are not only arrested but tarnished. The dogma of the Mystical Body is obscured by the rust of accidental and outmoded feudal concepts.

When the "Spanish Match" was broken off, poor Abbott broke off his poem. He was not heard from again. But perhaps he did live on in the later proponents of "throne and altar"—and in the incredible champions of "El Caudillo."

Crashaw, of course, is one of the innocents for whom history is something to be endured and, if possible, ignored. He does not degrade the great symbols by improper use. For him they are the cherished icons of the inner devotional life. Catholicism, continental Catholicism, with its bitter-sweet raptures and blinding surfaces, lifted Crashaw not only out of place but out of time. He is ravished by the sensuous surfaces of the Church. His Eucharistic poetry is faithful to the very accents of Aquinas. And he reports, as vividly as third hand allows, the ecstasy of the saint visualized by Bernini. Without doubt, he goes beyond Verstegen in his realization of the helpless humanity of the Infant Jesus. Crashaw's *Nativity* is profitably contrasted with Milton's in illustration of the wide gulf between a Catholic and a Protestant sensibility.

Yet in all these poems of praise and worship there is not one image by which the act of worship catches to itself any specifically human act other than the physical act of love. In the line of the conventionalized tradition of the Song of Songs, a tradition which had been given a new warmth by Tridentine baroque, Crashaw sublimated the passions of the flesh in the Passion of the Cross. He tells the "young gentlewoman,"

> How many Heav'ns at once it is
> To have her God become her lover.[11]

And "the undaunted daughter of desires" yearns towards the "finall Kisse" of the Heavenly Bridegroom.[12] Human love is made the efficient symbol of the divine love and by analogy is lifted to participation in it. But it is only in the symbolization of love that Crashaw can be said to create analogically. The nature image, insofar as it exists in his poetry outside the symbolization of the devotional act of love, is always metaphorical rather than analogical. These flaming fountains, weeping fires, starry seedtimes, and the Smiling May in the cheek, done in the wake of Elizabethan (and Italian) conceit, are, of course, beyond comparison with the dead and abstract metaphors of the "low" Anglicans. For wit is here happily at play, and, too, there is still a perfume to the flowers which Crashaw plucks from the great garden of things. Yet, in a real sense, Crashaw is shut in, rather than released, by the act of devotion. He worships indoors, in the church, in the baroque church. No sound is heard from the street. No one kneels beside Crashaw at the altar rail. He is indoors and he is quite alone. He never works like a gardener in the garden. His flowers are cut flowers sent in to be arranged to an interior design. He arranges them as a sacristan might arrange the linen and the candles of the altar.

Significantly, it is not until Catholicism has repossessed its roots that we get again, in the poetry of Hopkins, a proper realization of the integrity and analogical dignity of the "inscaped" thing. Crashaw had made of the liturgical public firmament a

---

11 "Prayer. An Ode, which was Praefixed to a Little Prayer-Book given to a Young Gentle-Woman." *Richard Crashaw*, ed. A. R. Waller (Cambridge, 1904), p. 281.

12 "The Flaming Heart." *Crashaw*, pp. 276–277.

private devotional domain. It was a domain to which few Englishmen for a long while would seek admittance.

The seventeenth century bequeathed the free, expanding firmament first improvised by Milton, a shifting firmament, pregnant with infinite possibilities (and contradictions), veering from rationalism to romanticism, from a doctrine of common sense to a quest for the over-soul of the philosopher and the under-soul of the psychoanalyst. It is only now in the wake of Gerard Manley Hopkins, that we can, with any certitude, begin to see the new outlines of an older firmament.

Clearly, poets like T. S. Eliot and W. H. Auden, novelists like Mauriac, Bernanos, and Graham Greene—to mention only a few of the better known names—constitute a unique constellation, a constellation which took shape slowly and is only now being observed for what it is. These writers are Christian writers, in the exact sense. They are not merely Christians who happen to write. Their art is consciously dedicated to the realization of a specifically Christian vision of reality.

This is not to say, of course, that a writer steeped in Freud or Einstein or Sir James Frazer is not a Christian writer. Christian art at its highest has never been, in the exclusive sense, pure. It is quite possible that a Christian today might find almost as much use for Freud and Einstein as St. Thomas Aquinas once found for the pagan Aristotle. W. H. Auden is a fine example of the capacity of the Christian artist in our time to digest and to employ the findings of the new psychology. T. S. Eliot's Christian universe is compounded, among other things, of the new anthropology and the new physics. I should say that it is precisely this capacity to meet, to grasp, and to put in order the magnificent chaos of secular thought which characterizes a genuinely Christian art in our time—or in any other time.

However, it is necessary to distinguish the specifically Christian experience in art from that literature of mythic religiosity now so prevalent. For there are literary critics among us who will pin the label "religious"—and even "Christian"—on any work of art which is not incarcerated within the sheer four walls of a materialistic determinism. Nowadays if any man so much as guesses out loud that mysteries may lie beyond the range of telescope and microscope, he is acclaimed at once as seer, mystic, prophet, saint.

And the conventional literary historian, trained in the fine art of reducing everything to neat categories, movements, patterns, schools, types, has, by his very method, helped to obliterate the real distinctions which must be observed between a specifically Christian literature and that undogmatic religiosity of feeling and vision so common in current writing.

True, it is no longer easy to isolate the specifically Christian work. No serious writer is able any longer, surely, to work within the limits of a flat naturalism. Even radical social change no longer seems enough to satisfy the artist's thirst for meaning or his craving for security. He has come to seek a metaphysical rather than a merely sociological kind of security. His sense of the mystery of the universe has deepened. So has his sense of the mystery of selfhood. He is no longer comforted when he says to himself—"I think, therefore I am." He is puzzled. He is, above all, *anxious*. His little umbrella of science no longer protects him against what seems to be the unpremeditated, unpredictable storm of being. This, precisely this, is the human situation as it is revealed in the lightning flash of our moment in time. The Christian writer today must be fully aware of just this situation, just this predicament.

It is in terms of *final* ends that we must draw our distinction between a Christian and a non-Christian art. In his pursuit of the mystery, the Christian artist will use every means at his disposal. He is not afraid to look into the subconscious world of desire and myth. He is not disturbed by Frazer's dying corn god, nor is he dismayed by the time-space concept of Einstein. The universe of Einstein will serve him as well now as the Ptolemaic universe once served him. The Christian has come to know symbolic knowledge for what it is. And he can use it.

The basic distinction between the Christian and the non-Christian religious artist in our time lies just here. The Christian is able or should be able to use the new symbols provided him by physics, anthropology, psychology. The non-Christian is used *by* these symbols. And it is just this point of distinction which the literary historian so often misses. For instance, Professor William Tindall, in his *Forces in Modern British Literature*,[13] has a chapter which he calls "The Hunt for the Father." The Freudian notion that all religion—and religiosity—is nothing else but the sublimated need for symbols of parental authority and protection is made here to apply equally to Eliot, Auden, Yeats, Joyce, Lawrence, Kafka—and even George Bernard Shaw! By this elastic formula, authentic Christianity is equated with various degrees of jungle myth, with the Lamarckian theory of creative evolution, with all forms of idealism, and even, in the case of James Joyce, with a forthright if painful rejection of Christianity.

Now it is true that in all these writers one may detect degrees of religious impulse and feeling. In only two of them—Eliot and Auden—is the specifically Christian note to be found. By different paths, Lawrence and Shaw arrive at a kind of nature worship, the adoration of the blood stream or the life force, as the case may be. Yeats concocts his own myth from many diverse elements. But the mythology of Yeats is an alternative to Christianity—just as William Blake's mythology is an alternative to Christianity, just as Huxley's romantic Hinduism is an alternative to Christianity.

A Christian writer like Eliot, as anxious as any of his contemporaries to break through the naturalistic surfaces to deeper levels of knowledge and experience, can afford, as these others do, to exploit the primitive myth, the content of the dream, the symbols of physics or of theosophy—and yet be able to create an art which

[13] (New York, 1947.)

[245]

is radically different from the art of Yeats, or Lawrence, or Kafka, or Joyce. Why?

In any approach to the contemporary Christian revival one must be aware simultaneously of the authentic sacramental Christian tradition and of the wounding of that tradition at its very heart by *both* Reformation and Counter Reformation. The wound is not easily healed. Nor can the Christian writer any longer proceed as though there had been no wound—or as though nothing since the wound has been valid and in health. Whether he be Catholic or Protestant, the contemporary Christian writer is forced to take account of the break in his own tradition and also of the brilliant and vital growth of secular traditions which may seem to be, but intrinsically are not, alien to his own.

Let us admit that with Protestantism there occurred in poetry an abdication of the physical and natural order, a retreat to "the Paradise within," which by the twentieth century was a paradise swarming with serpents. Its symbol is no longer the tree of knowledge but the psychoanalyst's couch. But surely there were gains, too, in all this. Man's knowledge of himself had deepened. And though it is true that Protestantism, in effect, delivered nature to the naturalist, it is also true that nature was thereby opened to enquiry as it never had been before. On the other hand, Catholicism, forced back on the defensive by the double assault of the Reformation and the new science, while able to conserve sacramental dogma as dogma, was, until recently, unable to insert this dogma persuasively either in the natural order or in the social order. For if Protestantism abandoned sacramentalism in principle, it is, I think, fair to say that Catholicism for a long while and to a large extent abandoned it in practice. Sacramentalism is an act—not just an idea about an act. One clear piece of evidence for the view that Catholicism did not always act sacramentally at the level of history is the famous papal statement that the tragedy of the nineteenth century was the loss of the working class to the Church.

If sacramentalism is the life of Christian art—and I think it is—its cultivation in our time must be made strenuous. If Christian art is to be wholly relevant today, it must not be merely pious. Above all, it must not be archaic, yearning nostalgically for the Ages of Faith. Is there anything more emblematic of retreat and even of defeat than the construction in the twentieth century of a Gothic church? (As though to engage in Christian worship one should withdraw into a distant age and shun the skills, the materials, the medium of this time and this place!) For a sacramentalist, surely, a new Gothic church is irrelevant. And it is therefore almost irreverent.

A fully sacramental Christianity must be able to penetrate again the whole world of knowledge. It must penetrate and reinfuse the historical order—not as it was, not as it might have been if there had been no Renaissance, no Reformation, no French Revolution, no class struggle—but the historical order as it is, as it has actually become.

If knowledge is indeed to be reordered again by Christianity, let us admit that no scrap or particle of knowledge can be ignored or dismissed. For sacramentalism must seek to take into itself its very opposite. It can exclude nothing. Even the spiritual, intellectual, and aesthetic fruits of the Protestant revolt against the sacramental principle must be sacramentally repossessed, or there is no sacramentalism. The whole literature of interior spiritual struggle from Bunyan to Kafka must be repossessed. Nothing must be lost.

The test I should make of the contemporary Christian revival in letters is a simple one. It is this: Assuming that this new Christian literature is dogmatically Christian—which it is—is it fully relevant? If it turns out to be nothing more than pious paper Gothic, it is worth very little indeed.

I think the relevance of contemporary Christian literature must be considered not only in terms of the idiom in which the Christian writer addresses us but also in terms of the actual dilemma of modern man. What, using the word in its broadest sense, characterizes modern secular culture? Preeminently two things

—fragmentation and alienation. Never as now has man known so much about the workings of nature. And yet the very science by which he knows nature threatens to destroy him. Never as now has man known so much about the workings of the self. But what he has come to know frightens him. Never as now has man known so much about the workings of society. But he is lost in society, overwhelmed by it. The diabolical newspaper headline has for him now the same fatalistic force as the muttering of the witch doctor once had for the most primitive savage. In short, modern man feels himself to be separate from, alienated from the universe. And he feels separate from, alienated from himself. Thus he is, literally, beside himself. The universe, society, the self—these have all become objects of knowledge, alien to one another and alien to the knower. The situation is the very reverse of any sacramental knowledge of reality. It is a situation which has been described before—many times. The point is, how is it to be corrected?

It is precisely to this situation that contemporary Christian art must address itself if it is to be relevant, if it is to be, in the deepest sense, Christian. One must recognize at once that such a situation presents enormous technical and semantic difficulties for the Christian artist. The long process of fragmentation and alienation that has gone on in our culture for over two hundred years has been destructive not only of the sacramental world view but of the very language in which the Christian sense of reality was expressed. The traditional frame of reference within which the Christian poet once worked has largely vanished. Milton could count on his readers to know the Scriptures. In the seventeenth century no man of twenty years would guess, as a student of mine recently guessed, that Moses was the husband of the Virgin Mary! And as late as Crashaw and Herbert, Catholic and Anglican poets could count on their readers to know the shape of the substance of the liturgy of the Church, with all its wealth of image and symbol.

It has been generally observed that one of the difficulties of a poem like T. S. Eliot's *Ash Wednesday* is this: Eliot here depends for his most significant effects upon an understanding of liturgy and ecclesiasticism not possessed in our day by any save professional churchmen and scholars. The poem may indeed communicate without being understood. Any sensitive reader of poetry is aware of the intensity and the integrity of this poem. Nevertheless, it is paper Gothic, although a very superior kind of paper Gothic. The way of the Christian artist nowadays cannot be this way. A sacramental re-entry into the experience, the knowledge, the sensibility, of our time can scarcely be effected by any effort, however fervent, to restore a Christian idiom appropriate to another and vastly different cultural moment. No one has realized this more sharply than Mr. Eliot himself. In the *Four Quartets* this kind of difficulty is in large part overcome. As Miss Helen Gardner [14] has pointed out, while the *Four Quartets* abounds in liturgical images and allusions, these are used to deepen and enrich effects already articulated by other means. This, then, is *not* paper Gothic. The building is modern, functional. And yet it retains, without being at all archaic, cross, candle, incense.

The great achievement of Eliot's *Four Quartets* is, of course, in the sacramental repossession of nature and time, things and history. In these poems the sacramental act is consummated through and by means of contemporary sensibility and contemporary knowledge. Mr. Eliot is fully aware, for instance, of the distinction we must now make between clock time and the baffling interior time of the stream of consciousness which cannot be measured at all by the tick of the clock. He is aware, too, of the idea of the continuum, of the sense we now have of reality as a flow, a stream without beginning or end. In these poems the concepts "beginning" and "end" become concepts of value, purpose, destiny, rather than merely chronological concepts. And the intuition of eternity is made to possess and to illuminate the

[14] *The Art of T. S. Eliot* (London, 1949).

personal and the historical levels of the time process. In the *Four Quartets* Eliot seeks to bring back into a pattern of meaning nature, history, the person. In *Dry Salvages,* the third of the *Four Quartets,* there is a fine realization of the recovery of authentic Christian symbol. The river and sea of this poem are actual river and sea. You could get wet in them, you could drown in them. They exist in their own unique right. Was there ever a keener sense of salt water than here:

> The whine in the rigging,
> The menace and caress of wave that breaks on water
> The distant rote in the granite teeth
> And the wailing warning from the approaching headland
>
> . . .
>
> And under the oppression of the silent fog
> The tolling bell. . . .[15]

Yet this is not descriptive nature poetry. This is not Masefield. In Eliot the river is a river. But it rises, through psychological and anthropological allusion to ethical and spiritual levels of meaning for the life of the person, just as Eliot's sea, actual and sensuously known at one level, is also at another level the symbol of the motion and the intention of history. And beneath its chaotic and complex rhythm beats "the unhurried ground swell, measuring time that is not our time," and touching both exterior nature and interior man with inscrutable but perpetual benediction.

I should say that Eliot as a Christian sacramentalist has, in the *Four Quartets,* overcome the fragmentation of contemporary culture by reabsorbing analogically the natural or cosmic myth in the historical symbol. And I should say that he has done so in the terms proper to our moment in time. The achievement of Eliot does not stand alone. Auden works in the same direction, and not the least important of his contributions to a modern Christian symbolism is the fusion in his best poetry of the Angli-

[15] (London, Faber and Faber, 1944), p. 26. Quoted by permission of Mr. Eliot's publishers, Faber and Faber in London, and Harcourt, Brace in New York.

can sacramental sense with the distinctly Protestant thought of writers like Kierkegaard and Niebuhr.

The recovery of the sacramental symbol by contemporary Christian writers is as yet by no means complete. I believe that despite the achievements which I have mentioned, there is some real danger that this promising cultural movement may be dissipated and lost again. I shall try to explain what I fear in terms of Eliot. Is it not the case that although Eliot has caught the necessary analogical relationship between nature, history, and man and has therefore helped to heal the rupture between these orders, he has not at all overcome the disease of alienation? Is it not true that although he is sensitive to the motion of history, he does not understand at all the content of history? He knows man—but not men. He does not enter into the concrete, the practical historical situation. Is this why the people of his *Cocktail Party* are so trivial, so ludicrously unrepresentative? Is this why he makes his lady saint die a sacrificial death at the hands of barbarous natives in some outpost of Empire? Here is nothing, surely, but ecclesiastical Kipling! Here is Christian sacrifice put in a Jungle Book vacuum. How irrelevant this is to the sacrificial demands made on the Christian by the intolerable practicalities of our specific moment in time. The corporate sense, the sense of living community, is absent in Eliot. It is absent in Auden. In Mauriac I should say that there is a feeling for the content of history and no feeling for its motion. Dostoevski was the last major Christian artist to possess fully the sacramental knowledge of man alive in a society that moves. Dostoevski in *The Brothers Karamazov* realizes symbolically the Christian fact of communion, and he places it in the living core of the historical process.

Without a recovery of this corporate sense, I suspect that Christian art can advance no further because it will have failed to cure the disease of alienation. The artist must do more now than absorb the cosmic myth into the historical symbol. He must insert himself into the historical process. He must stop hunting for the accidental social hierarchies of the lost Ages of Faith. He will be aware that within history only partial fulfillments of the Christian perspective are possible. But he must also be aware that without such partial fulfillments his art, and history itself, will vanish. This is the challenge for him now.

Index

INDEX

INDEX

INDEX